Roberta Kuhn, Jeffrey Kuhn's wife.

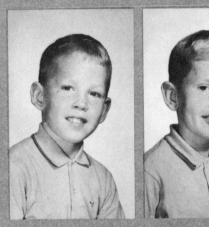

Tom and Dailey, Betty and
Ted de Angeli's sons.

Sarah de Angeli, Betty and
Ted de Angeli's daughter.

Michael, Peter, John and Danny,
Marianne and Maury de Angeli's sons.

BUTTER AT THE OLD PRICE

Books by Marguerite de Angeli

TED AND NINA GO TO THE GROCERY STORE

TED AND NINA SPEND A HAPPY RAINY DAY

HENNER'S LYDIA

PETITE SUZANNE

COPPER-TOED BOOTS

SKIPPACK SCHOOL

A SUMMER DAY WITH TED AND NINA

THEE HANNAH!

ELIN'S AMERIKA

UP THE HILL

YONIE WONDERNOSE

TURKEY FOR CHRISTMAS

BRIGHT APRIL

JARED'S ISLAND

THE DOOR IN THE WALL

JUST LIKE DAVID

BOOK OF NURSERY AND MOTHER GOOSE RHYMES

BLACK FOX OF LORNE

THE OLD TESTAMENT

A POCKET FULL OF POSIES

MARGUERITE DE ANGELI'S BOOK OF FAVORITE HYMNS

THE GOOSE GIRL

BUTTER AT THE OLD PRICE

Butter at the Old Price

THE AUTOBIOGRAPHY OF

Marguerite de Angeli

Doubleday & Company, Inc.   GARDEN CITY, NEW YORK

ISBN: 0-385-06813-1
LIBRARY OF CONGRESS CATALOG CARD NUMBER 77–116199
COPYRIGHT © 1971 BY MARGUERITE DE ANGELI
ALL RIGHTS RESERVED
PRINTED IN THE UNITED STATES OF AMERICA
9   8   7   6   5   4

This book is dedicated to all those who have helped me on my way. Especially to Maurice L. Bower whose encouragement started me and to Margaret Lesser who kept me going.

To my parents who set standards early in childhood and whose love was implicit in their care of me.

To my dear husband who always listened.

To my children. It wasn't all for them, but without them there would have been little point.

BUTTER AT THE OLD PRICE

Chapter One

My earliest memory is of morning stillness, the sun creeping through a little alcove touching the edge of a barrel top and shining on boxes that stood about the room as if we had just moved in. There was no one about but me. It must have been Sunday, though I wouldn't have known that any more than I would have known that the exciting colored chalks in their neat box were called pastels. I knew only that they were enticing and that I yielded to the temptation to try them—where?

Nearby, on another barrel top, stood a portrait my father was doing from a photograph. All around the edge it was unfinished, and whether it was because I instinctively knew that it was a desecration to touch the finished work or whether I couldn't reach it, I don't know. But I didn't touch the head. I used every color in the box on the empty corner nearest me.

What excitement to feel the soft touch on the canvas, to see the bright mark it made. Pink, fiery red, orange, violet, cool blue, and green. What wonder! I could not stop till I had tried them all. Even the gentle but serious talk my father gave me with my little hands in his could not erase the joy of that first experiment with color. From that day to this, eighty years later, the urge to draw and to paint has run like a bright thread through my life as the purple thread runs through heather tweed, now found, now lost.

I must have been somewhat less than two, because my mother has told me that we had just moved from Lapeer, Michigan, to Chicago, and we didn't stay there very long. Probably, my father had engaged the flat when he had gone on ahead to arrange work with a photographer to make crayon and pastel portraits, which were then in vogue. He had not considered that the neighborhood, with its noisy

Marguerite de Angeli's birthplace: Lapeer, Michigan.

saloon on the corner, was unsuitable for rearing two little girls. He was very young.

My father, Shadrach George Lofft, had married Mama, Ruby Adele Tuttle, when he was twenty-one and she was nineteen. Their first child was my sister Nina, who was fifteen months older than I.

Papa was easygoing and of a happy disposition, and like his father, Grandpa Lofft, gave one the feeling that the world was, on the whole, a happy place. His formal schooling ended with the eighth grade, but his constant and varied reading throughout his life gave him a fund of general information and a vocabulary that was quite remarkable. Because his memory was good, he could always give us at least a partial answer to our questions or direct us to a better source of information. He was an excellent mimic and story-teller and had a gift for drawing, which helped him in the photo-graphic work that gave us our living.

2

He had inherited from Grandpa a mechanical aptitude as well and could build practically anything. He enjoyed good food and in those days dieting was unheard of except when necessary for health, so my memory of him is as a big man, tall and rather heavy, pleasant-looking, bald, with fair skin that freckled in the sun. He had a good, light baritone voice and sang to Mama's accompaniment such old favorites as "The Kerry Dance," "The Lost Chord," "Twickenham Ferry," and others of the 1890s. To me it was blissful to hear, and a part of home. I think I have always had a need for reassurance, and this part of our family life seemed to provide it, along with his Sunday morning habit of smoking a cigar, which sent a fragrant wreath about his head. Perhaps it was because I missed him so much when he was away.

Papa would not tolerate the least suggestion of gossip among us, and when we occasionally discussed someone, not maliciously, he would say, clearing his throat, "Do you think it's going to rain?" Then we knew the subject was closed.

My mother was not perhaps what you would call pretty, but lovely. She had abundant brown hair and blue, blue eyes, which often I think of as gray. It may be that they changed according to mood or what she wore. Possibly I associate their color with times

Shadrach George Lofft, Marguerite's father.

3

Ruby Tuttle Lofft,
Marguerite's mother.

of severity: times when her strong sense of duty and upbringing, which was puritan, kept her essential kindness withheld.

Mama was tall for the time in which she was young, though not so tall as her daughters and granddaughters. Considering her dignity and reticence, it amused me to hear that in her youth it was she who gathered up the girls and took them to the ball game because she was in command of a horse and buggy and they were not.

My mother was an excellent cook and homemaker. Her needlework was exquisitely fine and she made clothes for us all while we were little and for us girls till we were able to make our own. Even then she made our best things. She was patient with us when we watched her make pie and let us have dough to make tiny ones in the lids of baking powder cans.

When she stuffed turkey I loved to watch while she sewed it with a big needle and trussed the legs and wings, and to smell the fragrance of sage and onion in the dressing.

Papa liked to be in the kitchen too, when he was home, either because he liked to help with the cooking or because he liked being with Mama. There was a beautiful relationship between my parents. Not only was there calm acceptance of the difference in their natures,

4

there was gentle affection and gracious appreciation—a good atmosphere in which to rear children.

Mama never called us "dear," although I often longed for that small sign of affection. One must not be effusive lest one's sincerity be questioned. Few compliments were given in our household. After all, why should one be complimented for doing her task well? But there was plenty of encouragement, especially from Mama in developing our special abilities.

"You can do *anything* you really *want* to do," she would say, and sometimes let me off the Saturday dusting to try the drawing I had in my mind. She was particularly at home with children and quietly let them know she expected only the best from them. They rarely disappointed her, and because they knew where they stood with her they loved her.

Besides the discovery of the joy of color, there are other scattered memories of Chicago. I remember too when our morning bath brought out the measles and a very serious burn covering my back when Papa came in to shake up the fire in the potbellied stove. Nina and I sat shivering behind it and, as often happened, I didn't immediately heed his "Come, girls! Get dressed." The delay, due to day-

Marguerite at age three.

5

dreaming, which I have done all my life, brought me in front of the stove just in time to catch the hot water from the kettle as the stove fell. Papa caught it and burned his hands, but nothing caught fire. I was in the hospital for weeks, and remember how kind the nurses were. It was impressed upon me that it pays to obey promptly.

The following summer at the World's Fair, I was often lost because I lingered to look at something and was not aware that I was being left behind. Although I was only four, some of the exhibits are still clear in my memory. One was a tiny locomotive run by steam, its bright brass driving rod smoothly turning three-inch wheels. Another, a doll-sized house of dark, unpainted wood with thatched roof and sliding doors, furnished scantily but to scale. I remember a tiny living plant on the doll-sized table. I was told it was made by people of Japan, who lived far away across a great ocean. Perhaps it was the exquisite perfection of the little house that gave me an appreciation of the miniature things I have always loved.

I remember women in foreign national costume working on Singer sewing machines like the one Mama used, and dark-skinned, turbaned men leading camels, and my hearing strange minor-keyed music. Once, when I stopped to gaze at a statue, I looked up to speak to Papa and found I was holding a strange man's hand. I was terrified but soon found my parents.

When I was about five I began to beg for a baby brother and was given to believe that I might have one if I saved up my pennies. When I had saved nineteen cents he arrived and was named William Arthur Lofft. For quite a while I thought he belonged to me and dutifully fetched and carried for him. Was not my nineteen cents gone from the bank? One day the grocer at the corner offered to buy him from me with a box of candy. I flew home to fetch the baby, but to my surprise my mother wasn't as tired of caring for him as I was. My greediness subsided, for I really loved him too, but I decided to turn the entire care of him over to my amused parents. I think I first learned to love and appreciate the wonder of a child through my brother Arthur.

On the Fourth of July, when Arthur was just a month old, we were to have a picnic in Lincoln Park. But the weather turned cold and windy and Mama thought it not safe for so young a baby, so we turned back home, two disappointed little girls.

"Never mind," Mama consoled us, "we'll have a kitchen-floor picnic." And so we did.

Mama spread a cloth on the scrubbed kitchen floor and we were as happy as if we had gone to the park. Who ever heard of a kitchen-floor picnic?

Arthur grew into a charming little boy full of tricks and antics as all children are as they learn to talk and walk and feed themselves. When he had finished eating he used to put his plate on his head like a hat. Why this was so funny I don't know. But it was. This set the pattern for enjoying each succeeding baby in the highchair at table and it has gone on and on.

Chapter Two

While Arthur was still a young baby we moved back to Lapeer, the Michigan town where I had been born five years before on a cold blustery morning, March 14, 1889, to be exact. I showed many of the characteristics of the month of my birth. Stormy and bright by turns, impulsive, changeable, highly sensitive, given to fierce loyalties, rushing into things headlong and as quickly abandoning them. I must have been a trial to my parents but I remember little punishment, only quiet and serious talk to set me on the proper path.

I was full of romantic fancies, which I carried out with my doll, dressing her as a lady rather than as a baby, turning up her real hair in a braid, which I doted on because my own hair was sparse, straight, and limp. When I was able to sew a little I ·made her long dresses, usually with two sleeves for one arm and none for the other.

More than anything, I loved to read. Before I could speak plainly I spent hours on the floor looking at pictures in books of my father's—books too large for me to hold but convenient to page through while lying on my stomach. One was Gustave Doré's illustrations for stories of the Old Testament, another was Dante's *Inferno*, terrifying but fascinating. Best of all was a volume of bound copies of the *Magazine of Art*, published by Cassel and Company, Ltd., London, 1885. It was an education in itself. It contained pictures in endless variety: engravings of the New Forest, thatched cottages, architectural drawings, homes and churches in London, studies in the drawing of drapery, costumes of different lands and periods. There were reproductions of paintings by famous artists: Hogarth, David, Caldecott, Andrew Lang, Burne-Jones, and many others. I learned about

8

the stars called Pleiades because I kept seeing a painting of them by Elihu Vedder; in later years I saw the constellation through the telescope at Kansas University. There were Japanese prints, drawings of Greek vases, everything! I still have the book and know it by heart.

Going back to Lapeer was really going home. Both my parents had been born there. Grandpa Lofft, with his parents, his brother, and his two sisters, Kate and Elizabeth, had come to Canada from England when he was eighteen. He brought with him his trade of blacksmith, which had been handed down for generations from father to son. Grandpa was a gentle man. He was a great reader and spoke well, with the diction of an Englishman. At work he wore a long leather apron to protect his knees from the hot iron and the horse's hoof as he fitted the sizzling shoe. The smoke curled up and the not unpleasant smell of the burning hoof filled the shop, and Grandpa assured me it didn't hurt.

Grandpa sang in the church choir and was able to fill in where any male voice was missing. He was meticulous in dress, and on Sunday wore the proper long-tailed coat and striped trousers, wing collar, and white tie. The joke Grandma played on him by sewing ball fringe down the seams of his trousers is told in *Copper-Toed Boots*.

As far as we knew, until a few years ago, the family had been English for hundreds of years and the men made anchors for the great ships built at Sheerness, at the mouth of the Thames. Grandpa used to tell us about it on starry nights in summer. He was indentured to his grandmother after his grandfather died. According to the indenture, his grandmother was responsible for his moral behavior.

For a long time I felt that Lofft sounded more Teutonic than English, and when my name and picture were in the Philadelphia paper one evening I had a call from a young woman who said her name was Lofft and that she was Danish. Aha! I thought, perhaps we came to England with the Danes in the ninth century. It seems reasonable.

Grandma Lofft was of Scotch and Irish descent. Her father, James Sloan, and her mother (whose name I never knew, but whose picture I have) came to Canada from the north of Ireland and settled

9

in Goderich, Canada. She was the eldest of six children: Margaret, Sarah, Lizzie, Kate, Sue, and William.

Grandma (Maggie) Sloan met and married Grandpa Lofft on September 6, 1862, in Goderich, Ontario. I have their marriage certificate in spidery writing on yellowed paper. They moved in early married life to Lapeer. William was their first-born and my father the second.

Our family on Mama's side is descended from the first William Tuttle, who came from England to America in 1632. Tuttle was first spelled Tut-Hill (the hill of watching) and goes back to the tenth century. Saxon? Welsh? Who knows. It is interesting to speculate about.

That first William Tuttle's grandson was Jonathan Edwards, the famous New England preacher. And his grandson through the female line was Benedict Arnold! Then on through the male line to another William Tuttle, who was my great-grandfather. His son was Columbus Tuttle, my grandfather. He owned a mill where window sash and blinds were made and where a kitchen table and big ironing board were made for Mama when she was married. Both were in use as long as my mother lived and the table now stands in a back room in my sons' shop.

Mama's mother was Eunice Hough, a descendant of Edward Hough of Chester County, England. William, his son, came to Gloucester County, Massachusetts, in 1640. His descendant, Walter King Hough, went to Michigan with his wife, Nancy Kelley Hough, and his family in about 1833 by way of the Erie Canal to Detroit, and from there to Almont by ox cart. There he and his four brothers hewed out the forests, built a log cabin, which is still standing and in use, and planted apple orchards that still flourish.

A later Walter King Hough married twice. His first wife was my great-grandmother. She bore him six children. When she died he married again and his second wife bore him seven more children. Of the thirteen I knew eight.

One of the six children of Nancy Kelley Hough was my grandmother, Eunice Clement Hough, who married Columbus Tuttle. She died just before I was born, but I feel I knew her because she left a legacy of kindness and good works about which I have heard all my life.

Lapeer (named La Pierre by the French explorers because of the flint stone found there) was a small town of about two thousand. It was the county seat and on the main street, called Nipsing (Nepessing, Indian), there was an imposing neoclassic building that was the court house. It stood on a grassy lawn on which were smaller buildings housing lawyers' offices; one of them was Uncle Ben Perkins'. He had married Clara Hough, my mother's aunt.

Across the intersected street was the jewelry store owned by Uncle Denny, who had married another of Mama's aunts, Emma Hough. Uncle Denny used to come to Chicago when we lived there to buy jewelry, so I knew and loved him. Across Nipsing Street was Uncle Charlie's grocery store. Uncle Charlie was Mama's brother. Next but one, and on the second floor, was the photograph gallery Papa had taken over.

Down the block, and on the same side as Uncle Denny's store, was Uncle Steve's general store. Uncle Steve had married Anna Perkins, Mama's cousin. The store was like many country stores, with yard goods in the front, china, crockery, and kitchenware in the center, and groceries at the back. There stood the traditional cracker barrel and the great wheel of yellow cheese.

Each Saturday the farm women brought in their butter and eggs to trade for other commodities: salt, sugar, flour, coffee, tea, and such. Aunt Ella Tuttle (Uncle Ben's wife) made such good butter that Uncle Steve gave her top price the year-round—sixteen cents a pound at that time, I believe.

Mrs. Desireau, who lived out the Davison Road, also brought her butter to trade. She was something less than a perfect house-keeper, so, as Uncle Steve used to say, you could find almost anything in her butter, even ashes. He never sold her butter.

One day she asked Uncle Steve why she didn't get top price for her butter as Mrs. Tuttle did. "Well," said Uncle Steve gently, "if you will be as careful in making your butter as Mrs. Tuttle is, I'll give you top price."

Mrs. Desireau went home determined to get top price the next week. It was summertime, but there was always a wood fire in the black iron range. There were no gas stoves then. Several little tads ran about the kitchen with nothing on but summer shifts. Mrs. Desireau sat working the butter she had made to get the water out of it. She had to get up to mend the fire, so she set the bowl of butter on the floor under the table. One of the little ones slipped and sat down in the butter. With a sigh of impatience, Mrs. Desireau picked up the child, slatted the butter off into the bowl, and mournfully said:

"Butter'll have to go at the old price again."

This became a saying in our family, and to this day when something has gone less well than one had hoped—a sleeve cut wrong while sewing, a pie crust not flaky, a board sawed to short measure, a drawing that is not up to standard—we console ourselves with "butter at the old price" and start all over again.

Chapter Three

Back in Lapeer, Papa took over a photograph gallery from the former owner, keeping a room at the back for a studio, where he did the crayon and pastel portraits. He was an excellent photographer with an artist's eye for composition and lighting. But he was too easygoing and trusting to insist on the payment of accounts, which is incompatible with having a stable income.

At first we lived in a cottage near Aunt Sarah and Uncle John Hough's. It was not far from Grandma Lofft's or Aunt Emma's or from Uncle Charlie's. Indeed, it was not far from anything, because the town was small. Nina and I slept in the one upstairs bedroom, but I insisted on having a light, so an oil lamp was left on the floor of the landing near the stairs. Which was more frightening, the dark or the immense shadows cast upon the wall, I don't know, but my imagination peopled every corner.

During the time we lived in Lapeer we moved frequently, sometimes to a better house, sometimes to one not so nice as the one we had left. I suppose it depended on how many people wanted their photographs taken or whether, having been photographed, they paid up. When I was about seven we moved to a much nicer house called the Moore house and Papa went to New York to work for a time. We saw him only at long intervals and it was a very lonely time for Mama.

The house, besides having modern plumbing and spacious rooms, was set about with gardens such as we had not had before. As spring came we found a bed of daffodils, jonquils, narcissus that, wonder of wonders, came up by themselves. Later, as summer warmed, a rose bed leafed out, lavish with pink, white, and deep red roses, dusky and fragrant.

Marguerite, age seven, and her sister Nina, age eight.

It must have been then that we fell heir to Grandmother's square piano. I was taking lessons from Mrs. Vincent and was to perform at the spring recital by playing "The Happy Farmer," which I had practiced mostly by whirling around and around on the piano stool to fill in the half hour's time assigned me. Mama wore a cluster of the red roses at the waist of her brown taffeta and looked lovely. I cannot remember how my playing went. I know only that Mrs. Vincent said to Mama, "You might as well save your money on that child. She learns the piece I give her the first time she plays it, then never looks at the music again. She will never make a pianist." And that ended the music lessons for me. Nina, however, practiced as she was supposed to and later studied with Aunt Grace Hough, who was a graduate of Oberlin.

My cultural education was continued in another field, however. I was sent to Mrs. Carey to study elocution. We were taught social graces and coached for a playlet in which I sang "Come and Buy My

Oranges." Part of our enlightenment was in being served light refreshment as we sat at a small table and were taught to behave as ladies.

By now I was in school at the little second ward schoolhouse where Matey Vincent taught. I admired her neatness and the paper cuffs she wore to keep her sleeves clean. I not only imitated her wearing the cuffs, but added a paper collar and a tie of my father's. By the next day all the children wore paper collars and ties.

When I was about eight I was sent on Saturday mornings to Mrs. Corkery, the minister's wife, to learn painting with watercolor. There were several children in the class and we were given pictures to copy, but not encouraged to originate anything. I loved the painting, but was not quite satisfied with copying, so this adventure, too, came to an end.

Sundays I went dutifully to church and Sunday school, enjoying the stories and the singing. But it troubled me that there were so many different kinds of churches. Why couldn't there be just one kind if we were all supposed to be Christian? Even my dear grandparents went to the Methodist church instead of the Baptist as we did. I must admit that Papa didn't often go. I remember sitting through a church

Marguerite, seven, her cousin Clara, and Nina—dressed to the teeth.

service once, trying to listen to what the minister was saying. But my mind wandered toward the scroll pattern in plaster around the walls, to the stained-glass windows, and to the tiny squash pattern in the new calico dress I was wearing. As I fluffed up the full sleeves of my dress, I remember Mama's hand on mine to quiet me.

The stories in Sunday school were better. I loved the familiar ones about Abraham and Isaac, and of Joseph and his coat of many colors, and the beautiful Rachel.

Some of the customs puzzled me, but I put it down to childish ignorance of the world or of God and His ways. Somehow, I thought even then, that ritual and dogma (though I didn't know those words) had little relation to the immensity of the scheme as a whole and that someday things would be more clear to me.

After Papa came back from New York and again took the studio, we moved to a smaller house. But Papa was back home and we were all together again. Near us was a Methodist church and around the corner the Catholic church. From the former we often heard on warm nights the singsong testimonies of the congregation baring their inmost souls. Embarrassing revelations to my mind, lacking in the dignity and the reverence due the Almighty. From the Catholic church we heard the lovely sound of bells mixed, unfortunately, with howls from the red setter Papa had brought us.

When we moved, I could hardly wait to see what kind of rooms there would be. How would the kitchen look? Where would Nina and I sleep? Would there be a garden and trees to climb? Would we have a hired girl as we did sometimes? Would she take me home with her for Sunday? Wouldn't it be nice to help some lady during the week and go home to a farm on Sunday as the hired girls did? Maybe I would even go to dances in the big shed at Lake Nipsing. But Mama's voice held disapproval when she spoke of those dances. Perhaps I'd better not be a hired girl after all. It would be better to be a milliner like Minnie Yorker, to trim hats with feathers and flowers, with velvets and silks. Yes, that would be more interesting.

But, walking home with Papa from the studio, my hand warm in his pocket with his hand, the late sun shining on a red brick chimney, our cloudy breath making patterns in the air, I thought nothing could be better than to make pictures with paint or pastel. Then it seemed as if my spirit were too big for my body. I seemed lifted off the ground and skipped happily home to supper. Perhaps there would be hot biscuits. Life was wonderful.

I was now in the third grade at the big school where Ida Turnbull was the teacher. It was she who first said to me, "Marguerite, you're dreaming again."

Trying to make a paying business of photography and crayon enlargements in a small town was uphill work. But how I loved to go there after school, go into the darkroom with Papa and watch in the dim red light while the image gradually appeared on the plate as he developed it in the chemical solution. I can see his hands as he patted the water to wash the plates clean, then held them dripping in front of the light to see how they had come out.

Sometimes I went into the room at the back where he did the pastel work, and I kept very still as he drew from a photograph, enlarging the figure to make a portrait in color. I longed to do it myself. But now I knew better than to touch things Papa used in his work.

In about a year, we moved again to a more comfortable house on Main Street. Once again Papa had to give up the struggle to make a living with the photograph gallery. He took a position with the Standard Dry Plate Company, traveling far to the west and south, and after every trip bringing back to us fascinating stories of the people he had met, and of the customs and dialects so strange to our little Michigan town.

By then Mama had taught me to sew fine stitches, putting pieces together for a quilt. She told us how her Aunt Louise had promised her and a friend a dinner served on solid gold plates if they finished the quilt they had begun by a certain time, but as her Aunt Louise had known beforehand, they never got the dinner. I was sure, however, that *I* would finish my quilt. (Of course, I never did.)

Somehow I found that Emma Smith, a maiden lady who lived across the street, would help me cut out doll clothes and teach me how to put them together. There were several tries before I learned that the sleeve must be sewed in as cut, with the high, rounded part at the shoulder so it would hang straight instead of sticking out at right angles. Still, I did make fairly creditable dresses for the doll, and I enjoyed the company of Miss Smith and other adults more sometimes than that of my schoolmates, whose whispered

17

comments didn't interest me at all. At Miss Smith's we talked quietly about our work or went into the garden or had tea with Mrs. Smith, who was blind.

Whatever the season, spring, summer, fall, or winter, there was always something interesting to do. In springtime there were wild flowers to gather in the woods just beyond Main Street and along the road leading to Nipsing Lake. How thrilled we were to come upon arbutus hiding under dry leaves, or an occasional lady slipper or dogtooth violet.

In the summer there were picnics at the lake, family ones or with the Sunday school when we went in a great carry-all and had to walk down or up the steep hill to save the horses. Usually we went with Uncle Denny's family or with Uncle Charlie's. We had no carriage of our own. I can still hear the gritty sound of the wheels in the dust of the road and the slap of the reins on the horse's rump. It seemed a very long way from home as dusk gathered, especially if Mama wasn't there. But it was not more than two or three miles.

In the fall Nina and I went with our cousins Harold and Clara Tuttle to find butternuts, hazelnuts, and hickory nuts in the woods, coming home in the fading light, tired and happy with our treasure, kicking through the dry leaves and guiltily stealing grapes from the vineyard we had to pass through.

Whether we were on such jaunts as these, or were celebrating some holiday or event—in summer, picnics, in the fall, going to the woods, in winter, Christmas—I always paused in my thoughts from time to time to say to myself, "It's still going on," to get the last drop of enjoyment from being with people. (I still do.)

Once Grandpa Lofft slipped and fell into the lake as he was getting out of a boat. Grandma insisted that he walk home so he wouldn't take cold, and I couldn't bear it that he must go all that way alone. Yet, I didn't offer to go with him!

It was always pleasant to go to Grandpa Lofft's for family gatherings, as it was with Mama's family, although I didn't know as many of them. Some of Grandma's people still lived in Canada. Grandpa's brother, Alfred, lived there too, with his wife, Aunt Kate, and their sons. Grandma's way of doing things, which was New England style, was somewhat different from the Hough and Tuttle way. I suppose it was because of her Canadian upbringing. A child knows these things even if she doesn't quite know why or in what way. In cooking, I remember, Grandma's cakes and pies were not as light as those my mother made, but when we happened to be there for breakfast we had coddled eggs in little oval dishes like bathtubs, and we had cookies.

The house was especially pleasant at Christmas, when Grandpa set up the tree in the parlor and trimmed it with ancient ornaments and with candles in weighted lead holders to keep them upright. It was beautiful when lighted and filled with small homemade gifts such as aprons or potholders for the women and mittens and beads or scarfs for us children. Once Grandpa made me a sled of hard maple with shiny runners. That was special.

Grandma's table for Christmas dinner was beautifully set with her best china from the cupboard, which opened into both dining room and sitting room, good English ware, some of which I still have. Off one corner of the sitting room was the plant room, from which one went down to the cellar. The tall bookcase was against one wall, a bow window took up the other wall, and on the wide sill were house plants, which sent their damp fragrance through the house. This small nook was different from any place I've ever known. On the bookcase was a stereopticon into which we slipped doubled photographs of the same subject. When shown through the magnifying lense the photographs became three dimensional. In the little wall space, as one entered, there was a carved shelf on which stood a scroll-like toy showing changing pictures as the knob was turned. No radio or television then!

Occasionally we slept at Grandma's, up the steep stairs where Papa and Uncle Will used to sleep as boys, when Papa longed for copper-toed boots. Later, when we were older, Grandma put us in the guest room off the parlor. The white-painted bed had an iron-framed canopy Grandpa had built and Grandma had covered with ruffled, snowy dotted swiss. One felt snug and cozy there.

The kitchen smelled of spice, of apples and wood smoke, and of the finely chopped creamed potatoes on the back of the stove. I loved to be there when Grandpa came home, weary from his day's work at the forge, but smiling and good-humored.

Beyond the rose trellis Grandpa had a garden of vegetables that supplied the table all summer, beginning with asparagus in May and strawberries in June. At the back of the yard were bushes of currants, red, white, and black, and gooseberries and raspberries, which Grandma made into jam and served with toast at breakfast.

Once in a while, when we were at Grandma's for Sunday dinner, dessert was served out on the lawn. It was ice cream from Mac-Elroy's Bakery, sent the day before, packed in ice and salt. It was delicious and creamy and like no ice cream I've ever had since.

Across from Grandma's lived the Yorkers. Mr. Yorker was part of the firm of Yorker and Kaiser, furniture dealers and under-takers on Nipsing Street. Mrs. Yorker was a handsome woman who always made us welcome. They had three children, two girls and a boy, roughly the same ages as Nina and I. Often when we went there it was to read aloud from one of the Alger books or a magazine the Yorkers took, scornfully skipping the disgusting parts about *love.* Florence and I made up stories with our dolls and had tea parties with her doll dishes.

I was now in Teresa Loughnan's class at school. How I loved to look at her. She was beautiful. I can still see how her eyes sparkled when she smiled, which was often. Sometimes, when my attention wandered, she too would say, "Marguerite, you're dreaming again." Arithmetic held no terrors for me then and it was easy to remember the multiplication table. Easy too to memorize "The Vision of Sir Launfall" and "Abou Ben Adhem." I wish it were that easy now.

Suddenly I was eleven, then twelve. I had discovered the beauty of Shakespeare and read over and over passages from *Romeo and Juliet,* remembering the prints in Papa's book of *Magazine of Art* showing the balcony scene and the scene of farewell in the tomb. I tried to draw faces I saw in my mind, but found it baffling not to be able to make them convincing. It didn't occur to me to copy any I had seen in the book.

The urge to draw or to write constantly bothered me, because I could do neither in any satisfactory way, yet felt I *must.* I was not always careful where I used my pencil. Good paper was not easily available so I used what I could find—the fly leaf of a photograph mount or of a book, though I was usually careful about books. Not infrequently I elaborated a pattern in the wall-paper or decorated the back of a piece of music. Still, my efforts were anything but good. Oh well, I'd think, I'll just do something else. At times, if it suited me, the something else was to scrub the kitchen. It was so rewarding to see the clean white boards instead of the boys' footmarks. But not for a moment was I tied to my lowly task. I turned myself into a nice old lady, poor but proud and honest, living in a thatched cottage with geraniums on the window sill. All my life imagination has served to lift me above present circumstance, be it irksome duty or deep sorrow.

Once in a while I went over to Aunt Emma's on Saturday morning to help her and to scrub her kitchen. I never elected dusting. That I couldn't bear. To touch a dustcloth was like touching the felt piano cover. It made me shudder. There was the reward of appreciation at Aunt Emma's even though it was only her dear smile, and Uncle Denny might slip a quarter into my hand at noon when he came home for dinner. The three boys teased me, the girls made much of me, and at Aunt Emma's I always felt at home.

In summer my restless feet took me at times to visit Uncle Ben Tuttle and Aunt Ella. They lived at the edge of town on a farm, where they kept cows and horses, pigs, chickens and ducks.

Uncle Ben was Mama's oldest brother, a great bear of a man, good-humored, but bluff in manner and speech. He allowed me to follow him around as he tended the animals, milked the cows or fed the pigs with the swill kept in a barrel. It consisted of sour milk, apple and potato parings, and a dash of bran. The pigs devoured it eagerly.

I especially loved the baby pigs, pink and white with their curly tails, and I loved the soft lips of the horses when they nibbled carrots from my hand. I too ate the crisp carrots pulled from the earth and brushed off. Aunt Ella was the kindest of women, but rather shy, quiet-spoken, and of few words. I loved milk and when I finally got up the courage to ask, she would say, "Why of course," and immediately draw it from the udder-shaped glass containers in the special icebox that held only milk. The containers were suspended from the top of the box and had small faucets at the base. I've never seen another icebox like it. In that day ice was cut from the frozen ponds and lakes and packed in sawdust in the icehouse on the farm.

The milk intended for butter was kept in shallow pans in the springhouse so that the cream could be skimmed easily. It came off the milk in a great thick blanket. I loved to watch Aunt Ella skim it, put it into the churn, then work the dasher up and down, up and down until the sound changed and she knew the butter had come. Then she gathered the yellow lumps into a wooden bowl and with a smooth wooden paddle worked the water out of it, washed it with cold spring water, then salted it and shaped it into rolls.

In a storeroom upstairs there were always hickory nuts to carry in my skirt to the wide flat stone by the kitchen door, where I cracked and shelled them and ate the delicious meat, occasionally putting some into the cup for Aunt Ella's cake.

When Cousin Eddy went to the far field to fetch the cows, I went with him, gathering thorn apples on the way or hazelnuts if they were ripe.

As I write these words it is a beautiful day, but the wind is high, moaning and crying around the house. It recalls to me one time when I was down at Aunt Ella's for a day or two. "Down" because it was south of Lapeer and about a mile from home. I was already homesick. In fact, I was always homesick when away from home, yet, always ready to go the next time. Adventure always beckoned.

The weather had suddenly turned cold and windy, too cold to sit outside to play with my doll or to follow Uncle Ben about. He was off on a far field somewhere. I discovered Hawthorne's *Wonder Tales* and was lost in the Greek myths. My loneliness and the misery of being away from my mother fled.

My way home, next day, led up the hill into town past the unpainted shack of the Spicers, a family of little renown except for their lack of intelligence and their pitiful yearning for recognition and for beauty. All the children were named for members of the royal family of England, and their sense of beauty was expressed in the riot of petunias in the front yard, otherwise untended. The only names I remember are Princess Maud and Prince Albert, a town character, unshaven, untidy, and foolish, the butt of jokes. For years I didn't associate my dislike of petunias with that ramshackle place where they lived. Then, suddenly, it came to me. I threw off my snobbish prejudice and began to appreciate the lovely, colorful blooms.

Chapter Four

My closest friend at this time was Belle Lincoln. She was gay and pretty and lived in the block next to ours in a lovely house set in a wide lawn. Belle and I made all sorts of plans for our grown-up lives. She was to be the great pianist while I would play a golden harp. This conflicted somewhat with my secret desires to become a painter of miniatures, but then there was time for all things, I thought.

One afternoon we went skating on the flats just beyond her backyard. I was to be home before dark, but Belle and I went into the shanty in the corner of the field to get warm. A family of immigrants lived there, probably Hungarian as I remember, who welcomed us and invited us to share the family supper that sent out such delectable odors as it bubbled on the stove. We accepted and of course I was late getting home. It was after dark and I had been disobedient, so I was sent to bed. But I had the memory of that deliciously different meal and the fascination of hearing the strange accents to console me. The seed had been sown when I first met people of different background from my own at the World's Fair in Chicago.

When I was about eleven I was invited on a visit to Detroit, where Uncle Will, Papa's brother, lived with his family.

Uncle Will was very different from my father, not so easygoing and without a sense of fun and mimicry, nor the love of people characteristic of my father.

Uncle Will took Kate and me for a treat to a place called Wonderland. Just inside the door was a cage of small monkeys, something I had never seen before. The strangely human antics of those engaging creatures so delighted me that I had to be dragged

23

away to see more wonders—for one, a room that turned upside down after we had entered. I left reluctantly, but thought to myself, Oh well, I can see them again when we leave. But Wonderlands are not like that. One is beguiled into leaving by another door at the rear. I was so disappointed that Uncle Will thought me ungrateful for his effort at entertainment and let me know that he was quite annoyed.

I didn't realize it at the time, but many, many years later it came to me that it was then I had learned that one must make the most of things as they come along. One cannot go back or repeat an experience exactly. When one of my books was published, at first sight of the printed copy I noticed only the faults in it. I wished I might go back and do it over. Suddenly the whole picture of that afternoon in Wonderland came flooding back and I knew a lesson had been driven home that day.

This was about 1901, and while I was in Detroit that week I saw *five* automobiles. Even then I wasn't sure I hadn't seen one of them twice.

In the spring of 1902, when I was thirteen, Papa was transferred to a new territory. The Eastman Kodak Company had taken over the Standard Dry Plate Company and had assigned Papa to Pennsylvania. Papa left immediately for Philadelphia, from which he would travel throughout the state, not as a salesman but as demonstrator of the new product. The old glass dry plates, which had been used until then, were now being discarded for film. He was an excellent photographer and was sent to advise about lighting, composition, and especially to show the advantages of the film over glass—easier handling, no breakage, durable emulsion, and less storage space. I remember his telling of one of his first experiences with the new product. After a short talk on its advantages over the old method, he went into the darkroom with the photographer he was trying to convince. They developed the image on the film, then put it into the water bath, and the whole emulsion simply floated off. Papa was stunned. He said not a word—simply opened the door, lifted his hat from the rack, and walked out!

But it was not always like that. He discovered what had been wrong with the process and became very successful in his work. He was with the Eastman Kodak Company for thirty-six years, until his death.

During that early spring of 1902 there was a period of nearly a month when we stayed with various relatives while our household goods were en route to Philadelphia. Sometimes I was at Aunt Emma's or with Mamie and Elgin Turnbull, who lived on the edge of town, down the road from the court house. There Elgin's father's grist mill stood by the mill stream.

I loved being there because Mamie had always been a favorite with me and Cousin Elgin teased me and made me feel at home. Grandpa Turnbull, as we called him, was kind to us children. He allowed us to go to the top of the mill while he poured grain into the hopper. Then we tore down to see the great post turning as the water of the millrace roared through the sluice, turned it and sifted the grain between the millstones, grinding it to powder (flour).

What an odd name—Turnbull. I have always been interested in the origin of names, and many, many years later I came across the origin of Turnbull. Robert the Bruce, with his men, was crossing a field on some venture. An angry bull came full speed toward them and would have gored Robert the Bruce had not one of the men rushed forward, grasped the horns of the bull, and with a twist thrown him to the ground. Henceforth the man's name was Turnbull. There is a record of the incident to this day on a pillar of Jedburgh Abbey. One of the Turnbulls has seen it.

Much as I loved my cousin Mamie and her husband I missed my brothers and sister and our usual home life, though we met often at various suppers given us in farewell. It was exciting to have so much attention and to eat first at Uncle Charlie's, then Grandma Lofft's, then at Aunt Anna's. Another cause for elation was my first new coat not a hand-me-down, and a gray tam-o'-shanter to wear, warm and snug over my ears, for it was still cold in Michigan. It was the first new coat I remember. Always before I'd worn hand-me-downs of Nina's or Kate's.

A dressmaker had been engaged to make us dresses suitable for the coming spring in Philadelphia. I had two. One a blue madras, sailor-style, the other of green wool trimmed with red soutache braid. It was much longer and more suited to my rapidly increasing height than any I'd had before. We had new spring hats too, mine of coarse beige straw with a floating chiffon veil. Very fetching to watch as I passed a store window, very grown-up. But once, while I turned to see the veil lifted by the wind as I passed Uncle Charlie's store, I stubbed my toe on an edge of the pavement and went flat on my face. I could hear Mama say, "Pride goeth before a fall."

Altogether, there was much coming and going, but I could hardly wait for the day when we would start for Philadelphia. What would it be like to live again in a large city? I had been too young to appreciate the advantages of a city when we had lived in Chicago, although I remembered the World's Fair, Lincoln Park, and riding on a horsecar, when Mama had bought me a bisque doll in a store.

Chapter Five

The weeks of waiting passed and finally it was time to leave on our long journey. It was nightfall when we boarded the train for Buffalo, where we were to change from the Grand Trunk to the Lehigh Valley railroad, going by way of Canada and Niagara Falls. It must have been a trying journey for our poor mother. Walter was not quite a year old. Arthur was eight and Harry, six. Nina was over fourteen and I, thirteen. We didn't have the luxury of a Pullman, but slept in our seats and ate most of our meals from a box packed by Grandma. For one meal, at noon the next day, we went to the diner. What a thrill! By this time the train was climbing the mountains, so it was a test of skill to walk through several cars to the diner and to manage food on a table that constantly jiggled. The swaying train caused a queasiness that took the edge from hunger. Still, it was a great experience to eat on a train.

Back in our places, we began to long for the end of the journey. Mama sang quietly to Walter, who went to sleep, but we others made countless trips to the water cooler. The car was over-heated for mid-April, the season more advanced than in Michigan, and my new wool dress was too warm. The dusty feel of the plush seat was unbearable. I stood on the platform with my face against the crack of the door to feel the cool air. The motion of the train as it went around and around the mountain near Tamaqua, where we stopped for passengers, was sickening.

Tamaqua? What a funny name. We took turns at the window to see the marvelous view; it was like being in heaven and looking down. Far, far below was the new green of April spread out in fields and woods, neatly squared off in orderly patterns, quite different from the countryside of Michigan, which was still in a more or less pioneer state, with stump fences quite common. Stump fences were made from the up-ended roots of trees that had been cut to clear the land. The houses too were different. They were of clapboard, like New England houses. Pennsylvania farmhouses were of stone, very plain but sturdy, as if they had been there for a long time, as indeed they had. We were all impressed. Arthur whispered, "Mama, is it the Promised Land?"

Would we ever come to Philadelphia? As afternoon passed we began to go through thickly settled country with factories and endless buildings and we knew we were nearing the city.

It was late afternoon when we reached Philadelphia and the great blackened shed where we got off the train and walked the long platform toward the station. And there was Papa. . . . How wonderful to see him again.

At last! At last we were here. Here in Philadelphia, where there were crowds of people coming and going, no one seeming to know anyone else. Stores and stores on both sides of the street and a trolley car marked "Baring St.," which was to take us home.

Home? Where was home? What would it be like? The boys sat quietly in the trolley, wonder-stricken. They had never seen a trolley before. In about three quarters of an hour we reached Fifty-fifth Street and Lancaster Avenue, our stop. It was still light, and I remember how we trailed down the poplar-lined street to the house that was to be our home, 1711. How could we be sure which was ours? They were all alike. But Papa knew. Row after row of red brick, with porches separated by a railing, some raised higher as the street climbed toward Lancaster Avenue, so when we reached our house the one next door was about three feet higher than ours.

I was so excited I could hardly breathe, but not too excited to see people on one or two porches who looked at us rather curiously, knowing we must be the new neighbors.

We stood for a moment while Papa unlocked the door, then went in through the tiled entry (later I learned it was called a vestibule), then into a long narrow hall where we dropped our suitcases and bags and parcels. Tired as we were, we must see the whole house right away. Where would the dining room be? The kitchen, the parlor? But here was the parlor just off the hall where we stood.

Papa had worked very hard to make the house seem like home. There by the window stood Mama's little ebony table with its pink vase. Just inside the door was our familiar old square piano with

28

its faded rose-felt cover. Along the wall was the green sofa, and standing on a new flowered carpet were the oval-backed chairs that had been Grandma Tuttle's. The big armchair that used to be in Papa's studio was by the window. Best of all was the crystal chandelier that Papa lighted to show its shimmering, glittering cut-glass pendants reflecting the gaslight. Gaslight! No more oil lamps to fill and clean? What luxury.

In the dining room at the end of the hall was more excitement. New furniture. A new square table instead of the old oblong one, and a new sideboard. It was almost dark there because the windows opened on a lightwell between the houses. Almost near enough to touch was the house next door. Over the table hung a Tiffany lamp with a large domed shade of colored glass that glowed with the light from the gas mantle. I saw one like it the other day in the window of an antique store for sale at a hundred dollars.

In the kitchen was a new gas range that needed only the touch of a match to get the fire going. Not only that, there was a coal range set into a niche and here Papa had built a fire that shed a welcome warmth on this chilly nineteenth of April, 1902. He had also put into the oven a roast of beef before leaving for the station. Next to the stove was a new icebox filled, Papa said, by a man who brought ice when needed.

The boys were ahead of us exploring the lean-to, containing an enclosed toilet and washtubs, where Papa had installed a new hand-propelled washing machine.

We followed out into the small backyard surrounded by an eight-foot-high board fence with a gate opening on an alley that led to another street.

There was still the upstairs to see. We children raced up the stairs, and by the time Mama and Papa followed we had already looked into the front bedroom and exclaimed over the new bureau, brass bedstead, and mirrored closets, where one could see one's whole self. This was to be our parents' room. In the room back of it Walter's crib had been set up all ready for him.

The bathroom with its tin tub was already familiar. We'd had one like it in the big house in Lapeer. There was another room at the end of the hall entered through paneled doors, a large sitting room that looked out toward Lancaster Avenue and the backs of the houses on another street. There wasn't much furniture: the marble-topped table with a lamp on it, a small desk, and one or two chairs. But there was a fireplace and a fire of coals, which made the room homelike at once. Here we could gather and read and, as I was to find out, do our homework.

We were all hungry, but wanted to see the rest of the house, for there was a third floor and it was there we children were to sleep. Nina and I in the front bedroom and the boys in the back room, where the one window looked out above the lightwell. We were fascinated with the tiny window shutters like those in the parlor, and it was only when the time came to dust them that we thought them rather a nuisance. But in summer we found them useful in keeping out the hot sun and letting in the air.

In the clothes closet I found my doll box, but suddenly I felt I was too old for dolls. It was sad, for I had loved the make-believe of playing with dolls. But there it was. I no longer wanted to.

We children entered Heston School, which was only two blocks away on Fifty-fourth Street. To our dismay we were each set back in a lower grade, I in sixth grade and Nina in seventh. I have forgotten what was missing in our list of subjects, but we had not had music as taught in the Philadelphia schools, or sewing, though when I sewed my stint to show the teacher I was far ahead of the others in fine stitchery. I just didn't know the various gores and gussets, pleatings and stroking gathers as taught in the sewing course. I soon learned.

I loved the teacher, Miss Massey Frailey, and things seemed new and exciting, just because they were different. For example, there was a pretzel man outside the school who sold soft salty pretzels for a penny. We had books provided by the school board, and my treasured geography, the first new schoolbook I'd ever had, was not needed. It was different from the one they used in Heston School.

There were many other things that were different from Lapeer, to be had for the asking. Wonderful things. A few blocks north on Fifty-second Street was the entrance to Fairmount Park. We were allowed to go there and to the 1876 Centennial Exhibition buildings still standing, Horticultural Hall and Memorial Hall. To enter Horticultural Hall was to have a foretaste of paradise. It was filled with a moist and fragrant warmth in which grew tropical plants, palm trees that reached the glass roof, orchids of many varieties, camellias, jasmine, and gardenias, none of which we had ever seen. I can still smell those exotic blooms, still see the ambient light enfolding them because of the glass walls and roof.

Memorial Hall was just a step away, and we found there more than one could imagine to gaze and wonder at.

In the large entrance hall were suits of armor, which time and story had wrapped in romantic fantasy. There were enormous vases from China, a marble sarcophagus with carved figures on the sides. Who had lain there? Where would it have been kept? In the center of the hall stood a marble pulpit with stairs leading up to the lectern. I used to marvel at it and wonder who had preached from that height and where. In adjoining great rooms were cases displaying chinaware, fragile and delicate, with beautiful decoration and design.

On a lower floor there was an exhibit of costumes, mostly eighteenth century, if I remember correctly. In one case was the dress worn by Hannah Penn, which was of great help to me many years later when I did the book called *Thee, Hannah!*

There were several ancient carriages of an earlier period, worn with use, the leather upholstery rubbed thin. In a small enclosure of its own was an exhibit of dolls with china or bisque heads, their dresses crushed into folds by a child's loving arms. Along one wall was a series of box-like arrangements with a peephole in the top through which one could see the ruins of Pompeii, bodies lying in disarray caught by the falling hot ashes. Gruesome, but fascinating. We went to Memorial Hall almost every Sunday afternoon.

Always I saved until last the exquisite joy of looking at the paintings in the art gallery of the museum. Oh, to be able to paint, to capture the loveliness of the hillside and woodland, the delicacy of shadow and light in a portrait.

Those Sunday afternoon trips to Memorial Hall always brought to the surface of my mind the need to draw and to write. I made many attempts to draw something meaningful, but had not yet learned that one must settle on a certain subject, work at it and stay with it until it yields to one's effort. Of course, one could draw anything. But what?

I should have remembered Jacob's struggle with the angel when he said, "I will not let thee go until thou bless me." But it took me a long time to learn that.

Usually, by the time we had come to the art gallery my sister and my little brothers were weary of looking but I wanted to stay and stay. Once, when only Harry was with me, I could not tear myself away so I told him to go on home by himself. He was hardly out of my sight when I realized what I had done to allow a six-year-old boy to go alone that long way home along Fifty-second Street and across Lancaster Avenue. I flew after him, but he was nowhere to be seen. I ran all the way home. But he had arrived before me. I know exactly what he looked like, in his knickers and long black stockings, his sailor collar and black tie. I can still see his mischievous smile at having outrun me.

Out of breath and disgraced for thoughtlessness, I listened ruefully to the deserved scolding. Enthusiasm and impulsiveness have always led me down the garden path. Sometimes to a rose bed. Sometimes to trouble.

We discovered the public library. It was not far away, just below Fifty-second Street, and on my first visit there I saw an original illustration in black and white of knights in armor that sent me into an ecstatic dream. Perhaps someday I could do a drawing as well. I remember it to this day. It was in the style of Howard Pyle, though I couldn't have known that then. I was given a library card and could take out books and keep them for two weeks.

It was a marvel to have access to a real library where books were lent as often as needed, where the librarians gave willing help to find the books one wanted. We'd had no library in Lapeer such as they have now.

My reading at this time was largely undirected and consisted mostly of romantic novels such as *Prisoner of Zenda, When Knighthood Was in Flower,* and others of a similar nature. Interspersed were Kipling, the stories of Kate Douglas Wiggin, and Andersen's *Fairy Tales,* which I had not quite outgrown. We had *Pearson's Magazine, Scribner's,* and *The Saturday Evening Post,* in which I read Corra Harris's "Circuit Rider" stories. They were particularly interesting because of the illustrations by Walter Everett and Howard Pyle, whose names became familiar and significant to me much much later in life.

Papa brought books home fairly often to add to our collection. One book on our own shelves was a recurring source of interest and amusement. It was called *Gems for the Fireside.* In it were all the nineteenth-century poets: Longfellow, Lowell, Tennyson, as well as stories in dialect, some in German-broken-English, whose titles are now gone from me. Two that stay with me are "Jimmy Butler and the Owl," and "The Little Rid Hin," known to today's children as "The Little Red Hen." We loved to hear Papa read them aloud, especially because the dialect lost nothing in Papa's reading. When I had children of my own, and we were living in Winnipeg, I wrote Papa asking him to copy out for me "The Little Rid Hin" so I could read it to my own children. He replied by sending an illustrated hand-printed copy. The illustrations were done in water-color and wonderfully alive. It seems a pity that he didn't make more use of his truly rich gift for drawing and illustration and all the rest.

Sunday mornings we walked to the Baptist Sunday school. It was a good mile from home, but we thought nothing of that. Mama had brought her letter from Lapeer and joined the Blockley Baptist Church after a call from the minister. He was a meeching sort of man from whom I fled in terror for fear he would ask me about my immortal soul and urge me to join the church and thus, in public, to bare my deepest thoughts. To me, one's prayers and thoughts about God were sacred and private. Saying one had been "converted" seemed ridiculous since I had always been not only reverent in thought, but had credited God with the moments of ecstatic joy that often filled me. The sickening, sentimental way in which Jesus was mentioned left me ashamed and disturbed. My thought was not clear enough to express, but to me the majesty with which He was clothed suffered from such bandying about of His name. Of course I didn't hear this at home. Grace at table was simple and natural and always the same.

Finally, joining the church seemed the thing to do. I was immersed, and with my sister became a member of the church. Not because I had become "converted," but to please my mother and to be done with it. So I became a Baptist, but I kept my own thoughts.

I had always loved the Bible, although I didn't read it con-sistently day after day or by chapter and verse. But the wonderful stories of the Old Testament fascinated me. I loved the majestic language of the King James Version and was able even as a child to make allowances for the apparent inconsistencies (according to our way of thinking and living), knowing that the accounts had been told and retold by human beings and were necessarily colored by human thought and experience. This was more feeling than conscious thought, but always there seemed to be a core of truth, a sense of universality that was comforting and sustaining. In later years reading and discussion helped to reveal my thought and to express what I had always believed.

Chapter Six

Spring in Philadelphia was quite a different matter from spring in Michigan, where the season came in hesitantly, as if shy about showing her glory. In Philadelphia it was sudden and often as warm as summer, with high humidity. School became a burden. So did our winter clothes. Children soon adjust themselves to new conditions, however, and the advantages of the city far outweighed the strangeness.

As spring warmed into summer the heat became really oppressive, with a heavy haze lingering through the morning. There were violent thunderstorms that first summer, which often left the air more still and hot than it had been, very different from the clear air and blue skies of Michigan. The poplars along the street dropped their leaves. Men in white suits swept the streets with great wide brooms, gathering the dirt and horse droppings, the leaves and sticks, into piles for the wagons to carry away. Sprinkler carts came along, spreading a cooling spray. Children ran out to catch the welcome drops, and for a little while there was relief from the heat. The horses wore straw hats with wet sponges underneath to keep out the heat, and at certain street corners water troughs stood where they could drink.

Hucksters called their wares all day long: "Banana-a-a-s!" "Fresh cor-r-r-n!" "Rags-and-ol-arn!"

Mama kept the wooden shutters bowed during the day to keep out the sun, and the semidarkness gave an illusion of shade and coolness. In the evening, windows and doors were opened to let in the slightly cooler air. We sat on the porch after dinner as did all the neighbors. Sometimes we talked with the people next door, but usually each family kept to itself, preserving an imagined privacy.

Philadelphia is well known for its conservatism, and at first Mama found it hard to make friends. She was busy with household cares and the church was too far away for her to be active in the women's services during the week. Papa was traveling throughout Pennsylvania much of the time, though he had a desk in town at the Eastman store.

We children were soon acquainted with the boys and girls of the neighborhood who seemed to enjoy coming to our house, where they always found a welcome. We girls were allowed to make lemonade, fudge, or taffy and there were molasses cookies to share. Sometimes in early evening we played games. Sometimes Nina played for us to sing around the old piano. There were picnics in the park and rides on the park trolley. It was delightfully cool as we sped through the fragrant moist greenery. It cost five cents for the round trip.

Papa introduced us to the pleasures of Willow Grove, which was a two-hour ride on the trolley, going through new and unfamiliar parts of the city and into the country. It was more than an amusement park. There was an open-air concert pavilion where Sousa's band or Victor Herbert's orchestra played afternoon and evening. Their music was tuneful and haunting, as different from today's rock-'n'-roll as were the ankle-length dresses from today's mini-skirts.

Nina and I were suddenly big girls and were required to do our share of the work: make beds, help with the dusting, set the table and wash the dishes, and help with the ironing, of which there was a good deal. The style of the times required the wearing of several petticoats, starched, and, in summer, ruffled and tucked dresses, and besides this there were boys' blouses, household linen, and shirtwaists.

Much as I loved cleanliness and order, I disliked the routine of housework, and as for disorder I was often the worst offender, leaving scraps of paper behind me covered with attempts at drawing or writing. Mama used to say, "That child! She leaves everything at her heels. It's heads or tails all over the house."

The crystal chandelier in the parlor was another matter. We loved it, *but*, periodically, it must be cleaned: every crystal removed, washed in soapy water, rinsed and dried, then re-hung. But oh, how it sparkled and shimmered!

I so well remember the many new experiences of those early

years in Philadelphia: how exciting it was to see Independence Hall and the Betsy Ross house, to imagine how the people looked and dressed as they walked on the very stones where we walked, touched the walls we touched, and wore the very shoes and clothes displayed in cases. I remember the feeling of awe as we first stood by the Liberty Bell and wondered what it had been like to hear it ring out in those exciting days when the country was new.

Many of the foods we ate were new to us. We discovered the deep, rich purple eggplant, its color and form as appealing as its taste. There was pepper pot and scrapple and sticky buns at a penny a piece to be eaten at recess; pretzels with coarse salt sprinkled over them, folded to resemble a child's hands crossed in prayer. Our Sunday roast was now pin bone instead of rib. It was less expensive and more tender, but one had to buy not less than seven pounds to make it worthwhile, because the bone was the same size whatever the weight of the roast.

I can still see my father as he carved the roast. He liked food and served it with a certain grace that showed his appreciation of Mama's careful cooking and a certain reverence for the bounty provided. We learned to go about the neighborhood to find the best place to buy: Seemuller's for ice cream carried home in a bowl; Scarlett's for meat, and for Louella butter, the Acme.

Once when a friend, Charlotte Roy, and I were on an errand, we passed a house on Lansdowne Avenue where, Charlotte said, there had been a tragedy during the summer. Daniel, the little boy, had been drowned in the heavy surf in Atlantic City. The sister, Anna, was deaf and away at school. The mother had been a girlhood friend of Charlotte's mother. As we passed she pointed out the sign announcing JOHN DE ANGELI, TEACHER OF VIOLIN. "The older brother," she said. "The father runs the Steel Pier in Atlantic City." Sad, the little boy drowning, I thought, never thinking I would one day know the family.

In our second summer Nina was sent back to Lapeer to stay with Uncle Ben and Aunt Ella to comfort them for the loss of their daughter. She was gone all summer. It was hoped that the dryer climate would improve Nina's somewhat delicate health. But, on the contrary, she became really ill. She had contracted tuberculosis, and had a gynecological problem as well. Today it could be taken care of very simply.

In the fall I was moved up with Nina to Miss Winnemore's

eighth-grade class. Nina excelled in all the things in which I was deficient: arithmetic, history, music. She found most difficult the things I liked best: drawing, composition, English. We studied about the Vikings, which fascinated me, and when we were asked to write a composition about their voyages and discoveries I received the highest mark in the class, but mine was the only one that was illustrated with drawings.

Many years later, when I was about to write *The Black Fox of Lorne*, I asked my husband, Dai, to go to Leary's, a famous old bookstore, to see if he could find anything helpful for me as research material. He telephoned me to say he had a certain book, but wasn't sure whether it would be of any help.

"Is it by Du Chaillu?" I asked. When he said that it was, I was astonished that I knew the name of the author. It had just come out without my thinking about it, but it must have been the same book from which we had studied in the eighth grade.

Chapter Seven

In the fall of 1904, Nina and I entered Girls' High School together, she in the general course and I in the classical, with Bryn Mawr as my intended goal for college. We had some classes together, and we went back and forth to school on the trolley.

Home from school, we began our study immediately after a snack of bread and peanut butter or cookies and milk, studying until midnight, with the exception of time out for dinner and dishwashing. It was a strenuous schedule; there was written homework for nearly all subjects. I was taking French, German, and Latin besides English and mathematics, all of which were everyday subjects, and botany, drawing, music, and gymnasium once a week. Papa used to help us, me with mathematics and Nina with composition. We sat in the second-floor living room near the coal fire in the grate or at the small desk or around the center table. Mama was often asleep on the couch after her long day of caring for the little boys, cooking and cleaning. On Friday or Saturday evenings we might have company if lessons were finished. On Saturdays there was baking to be done besides the other work. As we grew older I baked the bread, Nina the cakes, and Mama the pie. The bread was set to rise Friday night, then kneaded in the morning, divided into loaves, set to rise again, then baked an hour.

One day when I was looking for something of Mama's to wear with my shirtwaist, I opened her bureau drawer (a thing I had no right to do in the first place). I discovered there, carefully folded, tiny, new baby clothes. Then I knew. Another child was to be added to the family. Yes, I had noticed Mama's changing figure, that she went out hardly at all, but, ignorant as I was at sixteen, it hadn't dawned upon me that there was a specific reason for it. Anger flashed through me. I couldn't bear it. Another child, when there

Marguerite at fourteen or fifteen.

were already five of us? And I, a great grown girl. Gradually, I simmered down. There it was. I couldn't change it, so I accepted the fact. My anger evaporated. I began to look forward to the new baby.

The day of his arrival was just after we had gone back to school, but fortunately on a Saturday. Walter, who was then four, was taken over to Hopper's across the street. He was a special favorite there, and he loved the minister's great Saint Bernard. Nina and I were asked to take the other boys, Arthur and Harry, to the park to play tennis. Papa sent us off with a box of crackers and peanut butter and told us to stay all afternoon. When we came home there he lay beside Mama, another beautiful baby boy, perfectly formed even to his tiny fingernails. I marveled at his perfection. His name was John Richard Lofft, but we called him Dick.

Not long after this, one rainy afternoon, Nina was playing some of Papa's songs and I began to sing, making believe I was an opera singer, sending my voice deep down and holding forth in full volume as if to fill a great hall. It was fun. Nina nodded her head in approval and I sang louder than ever, one song after another.

She was an excellent accompanist, following the pause and emphasis of my singing. We had a great time.

Suddenly, the doorbell rang. I went to answer it and found there Mr. Hopper, our neighbor. I invited him in and started to call Mama, but he said no, he wanted to talk to me! He came quickly to the point. He had heard our little concert and thought I would fit into the quartet they were just forming for the Presbyterian church choir. Sarah Price, who lived in the next block, was to be the soprano. Horace Price (no relation) was to be organist. I would be the contralto, provided I began studying voice. Would I accept? *Would* I?

The elation brought on by the singing grew and my spirits soared. I couldn't wait to tell Mama and Papa. All thought of drawing or writing flew out of my head. I was to be a singer. I was to be paid a dollar a week and to begin as soon as I had found a teacher. A girl at school who sang beautifully recommended Madame Suelke, who lived and taught on North Sixteenth Street, not far from Girls' High School. Papa agreed to help pay for the lessons and I was to contribute the dollar a week earned from the church singing. I was accepted as a pupil and my life took on a new and exciting turn.

I found Madame Suelke a delightful, motherly type of person. Even I, inexperienced as I was, recognized her ability. She taught that singing should be a natural process, not forced, but flowing easily from an almost inexhaustible source of breath.

This afternoon, as I write, I have just been singing, at my husband's earnest plea, an old song marked by my teacher so long ago. It recalls her as she was then, a large woman, seated on the piano bench close to Marian Ritchie, the accompanist, erect and at ease, her arms outstretched, her eyes closed, her head moving slowly from side to side as she demonstrated for me the way to interpret a passage from the oratorio "Elijah, O Rest in the Lord." How to have endless resource in breathing, distinct diction, deep tone. Marian was always there with a supporting note when one was unsure, accommodating her playing to the singer's peculiar modulation and tempo. There was a tendency on my part to sing too slowly, and for a long time I couldn't understand what Madame meant by "lift."

"Never mind," she said, "it will come to you all of a sudden—sometime when you are doing something else, perhaps when you are washing dishes."

And so it did. Suddenly, singing as I washed the supper dishes, I expanded my rib cage as I had not knowingly done before. That was it! Lift. When I remembered how to do it, it seemed as if I could sing on that one breath, endlessly, easily, enunciating clearly and without effort. This was the secret of Madame Suelke's success in teaching—the ease in singing in contrast to a more forced method that would soon thicken the vocal chords and destroy the voice.

During summers, which she spent in Cape May, she coached such well-known singers as Madame Fremstad, Madame Sembrich, and others.

This was my introduction to the world of oratorio, cantata, aria. There were hours of practice, singing scales up and down over a fairly large range, though I was happiest in the lower register. Nina played accompaniments for me and taught me again the placing of notes on the piano, which I had forgotten. With her help I managed to keep up with the others in the choir.

There were Mite Society meetings at which I sang, sometimes alone, sometimes in duet with Sarah Price. These were held in church in the Sunday school room once a month as social events, mainly to keep the young people interested. Occasionally, I was invited to sing at other social gatherings, all of which helped to give me confidence in public singing.

Horace Price began to pay me attention and often walked to school to save his carfare so that he could treat me to soda or candy. He entertained us with his piano playing and accompanied me as I sang, but Nina was better at that. She knew instinctively where to pause and where to supply the right note at the right time, while Horace was more intent on his piano playing than upon following me.

It must have been the next June, after my seventeenth birthday, that Madame Suelke suggested I try out for the contralto position that was open at the Madison Street Methodist Church in Chester, Pennsylvania. Chester was only fourteen miles from Philadelphia and the church was near the station. I would be home from choir practice by 9:30 and would return to the Fifty-second Street station, where Papa would meet me so I would not be alone on the street at that hour. My tryout was successful and I began the routine of rehearsal on Friday nights and two services on Sunday. Margaret MacDowell was the soprano and she and I immediately became friends. The bass and tenor are vague memories, except that I was continually running on my way to and from the station to escape the attentions of the tenor, who also came from Philadelphia. Once he said to me, "I've been chasing that red skirt all the way from the station." But he didn't catch me.

It seemed best for me to spend Sundays at Mrs. Riley's boarding house. I met a number of fine people there, some who came only for Sunday night supper. Among them were Mary and Besse Howard, who were our neighbors in Philadelphia nearly sixty years later.

The minister's sermons were long and boring. I think he never preached a sermon without alluding to dens of vice and hells of iniquity, whatever they were. I didn't know what hells of iniquity were, but I imagined a group of reclining figures smoking opium, of which I had heard. It seemed an inappropriate subject for so highly respectable, upper-middle-class a congregation. It didn't occur to me at the time that he might be directing his remarks to the boys from Chester Military Academy, who sat in two straight rows under the pulpit, their gray-caped long coats sedately hanging from their shoulders, hair clipped and shining, grave, unsmiling faces looking straight ahead, chins in, shaven necks stiff, proclaiming their youth and—innocence?

I was always in a dither for fear I would miss the train either from Fifty-second Street or the connecting one from Thirtieth Street and be late for service.

One morning, as I was flying out the door, with Mama close behind to see me off, I caught my dimity dress on the door latch and tore it down the side a good six inches. It was quite new, and very pretty, Mama's handiwork, with lace set in at the neck and sleeves. I burst into tears. Mama was there in an instant with needle and thread. "There, there," she soothed, "it will be all right, the gathers will cover the stitches and it will never show." In no time I was off and made the train.

By fall I had met some of the members of the congregation through Margaret MacDowell, one of them a boy from the military academy. There were occasional dances at the academy to which he invited me. These affairs were well chaperoned and I was allowed to go with him and to stay the night at Mrs. Riley's, where I dressed before the party. One night I had some misgivings about the petticoat I had taken with me because the buttonhole was torn and my best one had not been laundered. I made do with a safety pin, which was contrary to all I had been taught.

Woe is me. Just when I was feeling quite elegant, whirling in a waltz with one of the boys, the safety pin gave way and down slipped my plain, untrimmed petticoat to the floor. I gathered it up swiftly and under the protection of Margaret, my chaperone, I fled to the ladies' room. I was mortified, as we used to say, but it taught me a lesson. Thereafter I mended my clothes after ironing, as I'd been told.

Quite a deep affection developed between the boy and me. I attended several other parties with him as the winter went on. It lasted half a year or so, until one day in a letter to me he spelled out plans that didn't include me. My pride was hurt. I didn't answer his letter for a while. Then, fearing he might think it mattered to me, I answered coolly, with plans of my own, such as going to Michigan to visit. And that was that.

I met several other young men at Margaret's house later who came to Philadelphia to beau me about, but formed no attachment to any of them.

The next summer when I was seventeen, I wanted to go to Lapeer to see my grandparents and other relatives. Vacation from choir would be in August. I couldn't expect Papa to pay for my train fare. The meager salary from the church barely covered carfare to and from Chester and to my singing lessons. I must earn some money. But how? Nina at this time was playing accompaniments for the pupils of a dramatic school. What could I do? When I spoke of getting a job, my parents discouraged me. "Your mother needs you at home," Papa counseled me. But I was heedless. I searched the newspaper for want ads and found that Snellenburg's needed "contingent" help for their white sales. Early in the morning I started out.

The day was hot as only Philadelphia in June can be hot, but nothing daunted me. I set out in high-collared shirtwaist and gray wool skirt to answer the ad. Mama again tried to dissuade me, but I was determined. Did I detect a slight smile on Mama's face as I flew out the door?

My application for work was accepted and I was taught how to make out a sales slip and told that it was the custom to wear a black skirt, but that for one day I could wear what I had on. Then I was put to work in the lingerie department selling corset covers at twenty-seven and a half cents apiece. Was I to deal with *fractions* all day? I was. Women flocked to the sale and I was

43

besieged with orders for two, three, a half dozen. Each time I had to deal with that half cent. All day long the floor manager shouted, "Where's that girl in the gray skirt?" I doubt if I wrote one sales slip without a mistake somewhere. Fractions had always baffled me.

The day finally ended. But could I go home? No. There were all those counters full of mussed garments that had been handled and left. They must be straightened and ready for the next day, and covered with striped dust sheets.

About six o'clock I left by the rear door, as employees were supposed to do, and emerged, a perspiring, exhausted wreck, into a pounding thunderstorm. I had no energy left for my usual terror of lightning and thunder, nor for irritation at waiting for the open trolley. I was numb with fatigue and sat all the way to Fifty-fifth Street in a state of oblivion, rain-soaked and bedraggled. As I walked the two blocks home from Lansdowne Avenue, tears of self-pity streamed down my face. I entered the house by way of the back door for fear someone would see me.

Both my parents were in the kitchen, where I slumped down into a chair and burst into sobs. Papa put his arm around me to comfort me and Mama offered a glass of milk, while I told them about the twenty-seven and a half cents. They both began to laugh, and I too laughed through my tears. I was so glad to be home. I could see how funny it was.

"Now," Papa said, "you see what we mean. You are much more suited to helping Mama, who needs you." And that was the end of my business career, except for a ride downtown to collect the dollar I had earned. Of course trolley fare was then five cents and a good lunch could be had for a quarter, so I was ahead a few cents at least.

Papa made it possible for me to take my vacation in Michigan, where I was most welcome and where I surprised everyone by walking down the stairs like a lady instead of coming down three steps at a time as I had done in the past. My singing was made much of, and I came home with a sense of having outgrown my childhood awkwardness. I returned with a determination to work hard at school, to make the most of my singing, and to act grown-up.

I found when I reached home that Horace Price's allegiance had switched to Nina. It was just right, as far as I was concerned. Later he married her.

When school began I hoped I would find it easier to keep up with the class in the two most difficult subjects I carried—geometry

44

and Latin grammar. But it became increasingly hard. A new ruling had been put into practice. If you failed in a recitation you must stay after school, study, then recite perfectly before going home to begin studying for the next day and preparing homework. For two weeks I managed to keep from failing. Then one day I failed, not in geometry or Latin, but in German, and was told to stay.

What should I do? It was the day for my singing lesson and I was due at Madame Suelke's in twenty minutes, just time to walk there. As the girls passed out on their way home, I was left standing alone in the corridor, miserably unhappy, undecided, and weeping. I couldn't bear to miss my music lesson and I was sick to death of the pressure of study: Latin declensions, German grammar, incomprehensible geometry. What would happen if I just walked out? I would miss the once-a-week drawing class and I would miss my English teacher, Miss Steele. But at last I decided that the singing lessons were more important to me. I left the building, determined never to go back. I remembered that now I couldn't go to Bryn Mawr, but it couldn't be helped. I only hoped that my parents wouldn't insist that I go back.

Tears kept falling all the way to Madame Suelke's, and of course when I arrived there I was in no condition to sing. My teacher was sympathetic and consoling, however, with quiet talk and advice.

She said, "You have a very fine voice and can go far, but I'm afraid you will be like your mother. You will probaby marry and have six children." How right she was!

After the hour's ride home I was a little more calm and was relieved when my declaration was received quietly and soberly, and with little comment. I'm sure that both Mama and Papa understood that the long hours of study and my difficulty with the precise requirements of Latin grammar and mathematics had taken their toll. I had grown very tall and thin, looking, as Papa said, like a yard of pump water.

Nina had already left high school for a business course, so my help at home was welcomed.

There have been many times when I have regretted that decision. Still, I have done a great deal of study on my own in research for my work, and while it was not the directed study at the same academic level it would have been had I gone to college, it has served its purpose. The more than two years of language study have been of enormous help in my singing, in my writing and reading, but especially in research.

Chapter Eight

In the fall of 1908 another change took place in my singing career and in my life. I learned through my teacher of an opening in the choir of the Presbyterian church in Overbrook, a suburb of Philadelphia only about two miles from home. I tried for the position and was hired, at a larger salary. This time it was to be five dollars a Sunday. I was pleased. The church was near home and the people were friendly.

As I remember that year it seems as if it had been all sunny weather. The choir was double quartet and I was the contralto soloist. One of the members invited me to join the music club to which she belonged. I was by far the youngest member, and was flattered that I was asked. The meetings were held in various homes, papers were read concerning music, then different members played piano or sang. Tea was served at tables beautifully appointed and spread with delicacies. Usually, I sang German *Lieder*, but sometimes I sang arias from operas in French while one of the ladies accompanied me. Here my study of languages served me well.

Just beyond Fifty-fifth Street at Lancaster Avenue, where the country began, there was a carpet mill. Autumn winds were high and the air was chill. Somehow a fire started in the mill, and before it was discovered it had become a furnace. The noise of the fire engines wakened everyone within miles. We stood at the windows watching the flames with excitement and terror. That fire influenced my whole life.

The next day, when I went to the drugstore for something, I met my friend Louise Jacoby and Anna de Angeli, whom I knew slightly. I was interested in her because of her deafness and the remarkable way she read lips. I had been to her house and had met

46

her mother, whom I liked very much. When I asked how her mother was, she said, "She is in bed with the grippe. She watched the fire last night and caught cold. But Brother is home."

I remembered that sign I had seen—JOHN DE ANGELI, TEACHER OF VIOLIN—several years ago when Charlotte Roy and I had passed the de Angeli house on Lansdowne Avenue. Now they lived on Fifty-fifth, not far from us.

"Tell your mother I'll come and sing to her," I said.

That afternoon when I went down to the de Angeli's to sing I was sure my motives were of the most innocent. Now that I am much older, I wonder. How much impression did that remark make upon me? "Brother is home." He had been but a vague figure in my mind, though I had heard Anna say that he worked in New York selling oriental rugs. This was the first time I had heard of his being in Philadelphia.

While I was singing he came in and was introduced as Brother Dailey. He was immediately friendly and I think we knew from that moment that each belonged to the other. He seemed to like my singing and got out his fiddle to accompany me with an obbligato.

John Dailey de Angeli, age eight.

I learned later that he liked my broad shoulders and the blue- and black-striped red blouse I was wearing, and to this day he remembers that I wore collar and cuffs of fine Swiss embroidery.

He walked me home and before he left me at my door invited me to go with him to a friend's house that night for music. It was the beginning of many such evenings both at home and with Dai's friends. They were many and varied, all older than I, as he was. But music was the thread that bound us all. He took me often to his house, where I met his father.

Dai called on me more and more frequently. Invariably, he left his umbrella, his violin, his scarf, or his rubbers. Finally, Papa said, "You can tell that young man he doesn't have to leave something here in order to have an excuse to call." He liked Dai, as we all did, and we enjoyed his playing. I had once said I would never marry a man with brown eyes, but Dai's became more and more appealing and his laugh more dear. I liked his clean-looking hands and his rosy cheeks, too.

He used to tease me because I once got off the Lansdowne Avenue trolley to walk home with him. But I didn't let Dai think he was the only man in my life, and I took care to accept invitations from others and to be very casual with him at parties. Still, we had a great deal in common, with our music, a shared sense of humor, and an appreciation of things pertaining to the arts. So, after six weeks' acquaintance, he asked me to marry him and I accepted. There was no prospect of immediate marriage, because he was looking for a more permanent job. For the time being he was paymaster for his father, going to Washington once a week.

In the 1890s, when the famous Philadelphia Orchestra was still called the Symphony Society, Dai was a member and played first fiddle. Fritz Scheel was then the conductor. It had been during this period that he taught violin and worked for Fritz and LaRue selling oriental rugs. From there he had gone to New York with the same firm and had attended Columbia University, where he took a course that gave him a background for his work. It also gave him an understanding of the people who wove the tapestry-like floor coverings.

He knew the symbolism of the designs and the value of the rugs according to their antiquity, the finesse of the weave, and the permanence of the colors. Although he has been in other lines of work since, and retired many years ago, he has never forgotten what he learned then.

Mr. de Angeli *père*, whose professional name was John E. Murphy, was the owner of Murphy's Minstrels on the Steel Pier in Atlantic City, and of a similar show in Luna Park near Washington. These were primarily family-type shows, attended even by those to whom the theater was too much of this world.

Through Mr. de Angeli's business Dai knew many people in the entertainment world; some he had known since childhood: Sousa, the band leader, Chauncey Olcott, the Irish tenor, Walter Damrosch, Victor Herbert, and many others, all well known in the early 1900s. Besides, there was Jefferson de Angelis, my husband's cousin (once removed), well known in musical comedy. I saw him several times and, with Dai, met him once in his dressing room.

The de Angelis came from Corsica, going first to France with the Bonaparte's, then with Joseph Napoleon to Philadelphia, where Benedict became a fruit importer, trading with the West Indies. Benedict's brother Hyacinthe (Iacinthe) and his wife, Emily, gave their daughter Giulia in marriage to the Count di Paraldi of Corsica and provided her with a dowry consisting of property on Arch Street at Ninth and on Thirteenth Street in Philadelphia valued at $60,000. Now it would be worth millions. All this I learned only a few years ago. We have portraits of Dai's great-grandfather, Benedict, and of his niece, Beatrice, painted by Bass Otis, a contemporary of Gilbert Stuart.

Dai's father not only owned the minstrel show but engaged all the orchestras, bands, singers, or comedians who performed on other parts of the Pier. Many of the artists who first appeared as professionals under his management later became famous. Among these was Frank Tinney, who came to Father when he was only a boy.

Father was very generous, not only to his family but to his friends, and often they took advantage of him. He was short and stocky like his Corsican forebears, but his blue eyes and fair skin were like his Irish mother's, Sarah Dougherty de Angeli.

Dai's mother's family came from northern Scotland. Her father, Jared Craig, married Nancy Orr, the daughter of a laird who wore fine clothes—knee britches and lace cuffs. They came to this country about 1813. Jared was a printer and had a shop on Chestnut Street. His father had been a teacher of Latin and English, and his name was Robert.

Jared and Nancy started a mission in South Philadelphia called Moyamensing Mission. They had three children, Margaret, John,

Mr. and Mrs. John de Angeli, Sr., Marguerite's parents-in-law.

and Kate, who was Dai's mother. When I knew her she was a tiny woman with large brown eyes, a quantity of graying hair, and a charming manner. In spite of having lost several children (one by drowning) she had a certain gaiety that sometimes came out in little skips and jumps, and a childlike faith that had its roots in her Presbyterian background. She took the greatest care of Father, protecting him from the importunities of actors who wanted to be hired or to borrow money. She gave him his meals at odd hours because of the demands upon him in his work. I came to love her very much and I think she loved me.

Dai's father died in 1924, leaving Frank Elliot to take his place with the minstrels. Dai was a little disappointed that his father hadn't chosen him to be his successor, but Father always thought the theatrical business too precarious to depend upon for a living. He used to worry about it from one season to the next.

There is no doubt, however, that a certain interest in and aptitude for dramatics has come out in our children.

Dai's sister Anna had been deaf since babyhood, as a result of scarlet fever. When she was three she was enrolled in the School for the Deaf in Fairmount Park. Dr. Alexander Graham Bell, who established the school, used to hold her on his knee. She was an attractive child and quick to learn, and when she was twelve she was taken to England to demonstrate the method of teaching the deaf to speak and to read lips. She had a certain imperious quality due to the special attention she had received all her life, but was merry and cheerful.

After our engagement Dai and I were frequently invited out for music. By this time I was able to play Dai's accompaniment if it wasn't too difficult. Sometimes Horace played the piano for Dai to play and me to sing from a book Dai gave me, especially arranged with violin and voice.

Horace was still playing the organ at the Presbyterian church, so it was natural that he and Nina had a circle of friends there, while I was drawn into quite another circle through Dai and his family.

I was nineteen when Dai and I met and I was still singing in Overbrook. A year later I accepted a position at Chambers Wylie Presbyterian Church on South Broad Street in Philadelphia. It was, and still is, an imposing building, and at that time well attended. The minister was The Reverend de Witt Talmadge, a preacher of local renown.

About this time Madame Suelke arranged for me to sing for Oscar Hammerstein I at the Metropolitan Opera House in Philadelphia. The day of my appointment Mr. Hammerstein and I were the only ones in the opera house beside the accompanist, as far as I know. I sang "My Heart at Thy Sweet Voice" from *Samson and Delilah*. Mr. Hammerstein stood in the auditorium and I was alone on the big stage. I'm sure I was frightened, but somehow, after the first few notes, the glorious feeling of letting out my voice to its fullest, to fill that great emptiness, released the tension and I sang on without fear. Mr. Hammerstein accepted me as a member of his chorus and gave me the time for rehearsal. He also said that the company was going on tour and in a few weeks would be singing in London.

London!

Marguerite at age nineteen.

I hurried home to tell the news, walking on air. To my surprise, my parents were not as impressed as I had thought they would be. But they said nothing much until I had been to the first rehearsal. Then they sat down and talked to me, pointing out that, if I pursued an operatic career, my life with Dai would suffer and when my voice began to age I would have little left. If I married Dai and reared a family my life would have more meaning, and in the end would be much more satisfying. I had simply been carried away by the glamor of travel and singing in opera and hadn't realized that I would be separated from Dai so much. As we talked about it I could see how wise and right my parents were. I never went to another rehearsal.

I continued to sing in the choir, by then in another church, Park Avenue Methodist, under the direction and musicianship of Rollo Maitland.

When I was nearing twenty-one Dai was introduced to an executive of the Edison Phonograph Company and offered a position representing them in Canada. He left for Toronto, where his head-quarters were at R. S. Williams Company. He traveled from there throughout the provinces of Ontario and Quebec, writing me every day and telling me about the excitement of selling, of hearing the new records, and meeting new people. He was very successful.

Since all was going well, we began to plan for our wedding. We had decided to be married somewhere away from Philadelphia, partly because neither of us wanted a big wedding and especially because of the difference in our families' religions. Dai's cousin on his mother's side was married to a Baptist minister and was living in Toronto. She invited us to have our wedding in her house. Neither Dai's parents nor mine made any objection to our plan, understanding that our basic beliefs were no different, but that some of Dai's more devout relatives might make it an occasion for dissension.

Chapter Nine

On March 14 I was twenty-one, and on the first of April I left by train for Toronto. A large company of friends and family attended me to the station. Father de Angeli presented me with a huge bouquet of white roses. I was pelted with confetti, and Horace, who later became my brother-in-law, took me aboard the train.

I learned the next morning, before our arrival in Toronto, that everyone had recognized me as a bride, but they had supposed Horace to be the bridegroom. He was thought to be very inattentive, as he was not seen again. I was told this by my seatmate, who was the American consul in Toronto. He looked after me until Dai arrived, somewhat late. The office force at R. S. Williams had delayed him with jokes and confetti. Besides, he had returned from a trip only that morning and had had to choose his wedding suit. He brought with him John Gill, who was also a representative of the Edison Company, to be best man. His long, lean looks recommended him to me and reminded me of Harry, my brother. Dai's good humor and gentleness took the sting out of my anxious waiting. We all went together to Dai's cousin's house, where we were made quite at home.

She insisted that I must rest and prepare for the wedding, which was to be at five o'clock. *Rest* in the *day*time at twenty-one on the day of one's wedding? Not be with Dai after so many weeks separation? Impossible. Still, I was a stranger to Jessie and must abide by her decision to keep me out of circulation until time for the wedding.

Dai and John Gill had gone to pick up the wedding suit and

there was nothing to do but pass the time until five o'clock. It was the longest day of my life.

I laid out my princess-style raisin-satin wedding dress and all the accessories. I tried to read a magazine, but it made no sense; I tried to sleep, but sleep was farthest from my thoughts. Jessie was busy preparing the wedding supper, so I couldn't bother her.

Her husband had been called away from town, so another minister who lived near was to substitute for him. The young girl next door would be my bridesmaid, and one or two neighbors were to be witnesses.

The afternoon passed. Dai and John finally arrived, the minister came with the bridesmaid and the neighbors, and it was time for the wedding.

The ceremony was performed. I remember little else except that John Gill's chin was damp with perspiration as he kissed me and that we had molded ice cream for the wedding supper. I remember too that when I tried to sing at the request of the wedding guests my voice would not respond; I couldn't sing for weeping. I was frightened, homesick, and a stranger in a strange land.

Dai took me in a hansom cab to the Hotel Mossop, where we stayed for two weeks while Dai worked in Toronto. Then we moved to a boarding house because it was cheaper and because Dai didn't know as yet where his headquarters were to be. He was being trained and tested for a far western territory.

There was another young couple staying in the house with whom we became friendly. The young man traveled through the week as Dai did, so we two young wives found occupation and entertainment for ourselves. I provided myself with material for embroidery, which was then in vogue, and found it absorbing and gratifying. In the evenings we sometimes went to concerts or plays, once to see Julia Marlowe in *Romeo and Juliet*. I never saw her again, but I shall never forget the thrill of that performance.

In a few weeks we moved to another boarding house where the food was better.

The days were long. I read and reread whatever I could find. I practiced the piano. I wrote reams of letters home. I tried to draw, even made an attempt at a self-portrait from my image in the long mirror, but the dismal results did not encourage me to go on. Sometimes I went shopping, but wandering in stores doesn't appeal to me as the best way to fill time.

Every day a letter came from Dai, from Quebec, from Ottawa, from London, Ontario, from Hamilton or Brantford. Every day I wrote in answer, sending the letter out into a seeming void, which even the map didn't turn into real cities. I was familiar with London, Ontario, because Grandpa's brother, Uncle Alf, lived there with his family, and once I had met him and Aunt Kate. But most of the postmarks on Dai's welcome letters were strange and unknown to me. One feature of the letters was a blessing, though frustrating. His writing was difficult to decipher, so the letter lasted me all day. I read it over and over, and finally discovered all the words and what he was saying.

At the end of June, Dai was sent to Winnipeg to open up a new territory in western Canada and establish new dealerships. He did not know how long he would be in any one place, distances between towns were great, and his trips might last for weeks. It seemed wise for me to visit my parents for a month or so until we knew more about the new and sparsely settled country and where Dai would set up headquarters.

It was hard to be separated again, but I missed my family and was glad to go home for a while. At the end of the month Nina was due for a vacation from the secretarial position she had with a wholesale grocery firm and agreed to go with me to Michigan. After our visit she would come back to Philadelphia and I would go on to western Canada, the specific place to be determined later.

We had been invited to stay with Uncle Alf and Aunt Kate in London, Ontario. It was on the way to Lapeer so we accepted happily. There were several young people in the family and we enjoyed the experience of getting better acquainted with Grandpa's side of the Lofft family.

Nina and I were more congenial that we had ever been; and now she was to be married to Horace.

By now I knew that I was to become a mother, and looked forward to the event with great joy, as did Dai. He seemed very far away, but continued to write every day. He had settled upon Winnipeg as our place of residence and his headquarters, but I was to join him in Saskatoon, Saskatchewan, at the end of August. After the few days at Uncle Alf's we continued on to Lapeer to visit Grandpa and Grandma Lofft and sleep in the little white-canopied bed in the guest room. There at the table in her place was Grandma in her rocking chair telling Grandpa how to do each thing he had done for sixty years. Warm affection between them took the sting away from "Now, William. . . ."

There were many other relatives to visit in Lapeer. We dined with aunts, uncles, cousins, and childhood friends, and the time flew by. At some gatherings I wore my wedding dress, but toward the end of the stay in Lapeer it began to be increasingly tight.

I was often annoyed by a disconcerting nausea, but my general attitude was that the bearing of children was a natural process, that one must keep that fact in mind and not give in to small inconveniences.

The day came when Nina went back to Philadelphia and I went on to Chicago, where I spent a day with Cousin Ernest Hough and Lillian, his wife. It was ninety-eight degrees that twenty-fifth of August when I left Chicago for Winnipeg. There was a change of trains in Minneapolis next morning, then a whole day's travel to Winnipeg. As we traveled north it grew colder and colder, and by the time we passed through the Dakotas it was freezing.

In Winnipeg I went directly to the Royal Alexandra Hotel to stay overnight, as Dai had told me to do. I had very little experience of hotels, so felt strange eating alone in the huge dining room and stranger still in the large bedroom assigned to me. How did I know that some evil person would not invade my room in spite of the lock? I'd heard that sometimes burglars picked locks. How would I know when to rise in order to get to the train before it left on its twenty-four-hour journey to Saskatoon? Would Dai be there awaiting me? Would I know him? Already his face was a blur. I couldn't quite get it clear.

Next morning I caught the train safely, and settled down for the endless journey. All day I was the only passenger in the Pullman. The only other person was the porter, who had little to do but bring me pillows, direct me to the dining car, and sleep, which he did most of the day. But, with or without pillows, *I* could not sleep. I gazed out over the expanse of countryside, which grew more and more empty as we traveled westward. Sleep eluded me until midnight, when other passengers came aboard and I heard their voices as they talked to the porter. Then I slept.

About seven in the morning we arrived in Saskatoon. Dai was there to meet me—and suddenly all was well. How could I have forgotten his brown eyes and his rosy color? The two months we had been separated vanished, as if they had never been.

For several weeks Dai and I stayed in and around Saskatoon. Dai traveled out from there to smaller towns, sometimes being gone overnight or for a few days. Sometimes I went with him. The cold weather continued and I was obliged to buy long winter underwear and a heavy sweater to keep warm, though it was still only September. By this time nothing but winter clothing could be found in the stores in any case. I learned later that even in August all summer things were put away and nothing but heavy woolen hose, felt boots, and fur-lined coats were to be had. It was like being in another world from the one I had known. The food was different, the people were different. The utter vastness in which the towns were set gave one the feeling of being detached from all familiar things. One could walk only a little way before coming to the edge of town, and beyond stretched the level prairie to a far horizon where grass and unfenced fields met the sky. When one looks at the map today it seems crowded with little towns, but sixty years ago it was pretty bare.

Night after night the heavens blazed with the magnificence of the aurora borealis, all the colors of the spectrum flashing and forming patterns from horizon to zenith. Perhaps I had seen the aurora before, but never in such intensity and never night after night after night. It was glorious. Many years later, in Pennsylvania, I remember a display to compare with those so long ago in Canada. It began in early evening. The heavens seemed on fire with patterns of color vibrating throughout the sky and all pointing to the zenith. We took cots outside to lie on so we could see without breaking our necks. But it was only that one night.

Chapter Ten

When Dai went on farther west I went with him, marveling at the immensity of the land, which had so few inhabitants. There was one train a day, one east and one west, so that it was later and later at each stop, until we were arriving at midnight or after at some places. The trains were crowded, mostly with salesmen going, as Dai was, to open new territory for business. Often I was the only woman in the car—sometimes the only woman on the train. The men rushed for reservations at the one country hotel, and sometimes there wasn't a room left for us. Then the men would double up to make room for Dai and me. Once a salesman slept on the billiard table so we might have a room. Dai tells of sharing a bed once with a Canadian Mountie who insisted on having the window open, and then found snow on the bed in the morning.

There were Dukhobors, a strange religious sect from Russia living in western Canada, who were sometimes aboard the train. They were already "sewed up" for the winter and it was not difficult to know when one was in the car. The children too, I'm told, were sewed into their underwear, which stayed on till spring!

The menus in these small-town hotels were pretty much the same everywhere. The cooks were all Chinese, and while the food was good, it was rather monotonous. In the middle of each table was a plate of soda crackers and it mattered little what kind of meat one ordered. It all tasted the same because all the meats were cooked in the same huge roasting pan and the gravy was a mixture of their mingled flavors.

In the larger cities, with the hotel and dealer cooperating, Dai gave concerts, using a record-playing cabinet that he had shipped from one place to another. Sometimes the dealer sent out invitations for Saturday recitals, which drew quite a number of people. Dai played recordings of the music of such composers as Beethoven, Brahms, Moussorgsky, and Mahler, or arias sung by Geraldine Farrar or Matzenauer. Sometimes he played semiclassics, which included songs popular at the time, such as "Macushla," sung by John McCormack, "My Ain Countree," sung by Henry Burr, or perhaps a comic record by Golden and Hughes. These were very popular affairs and very well attended because there was little other entertainment, and they contributed to Dai's success in his opening of the Canadian west to Edison phonographs and records. There was great competition with Victor machines, especially before Mr. Edison developed flat records. Dai won first place among Edison salesmen several times, and with his enthusiasm and easy friendly manner made friends wherever he went.

One of the trips we took from Saskatoon was down the Goose Lake branch of the Canadian Pacific, stopping at each town to sell or to establish new dealerships. The towns were all very new, very small, serving the pioneer wheat farmers who were turning the surrounding prairie into farming country. There were few women in the towns. The men who carried on the business of the community and those who worked on the railroad ate dinner at the hotel where we did. They were of all nationalities, mostly middle European, Czech, Hungarian, German, or Italian.

At one town I had quite an adventure. Sitting next to me at table was a big, raw-boned Scotsman, and across the table the town laundryman, who was Chinese. The Scotsman smelled strongly of Scotch whiskey and I couldn't bear his being so close. Whenever he turned to speak to me, which was often, he bent down close to my face. I tried not to notice, remembering that Dai was trying to convince him that he should become a dealer in Edison products. I thought he would leave after dinner as the others did, but when Dai left to make one more call he stayed on, making conversation until I became uneasy. I was too young and innocent to realize that he was trying to get me alone, until he suggested that I take a buggy ride with him out on the prairie. It was then that I excused myself, ran up to my room, and locked the door, hoping Dai would come soon. I knew the train was due to take us on down the branch line so I made sure all was ready to leave. In a short time Dai did come. We picked up our luggage and went to the train.

"Whew!" said Dai as we settled aboard. "What a relief! I thought we would never get away from that fellow."

I too heaved a sigh of relief, only then realizing that Dai, while trying to keep on good terms with his client, was well aware of the man's unwelcome attentions to me.

On down the Goose Lake branch we went, doubling back with horse and carriage in order to make two towns instead of one. Sometimes, besides going on to two towns and going back one, Dai went by horse and buggy cross-country thirty miles or so to the other railroad. Once, bundled up in a second-hand coonskin coat, he drove through snow and ice with the temperature at sixty degrees below zero to Prince Albert. I was not with him that time.

We arrived at Rosetown, the end of the line, on the eve of Labor Day. The next morning we knew from the noise that all the railroad hands were off for the day and were celebrating in the bar. Dai hurried me up to our room after breakfast, and before he left made sure that I locked the door. I could hear the noise from below, but got out my embroidery and set to work and wait. I was embroidering a linen shirtwaist for Nina's birthday in the style then popular and now coming back. There were hours of work on it and I found it fascinating to do.

It was fortunate that I had stayed in my room. One of the men in a fight picked up another by the shirt front and threw him through the plate-glass window.

The return to Saskatoon was uneventful and soon we were on our way to Regina, where we bought a camera, then on to Moosejaw, Swift Current, Medicine Hat, and Lethbridge, Alberta. At that time the railroad bridge was the highest for its length in the world. I sometimes wondered if it had been called Lethbridge because if one had fallen from it the sleep induced would have been eternal. But perhaps it didn't imply the "lethe" I'm thinking of. At any rate, one looked down from a dizzy height to the canyon below.

From the hotel window I watched Indians with their long black braids, wearing their striped blankets and moccasins, as they searched through trash in the alley for something edible or useful.

Often as we waited for the arrival of a train it seemed that the headlights were very close and that the train would arrive momentarily. Actually, it might be as much as thirty miles away, but the flat prairie, treeless and uninhabited, combined with the clear atmosphere was deceiving. This held true in the foothills of the Rockies as we approached them.

I shall never forget my first close look at the Rockies. I had just awakened in the Pullman and noticed the odd quality of the light. It seemed to come from high above instead of all around as it had on the plains. I looked out to see where we were, but all I could see was a dark wall that went up, up, and up, seemingly forever. I craned my neck and finally saw the top of the mountain, which appeared to rise from within arms' length and stretch away to the sky, piercing the blue and taking my heart with it.

The range of mountains went on and on as the train climbed higher and higher. We stopped at Banff and Lake Louise, then left the train at Field, British Columbia, where we were to spend the night. Steps led from the train platform directly into the Canadian Pacific Hotel. When we registered we must have looked very young, for we were given the bridal suite. This was no country hotel such as we had been seeing, but one of the finest, as were all C.P.R. hotels, and it was run for the convenience of its clients.

Morning showed a dramatic view from our window, a mountain, no less, as if it had been put there for our sole gratification. I decided I would walk to it right after breakfast when Dai had gone on the train back to Banff and Lake Louise. To my amazement I learned that it was unlikely that I could walk there. The mountain was more than fifteen miles away.

When Dai came back on the next day's train we went on to Calgary, the train stopping briefly at Golden to allow the passengers to get out to view the glacier, which covered a tremendous slope, seeming almost near enough to touch.

Dai had a number of places to go that he could reach easily from Calgary, so we stayed there for about a week, then went on to Revelstoke and down the Arrow Lakes by steamer to Nelson, B.C., the farthest point of our western Canada trip.

The colors of the landscape were unbelievably beautiful. We took pictures with our new camera, wanting to capture for all time the beauty we saw. But there were no color films then, so the pictures turned out to be flat and disappointing. Still, memory holds the color safe.

We went back to Calgary, and from there north to Edmonton, where we stayed for about two weeks, Dai traveling to surrounding territory and I putting in the days as best I could: writing letters, embroidering, walking.

It was in Edmonton that I saw and heard for the first time a band of Scottish pipers. They came toward me down Main Street, kilts swinging, gaitered boots in martial rhythm, bonnet ribbons fluttering.

The weird and piercing music of the pipes and the deep boom of the bass drum were tremendous. The brawny figure of the drummer, his back arched to hold the weight of the drum, tossing the drumsticks from side to side in a magnificent display of skill, lifted my heart and carried it with him till sight and sound were lost in the wide prairie. Since then I have heard pipers many times in Canada and in Scotland, but never will I forget that first time so long ago.

The occasion for the pipers' band was the opening of a new tract of land just outside Edmonton. If we had been more alert we might have stood in line all night, then sold our place in line for a goodly sum for the privilege of having a better choice of land. But this didn't occur to us till too late.

The land was to be had free if one filed a claim, but it was "first come, first served," and as always everyone wanted first choice for himself.

At the restaurant where we ate, we met girls who had been to Alaska. They told us of the fast-growing communities there, the opportunities for business, and about the new road being built, the Alcan Highway from Alberta through to Alaska. It was like the days of the Gold Rush. I suspect the girls were not the type one would meet under ordinary circumstances. They were always accompanied by men to whom they were not married. My worldly education was growing fast. Always, wherever we went in the newly opened country, there was an air of optimism and excitement that communicated itself to us. We were young, the world lay before us, we were happy, and Dai continued to receive letters of commendation from the Edison Company.

Chapter Eleven

It must have been October when we returned to Winnipeg. I remember that it was fairly warm again so we changed into more seasonable clothes. Awaiting us was an order for Dai to go to Minnesota to visit dealers and to establish them where there were none.

We rented an apartment in a house in Minneapolis on Blaisdell Avenue. There was a Murphy bed so we could move in even before we had other furniture. We ordered a round table that served for living-room and dining table, a large leather chair and one or two smaller ones, and a day bed in case of overnight visitors. We expected Dai's mother to come before the baby arrived.

There was a small living room, a still smaller dining room, and off it the bathroom and kitchenette. The kitchenette was hardly more than a corner cut off the dining room and it had no counter space that I can remember. I couldn't wait to learn to make a pie and to make bread, so I scrubbed the end of a packing case to use as a pastry board. The bread turned out well. I had made bread at home. But the pie was something less than perfect, so I made one every day for a week, until, when Dai came home from his travels, he pronounced the last I had made as good as those Mama made.

Dai was away all week. My letters came from Mankoto, Rochester, St. Cloud, all strange and interesting names. The time went slowly until he came home again. I began to try drawing, but the faces I drew had little relation to reality. It didn't occur to me that I could set up a still life and draw that. I might have kept up my singing but there was no piano. I made by hand baby clothes of dainty Swiss material and laid in a store of diapers, silk and wool shirts, flannel belly bands, flannel petticoats and booties. That's the way we dressed babies in those days.

What would the baby be like? Would it be a girl or a boy? What a mystery it all was. The child within was very active, and though I sometimes felt anxious about its delivery, and dreamed of all sorts of calamities that might befall me, I talked sense to myself. Had not my mother borne six of us safely? Had not every single living being come into the world the same way?

I read for hours on end, was bored with taking my meals alone, so ate what was easiest or most appealing. I discovered a market nearby to which I could walk, and sometimes I took the trolley into the center of town where I could shop and look around. Nights were endless, and because we were on the first floor I was sure someone would break in. I couldn't sleep. When I heard the milkman's wagon and the rattle of bottles I knew it was near morning, so I felt safe and slept.

Soon I became friendly with a Mrs. Lamkey, who lived down the hall, and I found her not only congenial but someone from whom I could learn a great deal. Later I met the people in the next flat, the Alfred Wallensteins. Mr. Wallenstein was then a member of the Minneapolis Symphony.

Thanksgiving arrived. Dai was home, making the rounds of the Minneapolis dealers, among whom was Archie Mathias. He was amiable and friendly and invited us to his house for Thanksgiving. From then on I was not so much alone.

I shopped for Christmas and sent things home to the family, but nothing seemed good enough. Packages arrived from home and were put aside for the day that had always meant so much to me. It was still easy to visualize the traditional scenes—the shepherds, the heavenly choir, the manger sheltering the holy family and the quiet beasts. Even now, when the accepted forms are being challenged and wider reading has acquainted me with the parallels among various religions, Christmas is still magical. I deplore the many Santa Clauses, and wish he had remained the delightful myth he was to me—unseen, as is the spirit of love.

To be away from my parents' home at Christmas for the first time was sad. But Dai was with me, so all was well. He had about two weeks at home.

The Mathiases came to eat Christmas dinner with us, which I had carefully planned and cooked; Dai took me to the theater and to the Minneapolis Symphony concerts, and the season passed happily.

It was much colder in Minnesota than in Pennsylvania, and we were surprised one morning to receive a visit from the landlord, chiding us for leaving the window wide open when the temperature was down to thirty degrees below zero. The pipes had frozen and it had caused him no little inconvenience and expense. January continued to be steadily cold. Dai traveled to nearby towns but was usually home on weekends.

We went to the Medical Building and chose a doctor at random. Happily, we chose well. He reassured me and told me to be ready to go to the hospital in early February. Toward the end of January, Dai's mother came, as we had hoped, to be with us when the baby arrived. I was pleased to show off the little apartment and my cooking skill, and Dai played records for her that we enjoyed. One I shall never forget; Mother loved it as much as we did. We played it over and over again and again. It was a Scottish hymn called "My Ain Countree," and sung by Henry Burr.

On February 6 all signs pointed to my going into the Methodist Hospital. The delivery was normal and usual for a first child. He was perfect in every way and bore a comical resemblance to my father.

We named him John Shadrach de Angeli for Dai's father and mine. He was as good as a child could be, and as he grew he seemed pleased with his world, for he laughed early and often. I enjoyed my stay in the hospital. I was perfectly comfortable and supremely happy.

Mother stayed to see that all was well and to help me get used to being a mother, then went back to Father de Angeli in Philadelphia. I missed her very much, but the baby kept me from being lonely. He was the most accommodating of babies, sleeping and eating at regular intervals, good-natured and friendly. Still, I missed Dai's companionship. I missed the coming and going of a large family, the clamor at table when everyone wanted to be heard at once, Papa's "Sssh! Lower your voices." I missed my sister and even the mud-tracking eternal racket of my brothers, especially Dick, the youngest. But when the blessed Friday evening came, bringing Dai home, all else was forgotten.

When Jack was about five months old, Dai and I were invited by Frank Tinney and his wife to come to St. Paul to the vaudeville theater performance in which he was playing. He had developed his gift for clowning so that he was in great demand as an entertainer and at this time was at the height of his career. Happily, Dai was at home and could go with me. I dressed the baby in his fresh white clothes and a little white serge coat I had made and we set out for the trolley ride to St. Paul. Frank had told us not to worry about the care of the baby. He would be looked after by the whole cast backstage and could sleep in the make-up trunk. We were flattered by the attention he received as he was passed from one to another. Everyone seemed so happy to hold him. He accepted the members of the cast in his usual good humor and so we left him. We had choice seats in a box and looked forward to the afternoon's enjoyment.

One of the acts near the beginning was a comedy team called the Empire Comedy Four, one of whom took the part of a little Dutchman with rosy cheeks, a red nose, and a small goatee. He was very funny. Next came Frank's act. He came onstage, greeted the audience, and made a few remarks, then said:

"Just let me get my little Dutchman friend from the Empire Comedy Four." He stepped into the wings and came out carrying our baby, made-up like the little Dutchman, complete with red make-up on his cheeks and on his nose, and a little black goatee. We were furious. But when the audience began to laugh and applaud, we laughed too. Jack seemed perfectly oblivious of the whole affair, and no wonder. He was sound asleep. And so we found him after the show, lying in a make-up trunk, still in his make-up, dead to the world. It was impossible to be irritated because his clothes were soiled with grease paint. What did it matter, even though we had to carry him home that way. He had been loved by dear, warm-hearted people. It was something to tell him later.

As he grew and flourished, Jack was more and more amusing and satisfying as a baby. Dai and I had made friends, I was busy, and except for the difficulty of saying "good-bye" to Dai on Sunday nights as he started out on his travels, I was happy.

We had found a Swedish woman, Mrs. Swedeblum, who came in once a week to clean, and who provided us with many a chuckle. She was so clean and fresh-looking it made one feel good to look at her. She had a wise philosophy delivered in an amusing dialect with its characteristic singsong inflection and she loved the baby. I would have liked to keep her for always.

At the end of June Dai was called in to the Edison headquarters at West Orange, New Jersey, to be brought up to date on new records, improvements in the machine, and for conferences with the other salesmen. This meant that I could go home to see my family and show off my child. Dai could come to Philadelphia for weekends.

It never occurred to me that traveling with a baby would be

difficult. Why should it? And it wasn't. Jack took to traveling as he took to everything in life. He ate and slept as usual. He didn't cry because he was well fed and well cared for and was content. We were indignant when we heard the man in the next compartment say, "I suppose that kid will cry all night."

What joy to be greeted by the family, to deliver Jack into my father's arms, to hug my mother and sister, and to see the boys again. They seemed to have taken some strange elixir that had elongated their legs and stretched their necks. Harry's nose had leaped out of his face and his jaw had lengthened. Arthur's body had become more like a man's, matching his already long legs, a fact of life that I was made aware of again when my own boys suddenly became grown-ups.

The Philadelphia summer was as steaming hot as ever, with a day now and then that seemed unendurable. My poor mother looked rather wan and tired and I feared it was too much for her with us there. But Papa got help for her and we had our traditional Fourth of July picnic up the hill beyond Lancaster Avenue on Beadle's farm. The Kriegers were there with their baby, Knut, who was just a week older than Jack. (Knut is now Dr. Krieger, scientist and professor of chemistry at the University of Pennsylvania.)

In later years, when both families had moved to Collingswood, New Jersey, the two boys grew to be fast friends. They had the same zany sense of humor, the same enthusiasm for *Alice in Wonderland*, Mark Twain, Stephen Leacock, and Robert Benchley. Even now, they celebrate birthdays together recalling old jokes, old saws, old radio programs and personalities.

Chapter Twelve

The six weeks we were home fled all too soon. The summer briefing was over for Dai and it was time to return to the west. Dai was scheduled to go back to Canada, so we returned to Minneapolis to pack our things for shipping to Winnipeg, where we moved into an apartment on Langside Avenue, paying what to us then was the outrageous sum of $50 a month rent. There was no Murphy bed, but a real bedroom with space for a crib.

The routine of Dai's traveling began again, the cruel good-byes of Sunday evening, the joy of return, not at each weekend now, but often after two- or three-week intervals, because Dai went farther afield, penetrating the remote towns. My daily letters (no pun intended) came from such places as Bowsman, Ochre River, Minnedosa, then from farther west, Kamsack, Canora, Humboldt, Regina, and Moosejaw. Some of these I knew from having passed through them on that first trip with Dai. Some sounded incredibly strange and far away.

Jack was beginning to crawl, not forward, but backward, often finding himself backed into a corner or against a table leg or chair. Then he howled for help. As he learned with my help to go forward, he became interested in things he was able to reach, one of them my Bible. I was of the school that believes a child should learn what he may or may not touch, so I left the Bible there, saying "No, no" when he dragged it off the bottom shelf of the side table. He sat up and looked at me questioningly as he fingered the thin India paper pages. So I took him on my lap with the Bible, showed him, at nine months, how to turn pages properly, without wrinkling, talked soothingly to him about the care of books. He listened as if he understood. He didn't know the words I said, of course, but he knew the attitude and the meaning of what I was trying to convey. I never let him tear magazines or newspaper because I felt he was too young to know one kind of book from another. I may have been mistaken about this, but I do not feel that I injured his little psyche. Even at this age he listened to nursery rhymes and learned to read when he was very young.

Winter closed in early in that northern country. By November we sometimes had temperatures below zero. It was the custom then to put babies out in the carriage to sleep during the day, so I bundled Jack up like a little mummy, with a hot-water bottle at his feet, and put him out on the back balcony for his nap. In the evening, at his bedtime, I rocked him to sleep as I had rocked my little brothers when Mama had reached the end of her endurance. I set the phonograph playing records I loved, such as the Bach-Gounod *Agnus Dei*, the familiar Mendelsohn *Trio* and lighter music such as John McCormack's singing of "Macushla" or "The Last Rose of Summer"—all comforting, all nostalgic reminders of evenings with Dai and with friends at home. Sometimes I sang Jack to sleep with my own remembered favorites. It took longer and longer to get him to sleep and he was restless and fretful, so finally I decided he should go to sleep by himself. I put him to bed, being sure he was taken care of and comfortable, then left him and hardened myself to his screaming. He stopped crying as soon as I appeared, so I knew he was simply spoiled. He cried for one hour the first night, three quarters of an hour the second night, and only fifteen minutes the third night. Then he never cried at all, but went to bed like an angel. It was what he had wanted all the time—to be put to bed and left alone to sleep.

While he was still a baby he caught measles from the child across the hall. He was very sick, but I followed my mother's procedure and he began to improve. I wired Dai, who came home, but he too was ill. So I had two patients.

One of Dai's customers in Winnipeg was Warren Fitch, who had a mail-order music business. He was very friendly with Dai and he and his wife invited us to their house for dinner. We took to each other immediately. Dai had been asked to bring his fiddle and I my music. Alice, Warren's wife, played piano and was an excellent accompanist. We liked the same kind of music so we played and sang to our hearts' content. Warren and Alice had three children, who welcomed Jack into their circle, and he accepted them and any kind of nonsense they chose to play. He let them dress him up in paper hats and put him on the rocking horse and he loved it all.

Soon we were spending holidays together, or putting our dinners together, combining whatever we each had on hand. Alice, coming from a Middle West background, Wisconsin, I think, cooked about as I did, although she was more experienced and was able to teach me things I hadn't tried before. She was like a sister to me and her friendship was very dear.

By this time I had found someone to take care of Jack while I went to choir rehearsal and Sunday service. I had become a member of the quartet in the church where Ralph Conway preached. He was the author of a book about the North Country.

Later I accepted the contralto position in a choir led by Mr. Vinen, an Englishman of splendid musicianship who played the organ in a large downtown Methodist church. It was a volunteer choir but the quartet members were professional. During the two years I sang with the choir I was often engaged for concert solo work. Once it was at a performance of the newly formed symphony society. The concert was held in an immense hall, the armory, I think, which held at least a thousand people. I remember that I wore a long black dress with a high red sash and that one of the town dignitaries, a Scotsman, said, as I sat down, "Madame, ye've a beautiful back."

Only lately, out of some collection of memorabilia, I found a review of that concert. Here it is, dated March 24, 1914, *Manitoba Chronicle:*

> Madame de Angeli was the vocal soloist. She sang two sacred songs in a beautifully sustained manner. Her contralto voice is of beautiful quality. She knows how to use it and she sings church music in the proper spirit. Consequently, she was well received. She was handicapped by a rather ineptly written accompaniment, but Mr. Haines had good success with the accompaniment to the other song. The audience was the largest that has yet been assembled. An indication that the people wish to have a symphony orchestra and to encourage Herr Stephani and the aggregation in their work.

Not many months after this I realized I was to have another child. Would it be a girl? I hoped so.

Toward spring Dai said I could go with him on the next trip to the far west if I could manage to travel with Jack and not carry more than one suitcase. I accepted eagerly and by careful planning condensed our clothing to a minimum. Jack, as always, was a help by being his own good-natured self.

The days were long on the train because, going out, we stopped only once or twice at larger towns until we came to Calgary, where Dai made his headquarters for two or three weeks, going from there to surrounding towns.

In our room in the hotel the manager had put up a crib for Jack. I spent my days taking care of him and embroidering. I must have embroidered a great many pieces of linen. In fact I still have the table napkins I embroidered for my sister before her marriage to Horace Price. There was a three-yard table cloth as well, of Irish damask. We didn't get to the wedding, of course, but Mama told me about it and how, contrary to most mothers who weep at their daughters' weddings, she was anxious only that the wedding guests didn't notice, as she did, that the sun shone through Nina's sheer dress, showing her legs. How shocking!

We soon became quite at home in the Calgary Hotel. The waiters, who were Chinese, as they were throughout Canada at that time, were captivated with Jack and provided him with a high chair and special attention.

I taught him to walk while we were there and already he was saying words and phrases. We found a nice Scottish woman who took him with her part of the time, leaving me free to go with Dai.

We went from Calgary to Edmonton, and were there when the terrible news of the *Titanic* disaster arrived. It was too shocking to take in. It was as if security in every moment of life had been threatened. Dai had received word of his annual visit to West Orange and we were to leave Edmonton in a few days. Would we travel safely on the train? Might it be derailed or have a collision?

Naturally, one couldn't continue for long in such a state of fear and uncertainty. By the time we had reached Winnipeg I was my usual optimistic self and did not share the anxiety of my neighbor about traveling as far as Philadelphia bearing a child so near the time of birth.

Before leaving for West Orange and the Edison plant, Dai arranged with Dr. Walker for me to stay at his house with a nurse for my lying-in. He promised to come back as soon as I called and to stay with me at Dr. Walker's.

How I hoped this child would be a girl. It wasn't. A little round boy was born on July 10, very early in the morning. At my sigh of disappointment when the doctor announced that it was a boy, he said, "Be thankful he will never go through what you have just gone through." And, of course, it made no difference whether it was boy or girl, as long as all was well with the child. He was held up for me to view, the funniest baby I had ever seen. All my mother's children and Jack, my own, had been very fair, blue-eyed, and blond. This baby had a cloud of dark hair, dark eyes, and a fuzz of whiskers down to his chin, and a scowl at being thrust into a cold world. My disappointment vanished. I laughed out loud. We named him Arthur after my brother and Craig for Dai's mother's name. The fuzz disappeared in a few days, but the fierce eyebrows remained and have been passed on to Arthur's Kate.

The summer passed only too quickly. Arthur was six weeks old and already on supplementary feeding. Jack seemed to love him and the whole family was amused at his different look and the small tricks he soon learned. I laugh when I read that a new baby doesn't smile knowingly until he is such and such an age. Mine all smiled very early and looked at us with understanding. Naturally, I talked to them and paid attention to them and they responded.

It was time to go back to Canada. The whole family was invited to attend my grandmother and grandfather Lofft's golden wedding anniversary in Lapeer. Dai and I decided to go from there by steamer, which we could take from Detroit to Fort William, then go by train to Winnipeg.

A marquee was set up in the garden to accommodate the guests and serve refreshments. Among the gifts was a sugar and cream set of gold china, which I still have.

We stayed in Lapeer only a day or two, then went back to Detroit to go aboard ship. Neither of us had ever traveled by ship, so it was exciting to find our cabin and settle in for several days' journey. All was fine until we were well into Lake Superior. There rough water took our appetites and made life scarcely worth living. We found the truth of the old saying about seasickness: first you are afraid you will die, then you're afraid you won't.

Back in Winnipeg we established ourselves in another apartment, with an extra bedroom for the children and a place for a girl to help me. We found a girl who was Indian. When Arthur cried she wrapped him tightly in a thin blanket with his arms pinned down, which distressed me, but it quieted him. "He thinks he is being held," she said. She was very good with the children, but we kept missing things, so we had to let her go.

As the days grew short and cold weather came, Arthur developed allergies that plague him yet. By now he was a beautiful child with the usual enchanting ways of babies and his own particular charm. Jack was into everything, including the discovery that he could open the icebox and that eggs when thrown made a nice crackling sound.

When Arthur was six months old I realized I was pregnant again. Now, with our fast-growing family, we decided we must move into a house with a yard where the children could play outside, where there would be room for a piano and I could resume my singing and accompany Dai with his fiddle.

Chapter Thirteen

We found such a house on Mountain Avenue, across town from where we had been living. To reach it one passed through a Polish section where the signs on store windows looked impossibly difficult to read but interesting.

It was still winter, so when the piano was delivered the varnish was checked and crazed from the cold, but the inside was unharmed. We took up our music again. I was able to play the simpler accompaniments for my songs and Dai's violin pieces. Through some channel I learned that there was a position open for a contralto soloist in the choir of the Methodist church. I applied and was accepted. The fact that it would be necessary for me to be absent for some time later didn't deter me. Other women took time out to bear children, why not I?

I stayed in the choir until three months before the baby was born, perhaps singing better than ever. The solo I sang that last Sunday in July was "He Shall Feed His Flock," from Handel's *Messiah*.

There was a natural respite for vacations in August and in September, I just didn't go back, but arranged with Mr. Vinen, the conductor, to return when I was able. He was a very understanding person as well as a fine musician.

As summer progressed we realized that Arthur was not walking as he should. We consulted a doctor who said he was undernourished because of a lack of protein. He was fond of potatoes and bread and the milk he drank didn't supply enough of the other elements required. The doctor prescribed cod liver oil mixed with malt, a thick, loathsome concoction, but Arthur loved it and licked the spoon. It must have been effective because in a few weeks he was entirely recovered.

Anxiety over him, reluctance to welcome another child, and homesickness overtook me, and I longed for Dai to be home to stay. There was no time to sit down long enough even to try to satisfy the urge to draw that so often came over me. Could I never be free to delineate what I saw so clearly in my mind?

A series of household helpers came and went, but mostly they went. I probably expected too much of them. One, a Swedish girl, neat and tidy who was good with the children and even with cooking, wanted to go to dances every Saturday night, just when Dai was home and wanted me to go with him to the theater. We were both very young. She left.

There was the daily round of babies' washing and diapers that had to be boiled for twenty minutes to sterilize them. There were no electric washers and driers then and no diaper service. Was this what life was all about? What would it be like when there were three babies to care for?

When *Good Housekeeping* magazine arrived I pored over the cover by Jessie Wilcox Smith, and looked in other magazines and books to find illustrations by Alice Barber Stephens, or Elizabeth Shippen Green, or N. C. Wyeth, all of the Brandywine School and students of Howard Pyle, whose work I had admired since I was a girl at home. Once I wrote to Alice Barber Stephens, hoping, I suppose, for some magic formula that would solve all my problems. She answered with the sound advice to draw what I saw and to keep at it. But the pressure of child care and household duties kept me from following her advice.

We found another girl to help me. She was Austrian, older than the Swedish girl and ready to do whatever was asked of her. She taught me how to make egg noodles and to cook other familiar things. She was a jewel.

About this time I prevailed upon Dai to take a position in the R. S. Williams store and cease traveling. I have often wondered if it was selfish of me, because nothing ever went as well with him after that. But it was heaven to have him home every night. Jack and Arthur were fascinating and lovable in their individual ways. I loved bathing them, unconsciously learning their anatomy while soaping their backs and seeing the movement of arms and legs, the small necks and comparatively large heads. Even then I didn't take advantage of this and draw them, but I learned more than I thought, all of which served me through the years.

Throughout the summer I established a routine of bathing the boys before lunch in a washtub on the sheltered back porch. They thought it a lark and so did I. When they had gone to bed for naps I made ice cream of fruit and top milk. I timed myself and spent only a half hour from start to finish, even to packing it in ice and salt for supper.

We were now friends with the people across the street, delightful people of English background. Two sisters lived next to each other, one had no children, the other had eight. There was always a welcome there, with afternoon tea, homemade bread, and jam.

Our next door neighbors were friendly too. One of the young women taught me how to improve my hat-making with such things as tie-tacking the trimming, binding the rim, and wiring the ribbon. It was she who found me a trained nurse to attend me when the baby was born on schedule, October 23, 1913.

The baby, happily, was a girl. She was tiny for those days, but perfect. We named her for Mother de Angeli and for my mother, Ruby Catherine, but called her Catherine.

The nurse who cared for me was very efficient. She had been trained in Guy's Hospital in London, was a licensed midwife, and had served as a district nurse in London slums. I found her Scottish dialect delightful but difficult to imitate. Her clear rosy complexion and crisp uniform were like a fresh breeze.

I had gone back to my choir singing and had many engagements to sing with the quartet in special programs at Christmas, Easter, and other holidays.

We found it difficult from the very first to find any baby food that Catherine could digest. She threw up at least half of what she ate and we were desperate.

In early summer Catherine became really ill. I discovered one morning that her little hands were puffed and swollen, and when the doctor came he pronounced it acute Bright's disease. I was terrified, knowing it to be a kidney malfunction of some sort and very serious. The doctor ordered a trained nurse to keep constant watch over the baby and, after discussing the feeding problem, prescribed cultured buttermilk as her diet.

She began to improve almost immediately, and with the doctor's treatment and nurse's care she seemed well again. The nurse was discharged and we kept on with the buttermilk, on which

Catherine thrived. But the illness had been a setback. Instead of the usual accomplishments of an eight-month-old child, she was more like one five months old. She couldn't sit alone and didn't try to crawl and was still very tiny, though she appeared well and happy. We hoped and expected that from then on she would continue to be so and that time would make up for the lag in her development.

Chapter Fourteen

In the summer of 1914 war had broken out in Europe, and while we read about the devastating progress of the German armies and were horrified at the ruthless destruction of life and property, I was so absorbed in my own small world that it seemed far away and almost unreal. Suddenly war was not far off; it was very near and frightening when Canada mobilized her troops and soldiers were everywhere. I have a clear memory of the day when we stood with everyone else, babies in the carriage, children clinging to mothers, men and women weeping as the Princess Pat Regiment passed on its way to embarkation for Europe and the war. Mothers, wives, and sweethearts ran alongside the marching men, sobbing, clutching at hands and sleeves for one last farewell touch of loved ones, most of whom never returned. One could not stay outside that harrowing scene.

We wanted to go home, home not yet troubled by the threat of war. Home to our families. We made immediate plans. We sent our furniture by freight. Dai had no job to go to but we had infinite faith in his ability to get one.

It was a long and tiring journey from Winnipeg to Collingswood, New Jersey, where my parents now lived. Traveling with three young children, keeping them amused and fed, was not easy. The memory of it is only a blur, like a nightmare one thrusts out of the mind.

Papa met us as always and carried the baby he had never seen. We took the trolley car to the ferry across to Camden. The trip to Collingswood didn't seem long after our train ride, and soon we were walking down Collings Avenue to the house we had never seen and to the family gathered there. Even Nina and Horace had come down from Philadelphia to be with us. The boys had grown even more. Arthur was home from his first year at Bucknell; Harry was just ready to enter. What a homecoming, and this time we were not going back.

We stayed with the family while we looked for a house and until our things arrived. Dai was soon settled in with the Cunningham Piano Company in charge of their talking-machine department.

The house we moved into was on a small street just off the shopping center and only a few blocks from my family. It was in a row of houses, traditional around Philadelphia, unimposing but sufficient for our needs. I took up housekeeping where I had left off. Now we were home. My husband came home every night as other husbands did. We were an established family. If people looked at me pityingly when I boarded a trolley to visit my sister with two children clinging to my skirts and one in my arms, I thanked them not. *I* was all right and managing very well.

In early March I noticed that Catherine was restless with a cold and seemed feverish for a while every afternoon. But knowing that she was teething and that the boys had shown similar symptoms while teething, I didn't worry too much. Since arriving from Winnipeg we had found no necessity to call a doctor, so we were unfamiliar with those in the town. One afternoon, when I was at Mama's, the fever seemed more intense, although it lasted for only an hour or so. We both decided that a doctor should be called.

The doctor came about Catherine's bedtime. He examined her, confirmed my opinion that the erupting molars were at fault, and said he would lance the gums next day if she continued to be feverish, but that lancing made scar tissue which in turn made it more difficult for the teeth to come through. He gave her a sedative and left. She seemed her usual self, smiling and happy, saying over her few words as we put her into her crib.

She never awoke.

Her poor little body was in rigor mortis when we found her in the morning where she lay in her crib next to me. Our frantic efforts to arouse her were in vain. She was gone.

My parents came over immediately at my call. Dai dressed hurriedly and carried the child to the doctor's house. He simply would not accept the fact of her death.

The doctor was stunned with the suddenness of the death.

There had been no sign of such tragedy when he had seen her. He couldn't account for it and wanted to perform an autopsy. In our grief and ignorance of its usefulness in other cases, we couldn't allow it. It was necessary under the circumstances to call the coroner, who pronounced it death due to the onset of pneumonia.

Despite the heartbreak, there were two little boys who needed our love and care. They must not be made to feel neglected. They were not much more than babies themselves. We picked up the pieces and tried to think only of them and to remember that there is no separation in love.

Everything in the house spoke of the child and the loss of her darling presence. I could not bear it. We found a pleasant old house near my parents and moved there, hoping the change would be salutary. It helped, and time itself dulls the pangs of grief, however sharp.

Spring brought to blossom the many varieties of azalea surrounding the house and the surprise of new green springing from the straggling vine over the porch, which later produced exquisite lavender flowers of wisteria. A bush at the back door burst forth in feathery smoke flowers, and all down the path to the strip of woods and the little stream below the hill were bushes of small fruits, rhubarb plants, and mulberry trees. Everything about us proclaimed the continuity of life and hope.

There was a tiny bridge across the stream leading into my parents' yard and perennial garden.

Our house was square-roofed and simple in design, built when the town was settled over a hundred years before, and across from the park given by Isaac Collings. It was a pleasant place to live and just right for the two boys, who played all day in the strip of woods when the weather warmed. There they were ambushed behind dead logs or hidden from Indians in cavelike hollows. Grandma's cookie jar was not far away.

Whooping cough attacked them that spring. As usual, when some children's ailment beset them both, Jack seemed to have some innate resistance to it and would recover quickly, while Arthur must endure it to the bitter end. He coughed so hard it was frightening.

As fruits ripened I made jams and jellies, using apple or currant to give flavor even to the flat-tasting mulberries.

I made bread and pies, sang or read the children to sleep for afternoon naps, then scrubbed the wide boards of the kitchen floor on my hands and knees. Gradually the blessedness of work eased the ache of loss. The fragrance of baking bread and the whiteness of the scrubbed floor satisfied my wish to be a good homemaker, and, as always, Dai's step upon the porch set the seal upon my day, whatever kind it had been.

It was a great consolation to live so near my mother and father. Besides, in the summer Nina and her husband moved down from the city and lived only a few doors from them. Nina was not well and needed their comfort and help.

She introduced me to a friend she had met while at the sanitarium, and through Edith Gaskill I met her sisters-in-law, Marian and Helen Gaskill, who took care of their father. We were close friends for many years and our children, now middle-aged, are friends still.

Some days I was busy sewing for myself and the boys. To keep them happy I allowed them to build a train of chairs where I worked so I could watch them.

My younger brothers, who were about seven and nine, often took over for me the care of Jack and Arthur. They and their friends were still young enough to play cops and robbers in the woods, find frogs and minnows in the stream, and invent imaginative games on the little arched bridge.

We enjoyed family gatherings in the park and the simple pleasures of small-town living. I had begun to sing again, this time in a church in Camden. It gave me an outside interest and the singing itself was very good for me. There is a feeling of elation in deep breathing and letting one's voice out to its fullest capacity.

A year passed. It was 1916. Dai's restlessness and dissatisfaction with his job began to show itself. Through a manufacturer he met in his work, he accepted a position in Detroit with J. L. Hudson Company. He left almost immediately, saying he would send for us soon. I couldn't bear to leave, but where Dai went I was sure to follow.

I often wonder how we survived move after move. But then we were young and strong and the grass seemed always greener in each new pasture. There were cousins and other relatives in Detroit on the Sloan side of the family (Grandma Lofft's) with whom to renew acquaintance—Kate, especially. She was married and had two boys, both a little older than ours but still young enough to be friendly with them.

We had not been in Detroit long before I found a singing position in an Episcopal church. Dai took care of the children while I went to choir practice and to services on Sunday.

As the war continued there was threat of its involving the United States, but it was another year before we entered.

Meantime, I discovered an art school with classes on Saturday morning. It was downtown, was not expensive, and it would be a beginning. What it would lead to I couldn't know, but I had been trying over and over to paint, and the sketches I'd made were just good enough so that I knew they must be better. I began to attend the classes. We drew quick sketches from the model and sometimes painted with oils. Dai had bought me a palette large enough to have been used in painting a mural. (He never did things by halves.) Sometimes the model was a woman, sometimes a man. They were nude, but there was nothing shocking about it to me, although I believe I was somewhat of a prude.

Mr. Wicker, the instructor, went from one student to another, and by way of criticism would say, "That's too cold, this is too warm." "What do you mean?" I would ask, and he would say, "Ask your palette." So we learned by doing and by reasoning. As time went on, one realized that red and yellow were the warm colors and blues and greens the cold.

The need to search for oneself led to many discoveries—rich color where one had never seen color, unexpected blue and green shadows in flesh tones, and the development of style, an originality, of one's own.

Life did not permit me to continue this delightful pursuit, however. It was now 1918. Ever since the U.S. had entered the war Dai had thought he should enlist, but I persuaded him that he could serve in some other way, so he went to work in a munitions plant. Food was rationed. I discovered I was again pregnant. Not only was I acutely miserable—food was the last thing I wanted. But I must prepare it for the family, must contrive meals from what we were able to get and try to eat it.

Then a letter came from Papa, a letter weighted with grief. He ended by saying, "If you want to see your sister again, you'd better come. She is dying. We have brought her over here and of course Horace is here too." I set out tearfully with the boys, leaving Dai to shift for himself.

·By late afternoon of the next day we arrived at Philadelphia, where Papa once more met us and took us by bus to Collingswood. My dear father always carried with him the reassurance of "All's well" even in this time of trouble.

As Mama met us at the door we shed a few tears, but Mama was a brave woman, accepting life as it was rather than as she would have wished it to be.

I tried to cover my shock on seeing Nina, emaciated and almost voiceless. Bathing her, which became my daily task, would have been unbearable except that she kept her dry sense of humor and joked with me all the while.

I tried to help Mama as much as I could in the house and in caring for my sister. It relieved tension and nausea. It seemed an endless time before death released my sister.

Flowers filled the room where she was. She gathered all her strength to get up and touch them, to smell their fragrance and admire each flower. She glanced out of the window. It was the first of April.

"Isn't it amazing," she whispered, "that the roses are blooming already in the garden?"

"Roses?" I said, running to the window.

"April fool!" she whispered, then dropped back into bed, shaking with silent laughter.

She died that night. The next day was my eighth wedding anniversary. How long must Dai and I be separated?

Chapter Fifteen

Spring came early that year after a bitterly cold winter. I wrote and asked Dai to come east to do war work and he agreed to come. He could rent the flat furnished until we knew what we were going to do. In a month he came and we moved into a small flat on the first floor of the Mathis house across from Mama's.

Mrs. Mathis provided us with some furniture, which we eked out with pieces from Mama's, and we set up housekeeping again. Dai soon obtained war work at the Philadelphia Naval Base.

After that bitter winter of 1917–18 there was still the deep involvement of the war, the threat of Harry's having to go overseas, and the possibility that Arthur might have to go. But my own life was much more serene because I was among friends and close family and most of all because Dai was with us once more. We sat outside in early evenings, listening to war songs being played on our neighbor's phonograph, songs sweetly nostalgic, sentimental, and a part of the sounds of a summer night.

By September the virulent form of the flu had struck down thousands of soldiers and civilians. The war was reaching its climax, but no one knew when it would end. When October arrived there was still the anxiety about the spread of the flu and its swift and uncertain effects.

One Sunday afternoon, when my mother and father were sitting with us on the lawn, Papa lined up the boys, Jack, Arthur, and Dick, thinking to keep them quiet and amused.

"Let's see how long you can stand perfectly straight at attention as the soldiers do. You know Uncle Harry has to stand that way sometimes for an hour."

They all straightened up, serious and unsmiling, emulating Uncle Harry. In about two minutes Arthur fell flat on his face. We all laughed, but were soon dismayed when he didn't get up. It was the onset of flu.

We got him into bed and called the doctor, who was already so harried by the increasing number of patients that he was delayed in coming.

By the end of the week, when Arthur had begun to improve, I was a victim, and by the second day had to be taken to the hospital for delivery. A large proportion of the nurses were themselves victims of the disease and were in an emergency ward. But all the misfortunes one might name could not stop the rhythmic contractions that bring a child into the world. Without doctor or nurse, and with only a fifteen-year-old volunteer to stand by, my fourth child was born, and she was a girl, bless her! We named her Nina, after my sister.

For me the flu turned to pneumonia, and for a few days I was scarcely aware of anything but the wracking cough. It wore me out and raised my temperature to an alarming degree. The nurses were beset with work and there was no time for special care. I remembered my mother's sovereign remedy and begged for a bowl of ice water and a flannel cloth. As always, it soothed the throat and I slept. In my fevered dream I thought how easy it would be to slip off into the long sleep. Suddenly I awoke to the realization that if I should die all my children, including the new baby, would be left to my mother's care. That must not be. She had already reared six children. How unfair to thrust three more into her hands. I began to fight furiously and to pray for my recovery. I began to perspire, and by morning my temperature was normal.

As I lay recovering I was still somewhat fearful. Through the window I could see the tower of a Polish church from which at short intervals the bell tolled the passing of one more victim. The keeper of that shadowy door had beckoned me enticingly only yesterday, but now I was turned toward life. I couldn't wait to go home with the new daughter. I still had the peculiarly bluish color characteristic of that disease, and I sometimes felt as if a grisly hand had touched my back.

When Nina was a month old the Armistice was signed. World War I was over. I shall never forget the early morning sounds of that happy day. Horns blowing, bells ringing, people's voices on the high note of joy. The end of the long, long tension. And we had our little girl.

Nina was a most satisfactory baby. From the first she seemed agreeable to everything and was the darling of the household. Her brothers adored her. The regular morning care, the ritual of the bath, which I had always enjoyed, was again a study in anatomy, a hymn of praise to the Creator of such wonders of perfection, a tactile joy in smooth skin, dimpled arms and knees and bottom, miniature fingernails. My large hands held her safely, so she loved her bath from the start. Like her brother Jack, nothing frightened or dismayed her. She was everybody's friend, and still is.

When Nina was nine months old summer had come and school was over. My brother Walter, then seventeen, went with me to Michigan to pack our household things and send them to Collingswood. We left the boys at Mama's. It was hard work, but fun too. Sometimes we were so tired we just laughed at nothing and couldn't stop.

While waiting for our things we found a house just across the street from Mama's. Father de Angeli came to our rescue and made a down payment on the house so we could buy it. It was a pleasant Victorian clapboard house with a useless square tower at the corner just for looks. There was no access to it. A wide veranda framed two sides of the house and a round window on the staircase filtered light into the narrow hall. The dining room was large and extended into an alcove connected with the living room, which, though rather small, was comfortable and homey. It had a fireplace in which coal was burned and a wide window seat that was a never-ending source of comfort and enjoyment for the children. It was there on the cushion that Nina sat to watch the people passing, where she and the boys took handfuls of cookies to eat while they read, where they sprawled when the world was not treating them as they thought it should. Only lately have I really known what the window seat meant to them all.

The kitchen was old-fashioned and spacious, with cupboards above and below a counter where the sugar and flour was kept. Nina's imaginary Mr. Jooger lived in the cupboard below and wordlessly answered her one-sided conversation. He sometimes took off on jaunts with his family or had the measles, but was usually receptive to Nina's visits as she sat on a small keg that had held apple butter. We had an old round table of oak where we ate breakfast and there was a combination coal and gas stove, which was very comforting in cold weather.

Chapter Sixteen

How could I know that in the summer of 1921 my life would take on a new and exciting turn beginning the fulfillment of the dream of years?

One morning when I was out sweeping the front walk I saw Mrs. Bower sweeping hers. She greeted me with a wave of the hand, then left her broom and came over to speak to me.

Had I known Mrs. Bower then as well as I knew her later, I would have been surprised that she came to speak to me instead of waiting for me to come to her. But I think she was so pleased with the news she had to impart that she felt she must communicate it at once. She told me that her son, Maurice, lately released from his post as lieutenant in the Army, had just signed a contract with the Hearst publications as an illustrator. *Illustrator?* My heart jumped.

"Illustrator?" I asked excitedly. "Could I meet him? I've wanted to be an illustrator all my life! Do you think I could really meet him?"

"Of course," she said. "I'll ask his wife to arrange it."

After a few more remarks we both went back to our work. Mrs. Bower across the street, and I where I was. But how lightly my broom flew! How bright the morning. How wonderful the world. It was as if everything had been transformed and had taken on a new look. But I hadn't met him yet. Perhaps he wouldn't like me or whatever drawing I might do.

That afternoon Polly, Maurice's wife, called and asked me to tea in the studio for the coming Saturday. When Dai came home I greeted him with the exciting news. He was as much impressed as I, knowing how much I wanted to draw and paint. He said he would take the boys and Nina to the circus so that I would be free.

Marguerite in her thirties.

All the rest of the week the housework went as if by itself. I sang at the piano, sang at my work, practiced my Sunday solo, thinking, planning what I should wear, how I would arrange my hair.

Naturally, I flew over to tell my parents of my good fortune. Mama was pleased about the invitation, laughing at my enthusiasm. Papa, on the other hand, was inclined to discourage me. He was fearful that I might get into loose company, perhaps neglect my family. Even though I had been a responsible wife and mother for ten years he didn't realize that never would I have been interested in unconventional behavior. He didn't insist, but thought he ought to caution me.

On Saturday we had the children ready early, the boys spick and span in clean shirts, hair slicked down with water, Nina in her little ruffled petticoat and Swiss batiste dress I had made. Off they went to the circus, while I took the trolley and ferry to Philadelphia. I can't be sure, but I think I walked up Chestnut Street from the ferry. Walked? Trod on air, rather.

Polly was already there when I arrived, and introduced me to her husband. It is hard to describe my mixed feelings that afternoon: I was ecstatic, yet timid. What had I to offer?

Mr. Bower showed me some of the reproductions of drawings he had done, some that were finished and ready for delivery and what was then on the drawing board for future publication. He showed me preliminary sketches made to clarify his thought, establish character and composition, each successive one coming nearer to what he had in mind.

The beauty of feeling, the careful handling of light and shade in the drawings, dissolved me emotionally. How did he do it? Could I ever learn?

I was too ignorant then to appreciate the telling accents that made the whole composition sing. That came later in my own experience. But I thought if I could come anywhere near the standard of his work, I would be the happiest woman in the world.

The talk went on about the ways of editors, the kinds of media employed, the dedication to authenticity. I listened to every word.

Mr. Bower had graduated from the School of Industrial Art and had been a student of Walter Everett, whose work I remembered from my girlhood. Mr. Everett had been one of a group of artists who followed Howard Pyle, N. C. Wyeth, Jessie Wilcox Smith, Violet Oakley, Edith Emerson, Katherine Wireman, Elizabeth Shippen Green. Henry Pitz is also of that school and his book *The Brandywine Tradition* tells the story.

For longer than I could remember I had admired the work of these artists, and to have them brought to life through Mr. Bower's talk was a little like having met them.

When I asked Mr. Bower if he would take me as a pupil, he said, "No"; he was too busy now to teach. He had taught at Spring Garden Street before going into the Army, but now work came in too steadily.

In that second before he went on, my heart sank. Was this to be only another disappointment? But he did go on.

"However," he said, "if you are serious and will go home and begin drawing on some chosen subject, doing the very best you can, I will be glad to give you criticism." What more could anyone ask?

"Remember," he said, "choose something that explains itself. Editors don't like to think." He laughed, but I'm sure he had someone special in mind. I have found in my experience that thinking and being helpful is an editor's principal characteristic.

I could hardly wait to begin. I left in exultant anticipation.

Soon after my arrival home, Dai came in with the children. But what was this? Nina in her petticoat? Where was the dress I had so carefully made? Dai held up inch-wide strips of the fine material. "She fell through the seat," he said laughing. "I caught her dress and it just unwound like this, but it saved her from a bad fall."

We all laughed. These days she would be considered well clothed in what was then a petticoat. And she was only two.

Then I had to tell the story of my afternoon—what we had talked about, who was there, what Mr. Bower was like.

"He's tall and very young-looking and friendly," I began, then went on to tell what materials I should have to start with, the type of drawing I should do for a beginning so he could see how much ability I had.

Dai said he would order the easel and the paper and long, thin charcoal such as Mr. Bower used. In a few days they were delivered and I set up shop in the alcove off the dining room. There I could

Maurice L. Bower: illustrator, teacher, friend.

work for a few moments at a time when something was baking, while waiting for the family to gather for dinner, while Nina was napping and the boys were in school.

At the very beginning I took Nina to the easel and showed her each thing and told her what it was for.

"This is Mama's work," I said, "and you *never, never* touch it." Nina shook her little head slowly from side to side.

"No, no, no," she said. And she never did.

What could I use for a subject? There was that old story Papa used to tell us about the Rig-jig-jag, and the witch and the long leather bag which we all loved. It was in the Grimm tradition. I took a scene from that and thus began the years and years of drawing.

Surprisingly, once I had set my mind on it, the drawing went rather well. Now to get Mr. Bower to see it and give his opinion. It seemed that I could never see him passing so I could call him in to look at what I had done. Later I knew the reason. He preferred to work late in the day and evening when the city was quiet, and sometimes he worked until midnight. I didn't know his wife or his mother well enough to ask about him.

Two weeks went by and I began to fear that he had forgotten my existence. Then one morning when I chanced to look out the window I saw him in the driveway fixing his mother's car. I crossed the street.

After a pleasant "Good morning," he agreed to come over and look at my first effort. I hesitated to ask him to look at my work, but he was kindness itself.

When he saw my drawing of the boy in the Rig-jig-jag story, he said, "*Well!* You *are* in earnest! I didn't really think you had it in you. I see you have." Then he went on to lay out a program for me to follow.

"I suggest that you choose three subjects to work on. Take subjects that are self-evident, that require no caption, and no explanation. Carry each drawing as far as you can until you can see no more to do to it. Then put it away out of sight, get out another one and start on that, then the third, taking them in turn for a whole year. I will help you when I can and I think by the end of the year you will be able to get commissions from an editor. I think too it would be better if you give up your public singing, or you will be spreading yourself too thin."

To this I agreed gladly. It had become more and more difficult for me to be calm in solo work and to meet the rigid schedule of rehearsal and performance. But a *year*? A whole *year*? But what was a year? I had longed for such a moment as this all my life. To have this encouragement toward the realization of that dream was like a gift from heaven. Nina stood by and listened to every word.

Mr. Bower looked down at her serious face and smiled. I think he took her into his heart right then, for her particular quality appealed to him as it seems to attract everyone. In fact he took to all the children and to this day he and his sister, Gertrude, seem a part of our family.

As that first year rolled on I sometimes became discouraged because I could not make my drawings look as I saw them in my mind. But even when they didn't go, there was always the belief that, in the end, all would be well. For the first time in my life I didn't stop even if a drawing turned out to be another example of "butter at the old price." I had chosen as one of the three drawings a family of five sitting around a Christmas tree, probably one of the most difficult things I could have chosen. Another was a girl making a cake; the third I've forgotten. When I just couldn't make the tree keep its place in the composition, or give each person in the group his proper amount of space, I called for help. Dai and I put the lamp in the front window and sat waiting until Mr. Bower came along on his way home, hoping he would sense my need for help and come in. He did. Then, as often happened, he worked for an hour or so on the drawing with the needle-sharp charcoal, making the tree mass, with here and there a detail of branch and twig and showing the small gifts and decorations in their proper value. It looked so easy when *he* did it. He talked as he worked, showing me how to emphasize this and minimize the importance of that, how to keep one spot the center of attention, and by proper use of light and shadow give atmosphere and oneness to the drawing.

I remembered how Papa used various means to keep the less important parts of a photograph subdued by shadow, sometimes holding a fan or magazine to interrupt the light, keeping the lower part of the figure in a lower tone than that above.

Little by little my drawings improved. I learned in drawing the clothing on a figure that one must make it describe the figure so it seems to be solid before putting on buttons or other decoration. Sometimes I seemed to be able to do it and sometimes I despaired of ever achieving anything. But I kept at it. I, who as a girl had seldom finished anything, kept at those three drawings for a whole year. My time was limited by household chores, by child care and by cooking, but there was always Dai's encouragement and the light of success shining ahead. I never doubted that someday I would succeed in doing illustration that would be acceptable to some publisher.

The day finally arrived when Morry, as we had learned to call him, sent me to Mr. Scheetz, the editor at Westminster Press. He told me to say that he would be responsible for having any drawing I might do ready for reproduction.

After examining my three drawings and nodding his head in approval, Mr. Scheetz gave me a story to illustrate for one of the Presbyterian Sunday school papers. I walked out of the building in such a state of elation that I could have floated on air to the nearest telephone to ask Dai to join me for lunch, so I could tell him all about it. Dai shared my excitement.

"Might as well make the most of this trip to town," he said. "Why don't you show your drawings to the Baptist publications as well?" And so I did. The editor gave me a story to do, but cautioned me that it was their only copy, so I musn't mislay it.

What a day! I was launched. There remained only the drawings to be done. But I had no doubt whatever that I could do them. It wasn't that I had any conceit about my ability. It was, rather, that I felt I had the inspiration at my disposal as has every other person—I must just dig for it within myself.

I gathered the children from my mother's and invited her to bring Papa for supper to celebrate. As always there was a great deal of merriment.

After supper I looked for the manuscript from the Baptist Publication Society to read it aloud. It was not to be found. We spent the evening looking for it. I was sure I hadn't left it on the trolley, but where was it?

When Mama and Papa had gone and I was tidying the house before going to bed, in despair at not finding the manuscript, I started to close the lid of the old secretary and there it lay. I breathed again.

Chapter Seventeen

From that day in 1922, except for a slowing down during the Depression, there had been an almost unbroken chain of illustration for Sunday school papers, magazines, and books. But it was fourteen years and two more children before I began writing my own books.

In those intervening years I illustrated stories by such well-known authors as Charlotte M. Yonge, Augusta Huiell Seaman, Elsie Singmaster, Dorothy Canfield, Elizabeth Vining, Cornelia Meigs, Ann Kyle, and others. Sometimes the drawings showed improvement. Other times I simply did the best I could and when it was time to deliver them and they were far from perfect, I simply said to myself, "Well, butter must go at the old price again."

The Bowers became our fast friends. Maurice we saw occasionally, but Polly began to join us often as we read to the children after supper. We read the Stevenson books illustrated by Howard Pyle or N. C. Wyeth, *Kidnapped, Treasure Island, The Master of Ballantrae*, and the Wyeth edition of *Robin Hood*. I bought Pyle's *Book of the American Spirit* and several of those illustrated by Arthur Rackham and by Willy Pogany. How I pored over those illustrations!

Besides the books, Dai read from the *Post* each week as it appeared, a series of stories about a freighter called *The Inchcliffe Castle* and the first mate, Colin Glencannon. We all found them immensely amusing, although I'm sure I would never have read them to myself and they weren't children's stories. Somehow Dai made them interesting.

Morry had re-married and with his wife had been living in Paris for almost a year. On his return he saw my work then in

Illustration from *The Torchbearer*, 1933.

progress, and said, with a look of surprise, "Pretty *good!* But you know this is better than you can *do*." Better than I could do? But I had *done* it. "I mean," he explained, seeing my crestfallen look, "it is better than you can do *consistently*." Then I understood. Many times my efforts have fallen below what I had done before. Sometimes I found that if I drew what wasn't there, the shape of a certain space, the thing I was trying to draw seemed to come out of the paper by itself. I suppose by drawing the space I became relaxed, which allowed my thought to come through.

Meantime, life in the family went on. The children had the usual mishaps that attend childhood, some of them contributing to the aging process. Ted fell on a knife and nearly put his eye out. Arthur was thrown over his bike handlebars and was brought home unconscious. Jack, playing mumbletypeg, stabbed himself in the thigh, but went to have it sewed up before telling me.

Nina was found to be allergic to the belladonna used to test her eyes and nearly died from the paralyzing of the intestine.

Sometimes, with the multiplicity of *things to do,* I threw up my hands in despair. What to do first? Then I said to myself and often, out loud so I would hear it, "Now, quietly, calmly, *think* what should be done first. One thing at a time, as if there were no others. *One thing.* Clear the table, make the beds, sort those papers lying there and do *one thing.*" Then I calmed down and little by little things were done and I could concentrate on the drawings or the writing that troubled me.

Dai planted a garden on the hill back of Mama's where my brother Arthur had bought ground for a house, which he later built, mostly with his own hands and to his own specifications.

Dai's garden grew well. He tended and watered it and was rewarded with the usual spring and summer vegetables, and they kept us supplied all summer long. There were literally bushels of tomatoes, which we served for almost every meal, still having enough to can for winter. We were especially fond of fried tomatoes served with cream sauce, a favorite even to this day. Mama used to tell with amusement how Dai groaned at every spadeful of potatoes he dug. The level of the garden was just about where she sat at her sewing machine, and through the open window she could hear his complaint. Once when he came home bent double with backache, Nina asked, "What makes Daddy hang over?"

Joy, to be appreciated, must be shared. So on every occasion, however slight, we gathered family or friends to join us. Our children always were a part of this and grew up loving their parents' friends, as well as their own, who were always welcome.

The house wasn't always in perfect order, because the children were allowed to feel it was their house as well as ours. The boards for extending the dining table might be in use as airplane wings, or the chairs as a train, or a blanket as a tent over a chair. But one place was inviolate, the sideboard in the dining room, part of a set acquired from a friend who had bought new furniture. I insisted that nothing, absolutely *nothing,* could be laid upon it except what belonged there. A deep blue Chinese bowl I treasured held the center and beside it were two pairs of brass candlesticks. On the upper shelf was a Japanese basket that held (out of sight) current receipts of paid bills. No keys or letters or any other trifle was allowed.

The children learned to respect this and I hoped that one tidy place would declare my real sense of order in the midst of the confusion created by the children's growing up. I had two rules: "Do it *now*" and "Never lay anything down."

In 1925 Ted was born—a long, lean little boy. We named him Harry Edward for my brother and Dai's father, but I didn't want him called Eddie, so immediately began to call him Ted. When he was born his ears were folded like small flowers that flew open at a touch. They never lay very close to his head. But who cared? He had his own special charm and sweet nature, which endeared him to all. By the time he was four he had a circle of friends among the neighbors and access to numerous cookie jars.

By this time we had a series of girls who came in to help every day. It was not always easy to find one who had enough interest in children to keep the youngest from clamoring for my attention.

The need for a studio became insistent. It seemed feasible to build one over the one-story kitchen, and my brother Arthur took over the planning and supervising of the work. He worked on it himself on Saturdays and holidays, but hired a mason to build the fireplace, which was the only source of heat. How impractical we all were. There was a large studio window that provided a proper light but was also a great conductor of cold. When I was engrossed in my drawing I never thought of the fire until I was chilled through.

A stairway led up from the alcove where I had worked before, but there was no door to close. I didn't want to be separated entirely from the children and what was going on downstairs. This was no ivory tower, but I had learned from the start to achieve a certain amount of concentration in the midst of the usual noises. I realize this is not the kind of atmosphere commonly thought necessary to creative work, but there it is. The family came first.

Dai had a genius for makeshift repairs. When we had tired of hearing the groans and squeaks of the spring on the shed door, he picked up one of his overshoes, stuck it behind the spring, and that ended the squeak.

When a bat got into our bedroom and I hid my head under the covers, Dai sailed around in his pajamas whacking at it with a tennis racquet until he killed it.

Our old Essex had one tooth missing in the starter ring gear. When it didn't engage, which was often, Dai got out the piece of oriental rug he kept for the purpose, laid it down on the ground, and crawled under the car to fix it.

When the studio was built we changed the kitchen, taking part of the space for a laundry. We put a new sink in place of the old blue one, leaving a two-inch hole where the old drain pipe had been, a perfect freeway for the mice that came in from the cold. Once, when they came skittering up through the hole and I jumped on a chair, Dai with his usual ingenuity grabbed the boys' baseball bat, shoved it small-end-down into the hole until it stuck, leaving a foot or so above the floor.

There it stayed. Every time the kitchen stool was needed, it had to be lifted up and over the baseball bat, then put back carefully under the drainboard and over the bat. It was a nuisance we got used to.

After six years, one Sunday night as we all sat in the kitchen having supper, one of us suddenly discovered the ridiculous makeshift and began to laugh, pointing helplessly to the baseball bat. We all caught the infection and Dai laughed until he cried, then got up and sawed the bat off at floor level, found a lid off a tin can and nailed it down.

When Ted was about a year old, and I was busy with illustration, we had a girl to help who was not very good at keeping him interested. He wanted to be with me. He called "Mama" from the bottom of the stairs in a way I could not ignore. I brought him up and put him in his playpen and as long as I was attending him he was quiet. But as soon as I sat down to work again he began to howl. So I took him out of the playpen and put the pen around the easel and me in my chair, letting him have the run of the studio. Then he was happy.

About this time a young cellist named Roland Hart came to see us to invite Dai to join a quartet as violinist. Wives were invited too and we were to meet first at the Mengers', who lived not far away in Oaklyn, New Jersey. Charlie Mengers played piano and violin, Edward Ryglewicz played viola, and Roland, cello.

After a period of chamber music by the quartet, Nell Mengers and I sometimes sang. Nell was soprano and Charles was the accompanist. It was a joy to sing with him. He followed every change in tempo or volume and was there to support us when needed.

The evenings ended with coffee and cake, an exchange of ideas, a comparison of backgrounds and stories, of which Charles had an inexhaustible fund.

As time went on there were intermingling groups, due to substitution of one player or another. Still, we all remained friends throughout the years.

Through Charles we met Harmon Robinson and his wife, who lived in Roxborough, a suburb of Philadelphia. Harm Robinson played viola and taught music and became a regular member of the quartet. Although I didn't realize it at the time, these happy evenings were to lead to two of my books years later.

Chapter Eighteen

After doing work for the Sunday school papers for a year or two, I branched out. Our fortunes had improved somewhat and Dai bought a Ford car. He drove me one day to New York with an introduction from Morry Bower to William F. Clarke, then editor of *St. Nicholas*. I showed him samples of work I had done and they seemed to please him. He gave me a story to do. I wish I could remember the story and how I illustrated it, but I can't. Evidently it was satisfactory, because Mr. Clarke gave me more and more to do over a period of years. Once, he said laughing, and pleased with what I had done, "Tell Maurice Bower to look to his laurels."

One serial I illustrated for him concerned knights in armor, castles and the pageantry of the Middle Ages and reminded me of that drawing I had so admired long ago in the West Philadelphia library. Was it as good? I wondered.

When Dai took me to New York to deliver some of those drawings he suggested that I show them to Macmillan before delivering them.

Louise Seaman was then children's book editor for Macmillan, when a special department of books for children, as such, was a new enterprise. They had begun a series they called Children's Classics, which included books by Charlotte Yonge. Miss Seaman gave me several of those to illustrate: *The Little Duke, Dove in the Eagle's Nest*, besides others on her list. The historical stories and books I was illustrating now entailed research. This meant that I must go to the library in Philadelphia, where I spent many hours over a long period of time studying costume, armor, houses and castles.

I shall never forget the kindness and patience of the librarian, who is gone now. She was French and spoke with a slight but charming accent. She is typical of librarians I have found. It seems as if they are never too busy, too tired, or too indifferent to give one help, but will go to endless trouble to find what is needed. I was introduced to Racinet and Viollet-le-Duc for costume and for architecture, to Rackham, Willy Pogany, and a host of others for illustration. Many of the artists I rediscovered, having known them through that old book of my father's, the year's bound copies of *Magazine of Art*, and often I found there some bit of background I needed. The Holbein prints from the stacks in the library were useful for costume as well as for characterization when I was given a story about Mary, Queen of Scots to do for *The American Girl*. But that was later. Gathering material was half the fun, but it was tiring too because of the intense concentration required.

Even with book illustration to do and *St. Nicholas* commissions, I still continued to work for the religious publications. Trips to New York for the day were fairly frequent because delivery was safer and quicker that way and recompense was swifter.

One day, before delivering my work to *St. Nicholas*, I took it to the Curtis Publishing Company. It was then on Arch Street. My recollection of the visit is vague, but I know I was given an article to illustrate for *The Country Gentleman*. I think it was by Corra Harris, whose stories of *The Circuit Rider* I had enjoyed years before when they had been illustrated by Walter Everett.

Not long after that first assignment I was invited to meet her at lunch. She was just the sort of person I had imagined her to be, humorous, tender, and down to earth. She told me of an amusing incident when she had been invited to Philadelphia to be entertained by the Curtis staff and was given orchids. She said they were so foreign to her way of life that she carried them hanging at her side, not realizing their value and delicacy.

Later I illustrated her *Circuit Rider's Widow* in a series that covered a long period of time, one a month. This was another step forward. During this time, when I went to deliver drawings to Curtis and sometimes had to wait awhile to see Miss Dinsmore, the art editor, I used to watch the young men and the girls who drifted past to the water cooler again and again, talking, giggling, wasting precious time. I thought to myself, They call this *work?* Time was so precious to me then. I made the most of every moment.

In later years, when people said to me, "You know, I think I could write if only I had time." I had to laugh, remembering.

When I began illustrating for Curtis they wanted me to do the drawings in pen and ink. I had never done pen and ink work and scarcely knew how to begin. I called Morry on the phone and asked him, "How do you draw in pen and ink?"

"I don't know. I never did pen and ink," he answered, laughing. "I would think, however, that you should follow the line of the figure and let your strokes follow the line of drapery." And so on. We both laughed and I went ahead. I chose to use gray paper as Morry did, only Morry used charcoal for the blacks instead of ink, using white Conte crayon to pick out the highlights. It was a pleasant medium in which to work, the gray paper giving a unity to the drawing that was effective. I used this method for a long time.

Some of the articles I illustrated were written by psychologists about the care and rearing of children. At that time permissiveness was the current theory and practice with children. I knew by experience that a too permissive attitude was not in the best interest of the child and certainly not of the parent. I had no academic training in psychology to back me up, but I had a certain amount of common sense, which told me that when a child goes out into the world he must consider others and not follow his own will without regard to his fellow man. This must begin in babyhood. A baby not more than a week old knows whether his crying brings the comfort of food or other needs or wishes or whether it doesn't. But, of course, I had nothing to do with the text.

All through the years of my life there have been wonders, moments when the spirit is carried far above one's ordinary self, moments that Elizabeth Vining calls "minor ecstasies." One such time, in early fall, after one of those blue and gold days rather rare in the Delaware Valley, Mama called us on the phone to tell us excitedly to come outdoors and look to the southwest. There was a tremendous flight of small birds flying south. She left the phone to run out herself for fear of missing what was left of the flight. She said it had been going on for over an hour. We hurried out to see it and it went on for another hour. A beautiful stream of small birds adown the sky, twittering and fluttering and holding together in a band that must have held millions of birds following

Illustration from *The Circus Pony* by Elizabeth Coatsworth.

that built-in knowledge of direction and timing. It was one of the most thrilling sights I have ever seen.

Once again, only two years ago, in spring, when I sat by my drawing table in early morning, thousands of wild geese flew right past my window. I rushed to the back door and watched until they had vanished into the north. What wondrous instinct impels their gathering and flight?

In the spring of 1927 the time had come once more to prepare for the arrival of another child. It was not easy to accept the fact, but there it was. The doctor consoled me by saying, "Just think. When you are old and the other children are gone, this child will be your comfort and support." As always I soon became reconciled to the inevitable.

Dai bought me a radio to which I listened for hours on end. It was still a marvel to pick sounds out of the air and to choose by turning a dial.

In January of 1928 the baby was born, another boy, beautiful, and healthy from the start, so well developed that Miss Eva, the nurse, brought everyone in to see him, visitors and patients alike.

Like Arthur, he had dark eyes and brown hair. We decided to call him Maurice Bower de Angeli. This would not repay Morry for all his kindness and help, but would show him our appreciation and perhaps, one day, our Maury would honor him with a good life. He has.

After a month of trying to satisfy his appetite, the doctor recommended extra food and from then on he was angelic and remained so until he was four, the self-determining age.

Both Ted and Maury, when they were small, begged at intervals to come up with me into the studio. I allowed them to come up and sit in the old rattan chair if they promised to be absolutely quiet. They promised, and in two minutes they fell asleep. They looked so appealing in their innocence that I *must* sketch them. So each has his own sleeping-baby portrait, Maury, when he was about a year and a half and Ted when he was about two.

When Ted was about three I was given a commission to illustrate an article on sledding or some such winter subject. I knew it was to be printed in black and white, but to make it more interesting to do I painted it in watercolor, using Ted in his little blue coat and leggings as one of the figures. When I delivered it the editor said in dismay, "Oh, but it is to be in black and white!"

"I know," I answered, "but it was more fun to do this way and I'm sure it has good black and white value." And it did reproduce well, but it was reduced to a two-inch-wide print in a back column.

Another commission I had for *Woman's Home Companion* was for an article about Joan of Arc. I was thrilled at the assignment and decided to do it in color and in oil. My brother Harry's wife, Peggy, posed for me, sitting on a pile of cushions astride a small chest as if on horseback. I had to imagine that she wore armor, but I found authentic material for it, and the painting turned out quite well. When I delivered it, after a month's work, I was dismayed to find that it too would be reduced to a two-inch width and be printed on a back page. Oh well, I was well paid for it and my brother still has it.

Our musical evenings went on and our circle of friends widened. Once, during a Christmas season, we gave a party in the studio. Morry Bower lent us his samovar to give the place atmosphere. We served supper from a chafing dish, then had a hilarious time with charades. Instead of acting out words, we used phrases and jokes we all knew.

One time when Dai had taken me to New York to deliver drawings, it turned very cold on our way home. It was late November and Dai was afraid the engine might freeze, so after bringing me home he took the car to get antifreeze put in. He hadn't been gone very long when he returned, and holding out the whisk broom to me said ruefully, "This is all that's left of the car."

I could only gasp. Then the story came out. As Dai had crossed the railroad track coming back the car had stalled, as it had done before, and nothing he could do would start it. A train was not far off, but Dai stuck it out until the train was almost upon him, then jumped clear, leaving the car to be struck by every passing coach. It was completely wrecked.

The car that replaced it was far from new and had crotchets of its own, but for a while it served.

Chapter Nineteen

At the beginning of the Depression, Dai had no work and it seemed as if all sources of income had dried up, except occasional commissions for Sunday school papers. Then May Massee, editor of children's books at Doubleday, asked me to illustrate a book by Elizabeth Gray Vining, *Meggy McIntosh*. This was a great help financially, but better still it introduced me to Elizabeth. We met at the Camden Book Fair, where we both spoke. Her loveliness, her dignity, and her established place in the book world kept me in awe of her for many years, although I longed to know her better. Later, when I needed material for *Thee Hannah!*, I went to the Friends' Library in Germantown where I met her sister, Violet Gray, who was in charge there. She directed me to helpful reading and I fell in love with her too. Our friendship deepened and has continued through the years.

This was in 1929, when Jack had graduated from high school. Arthur graduated in 1930. College was impossible for either of them, so both found work for a time, Arthur in the bookstore of Strawbridge and Clothier and Jack collecting and delivering for a cleaning establishment on a motorcycle. That job ended when a gasoline truck ran into him and threw him to the ground with the motorcycle on top of him. Arthur's ended when Strawbridge and Clothier found it necessary to cut down on the staff.

The problem of finding three meals a day naturally fell upon me, and while it was something to think about, it was a challenge to one's ingenuity to make a meal out of what seemed like nothing. Somehow, we always made it.

Early in the summer of 1931 a young cousin stopped to see us when college closed. She persuaded Arthur to go home with her

Drawing from *Ladies' Home Journal*, May 1930.

to Lapeer, where she was sure her father could give him work, which he did. The job was giving the Lapeer waterworks three coats of paint, and because of the Victorian gingerbread trim it took him all summer.

Payments on our house became impossible to meet, and as happened to so many, we lost the house in Collingswood, where we had lived for fourteen years.

Dai knew of a house in Pennsylvania in the country outside Jarrettown, where he felt sure we would be better off, where we could raise vegetables, where the children would be free to run. Why we thought this would improve our situation, I don't know. But in 1932, in very early spring, we moved to Jarrettown. Nina stayed on with her grandparents to finish the school year. I couldn't bear to leave her, but it was best. There were heartaches and doubts at leaving friends and family, the familiar school, and the home of precious memory. Still, unlike so many, we had no savings to lose when the banks closed, and no stocks to fall in value. We had nothing to lose. We had health and each other, the same stories to tell, the same music to lift our hearts, and boundless optimism.

As always, there was a certain excitement in moving, new friends to be made, new cupboards to be fitted out with dishes, pots, and pans, new settings for old furniture where everything took on a new look.

The house we had chosen was set back from the road and

about a mile from the village and school. It was square and dormer-roofed, a relic of the middle 1800s. The many rooms were rather cut up, but there was a center hall leading to an enormous kitchen, which was the heart of the house. Wide fields spread out all around and the view was typical of Pennsylvania farmland, which nothing surpasses in beauty.

As spring warmed, a variety of shrubs and flowers came into bloom: lilac, both lavender and white, lily of the valley, weigela, spirea, and old-fashioned sweet shrub. There were crocus and daffodil of many varieties as well—the garden was heavenly.

The barn and corn crib were a never-ending source of enjoyment for Ted and Maury. The chicken coop was the clubhouse for make-believe, and there was a swing hanging from a big tree at the back, which the big boys had put up for the little ones.

Dai and the older boys made a vegetable garden and planted all kinds of vegetables, including potatoes and celery, which proved to be a valuable contribution to the food supply.

Jack and Arthur helped the little ones to make kites to fly over the open field; the kitchen table was littered with paper and paste, with string and with rags for ballast.

Water was pumped from a well deep in the earth. It flowed cold and deceivingly clear, so it didn't occur to us to have it tested. . . . For a while, all went well.

We had not been long in Jarrettown when we received word that Dai's mother and sister, Anna, were in need of assistance. Although we had kept in touch with them we had been so engrossed in our own problems and decisions that we had not seen them for some time. It was a shock to hear they had come to the end of their resources and could no longer maintain their apartment in Atlantic City. We drove down in our car of many years use to rescue them and bring them to live with us. Without our knowledge they had quietly been selling some of their effects to buy food. There was almost nothing left. It was pitiful. We packed and sent by truck enough to furnish a bedroom and disposed of the rest, which paid for the moving.

Mother de Angeli, who was nearing eighty, took it like the gallant soul she was, and I was determined that all should go well. It did for a while.

Too late I realized that there was no good light in the house for me to work by. Mother and Anna had no concept of the concentration it takes to get a drawing out of one's head and down on paper. In Mother's desire to be helpful she constantly came to ask my advice about this or that, pulling me back from the world of imagination to reality. Anna complained because she had no money and because she was out in the country, not accepting the fact that *no* one had any money. Being completely deaf, she was cut off from the usual give and take that goes on among people.

It required a good deal of managing to feed nine people, provide needed clothing, pay for utilities and coal for the furnace. Money came in dribs and drabs, sometimes from photographs of school children that Dai made with our camera down in the city. Sometimes from odd jobs the boys found to do. Sometimes, but more and more rarely, from the drawings for *The Country Gentleman* or for Sunday school papers. I found it very difficult to do them because of interruptions. Dai agreed that a studio away from home was the only answer. Anna could look after the little boys and Mother, who was becoming more and more forgetful and childish. We engaged a room on Washington Square in Philadelphia, where Dai was going each day, hoping to find work. It was close to the Curtis Publishing Company, where I hoped I would find more work.

After three months' trial we found this arrangement extremely impractical. No work materialized and commissions for me lessened

Illustration from a *Country Gentleman* piece entitled "Herbs for the Kitchen," August 1937.

rather than increased. We gave it up. Once more I set up my drawing board in the dining room and moved the dining table into the kitchen, where there was more room. It saved steps and was more cheerful and pleasant in every way. There we gathered for the evening meal, which consisted of whatever was available. We made our own bread, which was very good, and often had vegetable soup, which was satisfying.

Here too we brought our day's experiences, our triumphs and disappointments, and always there were jokes old and new. Arthur told of meeting an old friend in Ambler who suggested the possibility of a job for the summer in a camp as a counselor. Jack would tell the joke he'd heard that afternoon. As he begins, Ted reaches for the bread and Dai hisses, "Sit down!" and helps him. Maury tugs at my sleeve and Jack goes on.

"Over the gate to heaven where Saint Peter stands is a sign saying HENPECKED HUSBANDS ONLY. There's a long line of men, each waiting his turn to be questioned. Farther over, there's another gate with no sign over it, and one lone man standing by himself. 'Hey!' calls one of the henpecked husbands, 'what ye doin' over there all by yerself?'

"'I do' know'—the little man shrugs—'my wife told me to stand here.'"

Everyone laughs. The little boys because everyone else is laughing and Mother for the same reason—"The wonderful works of a wheelbarrow," she says, which could have meant anything or nothing.

"*What?*" asks Anna, looking to me for explanation. And I with the conceit of one who thinks everything depends upon her, answer as best I can instead of delegating it to Dai or someone else. Anna's sense of humor was keen, but it was hard for her to follow a joke. I try to explain, but she shakes her head in uncomprehension and distress. She reads lips well but in group conversation talk moves too fast from one to another for her to catch the words.

Dai, to relieve the tension, recounts one of his oldest jokes told again and again, but still funny.

"I met a fella today who can jump twenty feet backwards," says Mike.

"Ah, g'wan now, nobuddy can jump twinty feet backwards!" says Pat.

"Well, 'twas yer own son Dinny," says Mike.

"Och, Dinny? Well *he* might," says Pat. Laughter again and

the same query from Anna, "*What?*" Then everybody talks at once and the confusion is deafening.

When I ask Ted what he remembers of that difficult time, he says, "It was *miserable*. But what I really remember is, everybody tried to make everybody else think that it *wasn't*." Which is comforting to know. He was just beginning school, walking a mile and a half each way with neighbor children.

Maury remembers nothing about it, but it took its toll of him because he was only four, when a child needs special attention and I was not free to give it then. It was some time before we realized that the reason he was behaving in a manner entirely foreign to him was because he didn't have his fair share in the company of so many adults. We began then to show him unobtrusive but special attention to which he responded slowly.

During the summer the garden Dai and the boys had planted produced a helpful supply of vegetables. The little boys discovered Far View Farm and Uncle Mike, who cared for the animals, the great barn, and the cow shed, and who told marvelous tales.

Arthur got a position as counselor in the camp in Chester County, but it was kept from me that due to a slight injury he had blood poisoning.

In fact, as summer came in, the whole situation worsened. It hadn't occurred to us to have the well water tested, or that the odd taste of the milk bought from a nearby farm was due to unwashed straining cloths. Ted and Maury became quite ill with all the symptoms of typhoid fever. I began to sleep less and less, and when they had recovered under a doctor's care I too became ill with almost the same symptoms, and with the added frightening feeling that someone had inadvertently piled books on my chest.

The boys' illness had been a strain, but more than that was the continual bickering between Dai and his sister. Dai scolded because she didn't do her share of the work and Mother, protective of her and of Dai, still her children, came to me and asked if I wouldn't be nice to Anna! I realized that she was confused and not fully responsible, but it was hard to take. The doctor's diagnosis that my illness was "only nerves" didn't seem to bring me back to health, and though I loved my mother and sister-in-law, a storm swept through me whenever they came into the room. I hadn't been used to the conflict inevitable in a family of differing generations. My mother and father came to see us and took me home with them. I walked from the car to the top of the steps and there I stopped. I could go no farther but stood there shaking and crying. Mama and Papa took me inside and led me to a chair where I stayed for hours and hours, keeping my eyes glued to the cherry tree with its ripening fruit, fearing that if I let go of that one point of contact with the world I would be gone.

Mama was finally able to reach our dear Dr. Sheldon, who gave me a sedative for one night, telling me I must learn how to sleep by putting everything out of my mind, emptying it of all concern or planning. He told me to come to his office next day for a complete checkup. I didn't see how I could do it, but with Mama's help I did.

After confirming his belief that my heart was sound, he told me I must bring about my own recovery. Knowing me, he was sure I could learn to rest and sleep properly, even fulfill my drawing commitments. But I must work only fifteen minutes at a time, dig in the earth for fifteen minutes, sit quietly for fifteen minutes, then go back to the drawing. The Curtis Publishing Company gave me another month to do the drawing for an article on gardening and so began my recovery, which the doctor said might take three months. Three months! It took a year and a half.

I stayed two weeks with my parents, then Dai came to take me home to try again. Both Mother and Anna did their best to help and I spent a great deal of time outdoors on a cot under a tree. There I could watch the wrens nesting and caring for their brood. They flew in with food and out again with waste matter, father and mother bird taking turns. If those tiny creatures had the built-in wisdom to care ceaselessly for their young, I must have it too. I must search within myself and find it again.

When things got too thick and I seemed to be falling apart, Dai took me to Bryn Athyn Cathedral, where we watched the masons working, choosing the stones carefully for color and fitting them together so that the lost-and-found line would rest the eye as it traveled up the corner of the building. The beauty of the scene, the doves flying in and out of the tower, the peace of men working at what they loved all helped. I went home quieted. Sometimes I went to my mother's again for a few days.

Chapter Twenty

In the fall of 1932 it became more and more contrary to reason to make believe we were country folk. How could Nina get to high school in Ambler? How could we afford to operate the car? We decided we must move again. This time to Jenkintown, where we could walk to all the necessary places, to school and to church, to shop for food, and to find the possibility of work. The rent for the house was almost half what it had been in Jarrettown. We moved.

The excitement and effort of moving took its toll, so while the furniture was being carried in I lay on a mattress on the floor in the center of things so I could direct operations. Everyone helped and soon it was home again.

This house too was rather cut up as to rooms, but the living and dining rooms were as one, and the seldom-used parlor was thus kept in order. In later years I was told how the boys climbed through the cubbyhole over the upstairs hall and out onto the roof. It is just as well that a mother doesn't know everything that goes on in a boy's life until he has grown up and become a responsible citizen.

As always, in a new setting, everything was going to be all right. Meals were usually one-dish affairs, scalloped potatoes, macaroni and cheese, spaghetti with perhaps a little ground meat in it, and once in a while yum-yum cake, large and spicy and filled with raisins, if available. For years I had made a pot of baked beans every Saturday, cooking them all day.

"Beanths?" questions Ted. "Beanths give me gath," and when we laugh, he says, "Well, they *do*."

Whatever I put on the table there was the satisfaction of

accomplishment. Food vanished as if by magic. The children learned that it behooves one to be on time at table lest there be nothing left. Homemade biscuits or bread or muffins made a feast of the commonest dish and one didn't worry about serving two starches at a meal. Nina tells me that we bought large boxes of prunes and apricots to offset the starchy diet. It is a good thing that they were cheaper than they are today.

Often the cupboard was searched and the icebox scoured to find one last bit to add flavor or nourishment. Was the peanut butter jar empty? No matter. There are two potatoes and one small onion and there is milk. We make potato soup for lunch. Are there no potatoes for supper? Way back on the shelf is a little rice and a can of tomatoes and a few stale crackers. We have a casserole.

Every meal is sauced with the boys' and Nina's recounting of the day's activity and Dai's wit, and we never missed a meal or went hungry to bed. But sometimes the confusion of voices drove me to take my plate into the quiet of the parlor.

It wasn't long before it became impossible for us to keep Mother and Anna with us. The doctor insisted that, for their own sakes as well as ours, we must find a separate place for them to live. I was heartbroken to have them go, but knew that it must be. Actually, they were homesick for Atlantic City, where they had lived for so many years when Father was alive. So Dai drove them down and found a place for them. Anna was given sewing to do through the Works Project and things went more smoothly.

Nina entered high school and Arthur joined the senior class as a postgraduate. A path through the backyard led directly to the school, which was only a block away. Just one more block away was the Baptist church, which loyalty bade me attend. I insisted too that the younger children go to Sunday school. They must learn at least the fundamentals of religion, even though my doubts about dogma and doctrine continued to increase. It seemed to me as though the churches tried to capture and hold in their stone structure a Being transcendently universal and spiritual, each thinking he had the whole Truth. Yet, I knew that neither Dai nor I had the wisdom to express what we felt at that time or to convey a proper sense of the immensity of the Creation in its infinite variety. There was always the fear of being thought pious and of offending the need of privacy inherent in us all.

One answer came when I heard of the excellent work of the

choir leader of the Episcopal Church of Our Saviour. I knew by experience that the Bible scripture set to music stays in one's memory and that what is learned in childhood is lasting. I entered Ted in the choir, and because he has perfect pitch he was soon promoted to soloist, a position he held for three years. Maury too joined the choir when he was six, and became soloist in his turn. Their clear flute-like voices turned me to water, and for some years to hear Ted sing "Oh, Holy Night" was very moving. At Christmas we all attended the midnight services and it seemed that angels did fill the choir loft instead of a number of little boys.

Dai began selling paper products, but it was a slow business. Few people had money to spend on even such small items as paper toweling, napkins, or tissues. Later, through a banker he knew, he took a job as night watchman in a warehouse on the Delaware River. How I dreaded to see him go each night and how I admired him for going.

One day in the fall I went down town to the street where the same banker lived and made a sketch of his house, then from the sketch made an etching of the house and sold it to him for a Christmas card.

Kind friends made us a present of food at Christmas, thoughtfully leaving the large package on the front porch. We discovered that it had been left by our old friends, the Gaskills, who suspected our need and quietly filled it.

The dreariness of winter was lightened by occasional quartets and symphonic music from the radio on Sunday afternoons.

Both Arthur and Nina became involved in extracurricular activities. Arthur was in the senior play, which was *A Midsummer Night's Dream*. He was given the part of Bottom and made it hilariously funny. Nina was active in the various things that took her back to school for rehearsals and basketball games. She had assumed the duty of washing the supper dishes, so, in order to be on time, she didn't allow much lingering at table for Dai and me. She snatched away this and that—"Through with this?" "Through with that?"— and away went the butter, the bread, and, at last, our plates were gone and we were helpless with laughter. The boys had their chores as well, shoveling snow, feeding the furnace, and sometimes running the vacuum cleaner. With all our hassle, I made it a point to have dinner on Sunday with proper dishes and proper behavior, so that the children would *know* the right things to do.

Often the heat was so meager in the back bedroom that I

brought my easel downstairs into the dining room. Not the best studio in the world, but it sufficed. One day, when Maury was old enough to go to school, he came home with his new book of poems by James Whitcomb Riley and asked me to read to him. I was busy finishing a drawing, so said, "You read to me instead while I draw."

"But I *can't*," he said, with almost a whimper. I was shocked. It hadn't occurred to me that he hadn't learned to read when he had passed his seventh birthday. I pointed to the first two letters and asked how he should say them—*th* I think it was. He sounded it out, then as I encouraged him, he went on, with my help, to the second line, then the third, chuckling as the words made sense. Each line came easier as he went along and by the end of the poem he could read! He fairly jumped up and down at his achievement.

Maury was far from being stupid, and had learned the alphabet at home, but the current method of grasping a word, whole, baffled him. It seemed to have no relation to the alphabet or to anything else. From then on he read everything and a new world opened to him.

We kept to the tradition of years' standing of going to my mother's for a Christmas Eve party, which was held early to accommodate the young children. Mama served supper for us all, and if all could be there, there were twenty-four of us. Usually chicken salad was the main dish. Papa was always on vacation for two weeks at Christmas and, as he liked to cook, he was a great help. We had no car for several years, so one of my brothers came for us and another took us home.

Our meager gifts added little to the pile on the table, but nothing could spoil for me the mystery, the joy of Christmas, the gathering of the family, the children, and the good will among people one met in the street or in one's household. Why could it not last throughout the year?

Nina, Arthur, and Jack were all good at theatricals and still are, though Jack dropped it long ago. Arthur and Nina have kept their interest in both acting and directing, but in amateur productions only.

Nina, who lives near Cincinnati, has several times been in professional productions in the Playhouse in the Park, and when the annual show is given for the benefit of the art museum it is she who writes many of the lyrics on contemporary subjects set to tunes that are familiar.

A neighbor who lived not far from us in Jenkintown, started

the York Road Players, inviting our boys to join the group. Through this activity, which was fairly successful, they met Elsa Frame, who directed the Wyncote Players. She, in turn, recommended Jack and Arthur to Leighton Rollins, who was looking for likely applicants for the summer session of his School of the Theater at Bar Harbor, Maine, and they were accepted. They found employment in a hotel to cover their bed and board, which allowed them to attend school during the day. The excitement of the work at school offset the boredom of whatever was required of them at the hotel, and from what they say, they filled in everywhere they were needed, even to cooking sometimes!

They were introduced to Greek plays as well as modern ones and had the thrill of performing before the summer audiences. Many famous actors and actresses came to the school as guest player, as lecturer, or as director of a certain play, among them Dame Sybil Thorndike, Maude Adams, Josephine Hull, Arthur Sircom, Phil Long, and Peggy Wood.

Jack Van Zanten was one of the students. During the summer his mother and aunt visited him, and in a conversation with Jack and Arthur it came out that they had lost their housekeeper. What would they do for help? Both were employed, Mrs. Van Zanten as assistant to a minister and her sister, Eleanor, as a librarian.

How it was arranged I don't know. But it was agreed that when September brought the summer session to a close and the school returned to New York, Jack and Arthur would go to live with the Van Zantens in Brooklyn. For this they would take care of the house, do the shopping and cooking, send out the laundry and care for it when it came back, and during the day would, with Jack Van Zanten, attend dramatic school. All this we learned through the boys' letters. The boys were to arrive in Brooklyn about four o'clock of a certain day. I thought the plan an excellent one, but of course felt I must go to Brooklyn myself to make sure the Van Zantens were suitable people for our boys to live with.

Chapter Twenty-one

I had been working all summer, off and on, painting in oil a subject I hoped would be acceptable for a March cover for *Good Housekeeping*. It was a little girl with a lamb in her arms. Early on the day that the boys were to arrive at the Van Zantens, I left for New York with my train fare and about a dollar more for lunch and carfare. Nina and Ted were in school and Dai was able to look after Maury until I came home.

I had once done an illustration for *Good Housekeeping*, and had met one of the executives, so went directly to the office with my summer's masterpiece and was kindly received. But, as I feared, it was not *just* what they wanted. Would I go home and try again? Perhaps next time? I left. What would I do with the picture? I was already sick to death of it, but it was on good canvas and not to be wasted. I didn't allow myself to be too disappointed, knowing there are certain requirements for cover design, although I didn't know what subtle thing was missing.

Because of the slimness of my purse, I walked over to Fifth Avenue, stopping on the way to eat a small lunch, wondering where I could put in the time until four o'clock. The Forty-second Street Library seemed a good place, but it might require a good deal of walking, of which I'd already had quite enough. A bus came along just as I had decided to go down to Greenwich Village to see Morry Bower. I had my foot on the step when I heard my name called— "Marguerite!"

I turned, and there stood my friend Ida Shafer with her friend Mrs. Bertha Spaeth and her daughter Helena. The bus went on without me. I explained where I had been bound and the reason for my being in New York, and my disenchantment with the painting I carried.

"Oh, don't go down there. Stay with us," said Ida.

"I'll buy it," said Mrs. Spaeth. "I'll give you five dollars for it."

It was somewhat less than I had hoped to get for it, but infinitely more than I felt it was worth at the moment.

"We can talk while Ida shops," she went on. "We've just come over for the day from Seaside Park."

That in itself was remarkable, that we should meet on Fifth Avenue. But more was to follow. As we sat in a store while Ida shopped, Bertha asked me my birth date and name. I wrote Marguerite de Angeli, March 14, 1889.

"Let's see if we can tell what is in store for you," she said, making marks on the letters I had written.

"Do you know," she said excitedly, "your life is going to take a new turn almost immediately. Yes, it is very clear. It will be quite soon."

Knowing nothing of what she was doing, and being skeptical, but enjoying the fortunetelling, which is always fun, I accepted politely what she said. It was pleasant to be with friends and I hadn't been sure that Morry would be in his studio anyway. Besides, I was five dollars richer, and the prospect of a change could be only good. I had always been a believer in the influence of forces in the universe on human life as well as upon everything else. My thought was not clear about it, but I was receptive.

Perhaps, I thought, this new venture of the boys' will turn out well, and surely the Depression must end sometime.

We had tea somewhere, then I left and went by subway to Brooklyn.

It was so good to see the boys again and to meet their friends, the Van Zantens. They had grown and had become more sure of themselves after a summer on their own.

Mrs. Van Zanten begged me to stay for dinner and to spend the night, saying that in the morning the boys could take me in her car to call on publishers and perhaps find some illustration to do. For some reason I can't explain, instead of going to one of the publishers for whom I had done work, I looked up the address of another, Longmans Green, I think it was. Perhaps it was because I hadn't heard from any of the familiar ones in a long time and I thought a new approach would be more effective. Perhaps it was fate.

Drawing from *The American Girl.*

When I entered the building and looked at the list of occupants, the name of Helen Ferris, Junior Literary Guild, was near the top. *Helen Ferris!* I had wanted to meet her for years. I had done many drawings for her for *The American Girl* and received many kind letters from her, but had never met her. Now I would go right up and introduce myself, never for a moment doubting my welcome or that she would be there.

Miss Ferris welcomed me as I had hoped, then said, "Why you are the very person I wanted to see. I have been getting letters asking for books suitable for very young readers—something they can read to themselves in the first grade. Why don't you write one? You have five children. I know you can do it!"

I took a deep breath. "I know I can too!" I exclaimed. "I *know* I can."

How could she know that I had carried scraps of paper in my purse for at least a year on which I had recorded my children's brilliant remarks, hoping I could use them sometime. So far they fitted into a story about as convincingly as those French phrases we used to see in textbooks fitted into a conversation—"La plume de ma tante est sur le bureau de mon oncle." Still, I had wanted to write almost as much as I had wanted to draw, and felt that I could easily write a story for a six-year-old. It was only a matter of settling on a subject. Miss Ferris took care of that.

"Take a subject familiar to most children, say, a trip to the grocery store or some other everyday adventure. Make a dummy showing sketches and text and send it to me," she said.

I was so excited at the idea of being asked to write a story that I could hardly wait to get back to tell the boys. They shared my excitement and felt as I did, that somehow I had been led to that office building.

Was this the new turn my life was to take? Perhaps it was, I thought. And so it proved to be. I couldn't wait to begin. The boys took me to the station and soon I was on my way home.

I was, in fact, excited to the point of nausea. The day had turned warm, the train was stuffy and noisy. I closed my eyes and thought about the story, trying to shut out all sound, and I learned something I hadn't known how to do before. Somehow all outside noises withdrew from my consciousness and I was removed to an inner place of infinite quiet. Many times since this discovery has come to my aid.

Helen Ferris had told me that the book should not be more than thirty-two pages. There should be a picture of some kind on every page and both boys and girls must be represented so that both would read the book. I already knew that boys would not read girls' books.

All the way to Jenkintown I thought about the story. What should I name the children? There were Bettys and Peters all over the place. Why not use two of our own children's names? *Ted and Nina*. I could change them later when the book was accepted. I didn't want to leave Maury out, but his name was not as easy to read as the others, so I would use his size and shape and call him Ted.

Because any kind of excitement was still very wearing, I found it necessary to go to bed for a week and let the family take care of me. This didn't prevent me from beginning the book, however. I gathered pencils and sheets of paper, cutting and folding them as we used to do as children and sewing them together at the back, so I had thirty-two pages. I didn't realize until later that this is what publishers and printers call a dummy.

Then I began drawing a little and printing the words, just as they came to me and as I might tell a story to the children.

By the end of the week I had a little story with pictures. I sent it off hopefully to Helen Ferris. In a few days I had a reply. She approved substantially of the dummy, but said I had spent too long on the way and not enough time in the store. Would I do another one, keeping all the bits of fun and style, but spending more time in the store. *Would* I? I set to work at once, and somehow I couldn't change the names of the children. The names had a sort of rhythm and Ted and Nina had already become other children in their own right.

The reply to my second dummy came swiftly. "This is just what is needed," the letter said. "Now, where shall I send it? I suggest Margaret Lesser of Doubleday. She has just been made editor of their children's book department. I think you will like her."

Hooray! Of course I could think of nothing better, and wrote Helen Ferris to that effect. I hadn't long to wait. Miss Lesser too liked what I had done and asked me to come to New York to talk about how it would have to be illustrated.

Would Miss Lesser be friendly? Yes, from the tone of her letter I was sure she would be.

Still, doubts plagued me. By the time the train reached New York, I was convinced my trip would be fruitless. That young editor would have second thoughts and would return my little book.

I need not have been afraid. One look at Margaret Lesser, one sound of her voice, reassured me. An instant friendship began that has lasted through these many years and still continues.

It is difficult to describe the joy with which I returned home that afternoon. I was scarcely able to contain my elation, which kept bubbling out in secret smiles.

The months of work ahead were as nothing. If others could do drawings by that strange method called making "separations," I could do it. The process required doing about seven drawings for each color illustration—more if my first sketches were not successful. But the process saved the cost of an engraver's work, allowing the publisher to sell the book at a more reasonable price.

The process was lithography, but the drawings were to be done on glass instead of on the heavy stones formerly used. The process had been originated by William C. D. Glaser, who provided the sheets of glass when I needed them.

In drawing, when I had decided on a subject, it was quite clear in my head. Getting it out on paper was another matter. Sometimes I made a dozen sketches before I had one clear enough to follow and enlarge, the figures substantial, the composition satisfactory, and the detail sufficiently thought out.

What a joy then it was to do it, to see the picture take form. Once in a while it seemed as if the figures came out of the paper by themselves, taking on a life of their own. That is exciting. Often the enthusiasm of beginning carried me to a point, then a period of just plain work set in. The first flush of beginning was gone, and the end not yet in sight. So, as in everything else one does, work is the only answer. Nevertheless, I should say that the rewards offset the failures.

Miss Lesser asked me to come back to meet Mr. Glaser and to spend a few days in the printing shop working under his supervision until I understood the method. So I did.

All this took weeks to accomplish. For example, in the drawing where Ted is hammering, I had to make the pen and ink finished work showing him hammering with his left hand, so that when it was printed in the book he was using his right hand. Each color drawing had to be done with preliminary sketches, drawn carefully in pencil, reversed, then drawn in pen and ink. These were then printed in light blue on the sheets of glass, about twelve of them on a twenty- by thirty-inch piece of finely ground glass. There were four of such glasses with the same drawings, each to be printed in a separate color, but drawn in black, the density of the color depending on the amount of black pencil used. Down in the right-hand corner of each glass I filled a square of black pencil and named it red, blue, yellow, or black, indicating the color that should be used in printing it. Thus, when the images were superimposed, the pictures appeared in full color. Where I wanted green I had to fill in the space on the plates marked both blue and yellow. Where I wanted violet, as in some shadow or a boy's shirt, or deep red, I had to fill in the space on the plates marked blue and the one marked red. If I needed brown, or some other mixed shade, I had to use my judgment as to which plates I must use and what amount of pencil strokes, whether heavy or light. Of course I never saw the color until the book was printed.

I'm sure this is not very clear, but at first it was not clear to me either. I learned by doing.

Dai made a new top for my drawing board with an inset of glass so I could see what I was doing. I took over the parlor for this work in order to have a place to lay out the glasses so I could compare as I worked. The piano was broad enough to hold several glasses at once. In the next book, *Henner's Lydia*, the most tedious drawing of all was a small one showing canned fruits and vegetables and jars of jelly on shelves in a cellar. I wanted grape jelly in some and currant in others, so I had to have blue with red in some and a little yellow with the red for the currant, as the red was too sharp by itself to look like currant. The jelly glasses in the drawing were less than an eighth of an inch high, so it required a great deal of checking to make sure I was working on the right shelf and the right glass.

It took me all fall and winter to do the drawings for *Ted and Nina Go to the Grocery Store*. It wasn't easy, but there was always the excitement of knowing that someday there would be books.

Before I had gone very far, Miss Lesser asked me to do another book of the same kind. Another artist, Florence Bourgeois, was doing two books with the same format and, if I could do another, all four could be printed at the same time. This would cut printing costs enough so the books could be sold for fifty cents each. This was still during the Depression—1934–1935. I suggested a "rainy day" book, remembering my grandmother's attic. And so it was. I called the book *Ted and Nina Have a Happy Rainy Day*.

Chapter Twenty-two

When Margaret Lesser took me to lunch to celebrate the completion of the Ted and Nina books she asked me if I knew anything about the Pennsylvania Dutch, saying her mother's family had come from near Reading.

Indeed I did. My father traveled through Pennsylvania a great deal as representative of Eastman, and we had loved his stories of the amusing expressions and turned-around sentences, of the good food and traditional customs. He couldn't say enough about the beauty of Pennsylvania.

"How about a book on the Pennsylvania Dutch?" she said, with her head on one side. I needed no more persuading. I went home, as I usually did after seeing Peggy, with my head in the clouds and an assurance that I could do anything, whether it was to begin a new book or to correct one I had done. This time I had an even more interesting subject, one that would require research. As I recalled some of the stories my father had told about the Dutch country I had a conviction that I should stay with a family and learn to know their ways for myself—what they ate for breakfast, how they behaved toward each other in early morning, their attitudes toward people, their habits of work. One learns to know people better after a few days of close association than after months or years of casual meeting.

We had no car at that time so Dai and I couldn't just wander about the country as we once had done. I hardly knew where to begin, but felt something would turn up. It did.

Naturally, I told my family, my brothers and their wives, about my new project, perhaps secretly hoping that one of them might give me a lift.

Sketch of Ted and Maury engrossed in *The Boy Mechanic* one Sunday afternoon in 1935.

Meantime, I read books from the library and bought a book about the making of Pennsylvania. I learned that most of the early settlers had come to America for religious freedom and had followed such leaders as Menno Simonds and Zinzindorf. The groups had split into the many sects we now know, due to some small difference of opinion about daily practice, such as which was considered too worldly for dresses, the use of small-figured prints or plain, bright-colored material. Or whether the bonnet worn by the women should be one shape or another, or whether men should wear buttons on their coats or hooks and eyes. Or whether men should have beards or be clean shaven. There were other differences too.

I knew by now that it was the Amish sect I wanted to portray, because only the Amish dress the children in the old-fashion, plain-colored clothes. The book was very helpful, and after reading it I felt I was ready to go up into the country to see for myself.

But where? I couldn't ask at the train station for a ticket because I didn't know where it should take me. I had thought it would be exactly right if I could stay with a doctor's family. His patients would trust him and accept me. But I knew of no doctor and it did not occur to me that I might have found one in a doctors' registry in Philadelphia.

Then one day my brother Dick called. He was going up through Pennsylvania. Why didn't I go along? He would call for me at 6:30 on Wednesday morning and would return on Friday afternoon. Would I go? Of course I would.

Nina promised to be home from school when the little boys came home, and to look after the house and prepare the meals I planned for the three days. Dai, as usual, was cooperative and willing to do what he could. The older boys too were happy about this opportunity for me.

Dick and I planned to meet on Friday in Lancaster at the bus station, if possible, when he would drive me home, and we agreed that neither of us should wait too long for the other. I felt that something would lead me to the right place.

Wednesday was a beautiful morning in mid-October. Trees were ablaze with fall color, it was quite warm, and the ride delightful. The farther we drove from Jenkintown the lovelier the country. We had lots to talk about and the time flew.

Suddenly, at a crossroad, I saw a sign saying CHURCH SUPPER. "Oh," I said to Dick, "I must have a church supper in my story," and noted it in my little book, not remembering that the "house" Amish have suppers in their homes.

Another time, I saw geometric signs in brilliant color painted on a barn, and then a little girl running down a hill after a tiny pig. I put it all down.

Suddenly, we realized we were entering Reading, a city, not the country. In our eager conversation and interest in things we saw, we had perhaps overshot our mark. What should we do? We consulted the map.

"I have to go as far as Pottsville today and will be busy there until at least two o'clock on Friday. Here's a town called Womelsdorf that sounds Dutch and it's on my way. Let's go there. It's only twelve miles."

Womelsdorf proved to be like the "tidy towns" that used to advertise soap. It was scrubbed and polished and swept as if it had just been built. When we came to the turn in the road where Dick must go on, I saw a woman sweeping the walk.

"Let me off here," I said. "I'll find some place to stay, then get on with my research."

Dick stopped and, knowing that I was still not very strong, said, "I just hate to leave you here and not know where you will be and how you will be cared for, but I must go on to my appointment." I knew I would be all right so waved him on and turned to speak to the woman.

"Could you tell me where I might find a family to stay with for a few days?" I asked. "I want to write a book about an Amish child and I must visit with a family so I may see how they live."

"Amish?" she questioned. "I don't know of any Amish around *here*." I was taken aback. No Amish? What would I do?

"Do you know where I could stay till I find out more about it?" My bag was heavy and my coat too warm.

"Well," she said thoughtfully, "you might try next door. She used to take in boarders, but lately she ain't been so vell, but you could try." She watched as I went next door and rang the bell. A woman on crutches came to the door, but at my request she shook her head emphatically, no.

"But," I begged her, "I will take care of the room, make the bed and be no trouble, if only you will let me leave my bag and coat and know that I have a place to sleep."

"Oh vell"—she nodded—"I guess you can stay." Painfully she led me up the stairs, where I left my things. Then I asked where the school was. She directed me to the school building, only a block or so away. I went straight to the office of the principal. He was very kind and much interested in my project.

"But," he said, confirming what I had already heard, "you are in the wrong country. You should be in Lancaster County, where most of the Amish have their farms. Lancaster County is the other side of the mountain. You will need to go back to Reading. And I suggest that you go to City Hall and to the office of the Register of Wills. He will know some of the Amish families in the county."

This was a blow. My first day almost half gone and nothing accomplished. The bus for Reading, they said, would stop at the corner where Dick had left me, but it wasn't due for about an hour. What should I do?

First, I went sadly back to the house where I had engaged

the room and told the lady I could not stay after all. I said I would like to pay her something for giving her the trouble of preparing the room.

"Vell," she said, "you can giff me a quarter," which I did.

Where should I go? What should I do while waiting? I felt the need of food, so went to a lunch counter and ate a sandwich, then to the corner to wait for the bus. The hour wasn't nearly gone. How long would I have to wait?

In a moment a nice, fresh-faced country boy drove up and stopped for the light.

"Is this where you get the bus for Reading?" I asked.

"Sure," he said, "get in. I'll take you." He wasn't more than seventeen, younger than my own boys, and he looked as honest as a boy could be. I got in, telling him I had been advised to go to City Hall. He nodded.

"I'll take you there," he said. He seemed very shy and not talkative, but was very kind.

When I reached City Hall and found the office of the Register of Wills, the man I wanted to see was just leaving for lunch, putting his hat on as he walked, but he listened to my story and said, yes, he would help me, but to please come back after an hour when he would possibly have better information for me.

After lunch he was indeed helpful. He gave me the name of a friend who worked at the Dodge Agency and lived in Morgantown, the center of the Amish district.

"No doubt, if you go to see him he will take you there when his day's work is over," he said kindly. Off I went, feeling that at last I was nearing my goal.

His friend was very pleasant. Yes, he did live in Morgantown, he did know many Amish people and would be glad to take me there, *but* tonight he had to go north to see a customer. However, there was a train leaving Reading about five o'clock. Of course it didn't stop at Morgantown. It stopped at Joanna, which is only two miles from Morgantown. Before I had time to frame the question, How could I walk the two miles? he went on.

"There will be a postman there to pick up the mail, and if you ask him he will take you to Morgantown. Tell him you want to go to Mrs. Herr's and tell her I sent you and I'm sure she will allow you to stay with her."

I thanked him, hoping I could remember all the directions he had given. I went first to the station and bought my ticket for Joanna, then hunted up a movie where I spent several uneasy hours. I ate a small meal somewhere and arrived at the station long before train time.

Finally, I was aboard. Because it was well along in October, the afternoon had faded and gone soon after we left Reading. The train was a local and seemed to stop at every fence post. Each time I started up when the conductor came to announce the station, thinking it might be Joanna, until the conductor said, in exasperation, "Lady, I'll *tell* you when we come to Joanna."

Where will I sleep tonight? I thought, then talked severely to myself. What nonsense to worry. It is warm enough to wrap up in my coat and sleep outside! Stop fretting. I calmed down.

"Joanna! Joanna!" called the conductor as he opened the door and smiled at me. I got off the train in pitch darkness, but one lonely lightbulb shone from the country store. Several people got off with me and went toward waiting cars. But one car seemed to linger. Was it the mail car? Then I saw a man carrying a mailbag to the car. I asked him if he would take me to Morgantown.

"I'd be glad to, lady," he said, "but I have another passenger, and tonight I have only the roadster. My other car is being repaired." He gestured toward the other passenger who was a woman, rather larger than I. She looked at me pityingly.

"Oh, we can manage, I'm sure," she said. "Get in." She moved over and I sank into the seat with relief. Then began my oft-repeated tale of why I happened to be in that part of the country and that I needed a place to stay with a family. I told them I was to see Mrs. Herr, hoping she would take me in.

"If she won't," the lady said, "come back to me and I will see that you find a place." I never thought about a hotel until long afterward.

Soon we had arrived in Morgantown, left the lady passenger at her house, and gone on down the village street to Mrs. Herr's. The postman knocked and delivered my request, but Mrs. Herr shook her head. I got out and added my plea.

"No," she said, "I'm making pickle. I'm too busy."

So we went back to the car and to the lady who had offered her help. She took me next door to her neighbor where I was promised a bed and food for two days. I sighed with relief and went straight to bed. It had been a long, long day.

131

The next morning I was up bright and early, in time to have breakfast with Dr. and Mrs. Zuk. *Doctor!* Why I was just exactly where I had wished to be! In a doctor's family. It seemed a miracle.

As I had hoped and wished, the doctor said he would take me on his rounds, but first to the little red schoolhouse, where he left me until recess. There was a buzzing of whispers as I sat down at the teacher's invitation, then lessons went on as usual. The teacher was Mrs. Lincoln, the boys and girls were nearly all Amish and dressed as they might have been dressed two hundred years before—"plain," which meant material with no figure in it, though for the girls' dresses and the boys' shirts it could be of any color—usually a bright one. The boys had bowl haircuts and wore trousers down to their boot tops. The girls' dresses came down to their shoe tops, and their sleeves to the wrist. The broad-brimmed hats and girls' bonnets and shawls hung on the wall at the back of the room and I learned later that each shawl was embroidered with the name of the girl to whom it belonged.

While the children recited their lessons at the front of the room I made quick sketches and wrote down a list of the colors worn in dresses and shirts. I noticed that the boys' jackets were fastened with hooks and eyes rather than "worldly" buttons.

When time for recess came the children crowded around me with "Oooh's and Aaah's," speaking in the Pennsylvania Dutch dialect peculiar to Lancaster County. I showed them the sketches I'd made and asked their names. There were twenty-six children and, if I remember correctly, twenty-one of them were named Stolzfus.

There were four Lydias, three Johns, and four Yonies. The girls were distinguished one from another by the middle initial, which was the initial of their mother's maiden name. The girls showed me their shawls and there it was in tiny cross stitch—Lydia B., Lydia S., etc. The boys were distinguished by various means. One was Duck Johnny because his father had a pond in which he kept ducks. One was Silo Johnny because there was a silo beside his father's barn! Yonie is short for Jonathan.

In no time, recess was over. The doctor came for me and I left with warm affection for them all, including Mrs. Lincoln, who asked me to visit her in Churchtown. Much later I did visit her one afternoon when a friend drove me to Morgantown. After midday dinner with the Zuks, the doctor took me on his afternoon rounds. The dinner was hearty and good, with a variety of "sweet and sour," which, I was told, is typical of Pennsylvania Dutch food.

At two or three homes where the doctor stopped he took me in, introducing me as a friend. I kept very quiet, but I saw the bare floors, the curtainless windows, the folding doors between rooms, which the doctor said allowed for Sabbath meetings, for these people were "house" Amish, believing that even a church building was an expression of pride in worldly possessions. I also noted the extreme cleanliness. Once I was allowed to see the new baby.

Next day, when the doctor called at this same house, he suggested that I wait outside for him, so while he was busy I stood beside the car and sketched the buildings on the farm lying down below a field. It seemed the epitome of Pennsylvania farmland—the stone barn, the solid, well-built house and outbuildings, the turning weather vane. I used my colored pencils to catch the brilliant foliage, the amber stubble in the field, and finished it before the doctor returned.

When Dr. Zuk saw my sketch, he said, "Henry Stolzfus lives there. That barn is over two hundred years old. This part of the house"—he pointed out—"is where the grandmother lives. She can be with the family or by herself, whichever she pleases." Which seemed a good arrangement.

I had a number of other sketches I'd made, sitting beside the road on a stone. One was of a house and barn where I knew a cider press stood at the back. I had seen the children crowding around and being given sips of cider. I had wanted very much to be invited into the house, but though the man running the cider press was friendly, he didn't ask me to go in, nor did his wife.

Time came for me to take the bus for Lancaster. By the time I reached Lancaster, where I hoped to meet Dick, a severe thunderstorm was in progress.

I waited for about an hour, but Dick didn't appear. I was afraid I would be very late getting home if I didn't take the bus then ready to leave. There would still be the train ride from Philadelphia to Jenkintown. So I left. As we approached Coatesville, I looked out of the window at a passing car and there was Dick, oblivious of me, and soon far ahead.

It was nearing six when I reached home. Everyone was eager to hear how I had fared, but *please,* let's have supper!

For about two weeks the whole experience was a jumble of unrelated facts. Then a letter came from Mrs. Zuk telling me that lightning had struck the two-hundred-year-old barn that I had sketched in colored pencil that afternoon while I waited for the doctor and had burned it to the ground, killing a number of the animals. She was sure I would like to use the dramatic incident in my story. I told my friend Edith Gaskill about it and she suggested that we drive up to see the ruins and perhaps I would get more material for the book. I was very happy to go of course. When we arrived at the Stolzfus farm all the men of the community were there helping to clear away the debris from the fire and the women folk were cooking and making a kind of frolic out of it.

When they saw Edith and me near the well, where we found a seat, they all gathered around us. I showed Mrs. Stolzfus the drawing I had made of the barn the very day that it had burned. She was impressed that I had happened to do it that very day and with the others was surprised that I was able to make a recognizable sketch of the little boy they called Yonie who had come along with his red wagon filled with wood for the kitchen fire. Then it seemed all right for me to ask Mrs. Stolzfus if I might see the inside of the house. I told her I wanted to make a true picture of a way of life I thought might not last too long. She was a little hesitant, but said, "Vell, yes, you can come in."

The house was immaculately clean, even with all those women working there that day. Mrs. Stolzfus showed me a little hooked rug her daughter was making.

"Teach a child to vork when he is little, and vhen he grows up, he likes to vork," she said.

As we left the farm the women waved good-bye in friendly fashion and I felt I had a little more to go on. Yonie would certainly go into the book and could be Lydia's little brother.

For some time after this I was still hesitant to begin, fearing that I might exaggerate some phase of Amish living or say something I shouldn't. But I kept trying with sketches and some hand-printed text, limping along.

Then one day, the telephone rang. A strange voice said, "You don't know me, but I hear you are writing a story about the Pennsylvania Dutch. I think you ought to meet my tenant who lives upstairs. Her husband teaches at the high school and through one of your children we heard about you. Why don't you come up and meet her? Her name is Mrs. Martz and she used to live in Lancaster County, where the Amish live."

It didn't take me long to get to the house in the next block where Mrs. Martz lived. When she asked me what I would like to know, I said, "Just talk."

She began by telling me that her father had a country store in Blue Ball and that, because most of his customers were Amish, he carried a large supply of the kind of merchandise they particularly liked, especially bolts of dress material in bright colors and black, but having no pattern printed on it. He kept lawn for caps, which could be laundered, and long black stockings and heavy shoes.

How I listened. This was exactly what I needed to clarify what I had seen and heard—to sort it out and be sure that my memories were right. Then she went on.

"He was tending the horses belonging to John's Henner—no it was *Nate's* Henner—"

"Aah!" I said, "now I have it."

"You have *what?*" questioned Mrs. Martz.

"The title for my book," I answered. "Not John's, not Nate's, but *Henner's* Lydia." And that was that. We talked for a little longer, but I was eager to get home and get to work.

Now the story moved. I had already chosen Lydia for the name of the central character. I liked the name, and there were so many Lydias in the class I visited that it seemed natural to choose it.

I made a dummy, such as I had made before, with drawings and text alternating, and sent it off. Imagine my delight when a telegram arrived from Peggy saying, "Thrilled with Henner's Lydia."

While I was writing the story, or rather, printing it by hand, Nina came down with tonsilitis and was in bed for several days, a captive audience because a part of the story was written as I sat by her bed. One page was done as I sat in the kitchen with my feet in the oven because the furnace was on strike, and while I watched the bread rising. Each page is woven into the life of the house and the care of the children.

By the time I was ready to sketch the end paper, Maury was eight and could help me by arranging matchsticks to show where the road should wind, because it must be drawn in reverse as before. Later, when the book had been published and he was wondering what to do with himself one Sunday afternoon, I asked if he had read the book.

"No," he said. "It's too peaceful."

About the time I began to work on *Henner's Lydia* the first royalty check came in from the sale of the Ted and Nina book. I had received an advance on the book, which had been absorbed quickly by bills and current expenses. But when the semiannual check arrived it was like finding money, and there was great rejoicing. As for me, the exultation of being recognized as an "author" lifted me off the floor—literally, much to the amusement of the whole family. But they knew me and had been a part of my first book. Our fortune had improved in other ways as well and we had weathered the Depression.

The work on *Henner's Lydia* continued with making the drawings and the separations, and it was finished by spring and published in the fall of 1936.

When I finally saw it printed in color I found it nearer to my intended color than I had thought it would be. Some color was more intense than I could have wished and in some places I had not retraced the black, so the color was indefinite. But on the whole it was not bad and was pretty exciting. The color in the Amish women's dress *was* intense but once I had seen a baby with a purple bonnet on.

Chapter Twenty-three

Although I had the two Ted and Nina books published and doing well they were small books for very young children. With the publication of *Henner's Lydia* and an accolade from Hendrik Van Loon and other good reviews I began really to feel like an author.

Hendrik Van Loon had written a long review in the New York *Herald Tribune* children's book section that gave me a certain confidence. He said, among other things, that I must have raised dogs to know so much about children! Naturally, I had to write and tell him that I had reared children, not dogs, and that my natural aptitude for absorbing the traits, the speech, and even the gestures of those with whom I associated was probably a great help.

Another thing he had said was, "She has broken one of our most cherished traditions. There is quite a lot of German in the book and not a single mistake," which pleased me. He answered my letter and sent with it the drawing of a saint that had been intended for use in the newspaper review and also a box of cookies from Holland for the children. This was the beginning of an exchange of letters that lasted until his death. I met him only once when, at his invitation to stop any time we could, we called on our way to a regional library meeting at which I was to talk and received a warm welcome.

Soon after the publication of *Henner's Lydia*, I had a letter from Cornelius Weygandt, then professor of English literature at the University of Pennsylvania. He wrote that, when he was given a copy of the book by a friend, he sat down on the stair and wept because it took him back to his childhood in the Dutch country.

I discovered later that Maurice Bower had attended his classes, and when our own Maury was grown he too attended Dr. Weygandt's classes. A nice coincidence. Later, in one of his books about Pennsylvania, *The Red Hills,* Dr. Weygandt dedicated one of the chapters to me as the author of *Henner's Lydia.*

Lancaster booksellers did very well with *Henner's Lydia* and the publishers were amused and pleased when a shop in the bus station began to order the book by the gross! One of the best customers at Herr's Bookstore was the Amish grandfather who bought fifty copies because he felt all of his grandchildren should have a copy.

Each book brought with it a circle of new acquaintances, many of whom became our friends. Through *Henner's Lydia* the world widened to include librarians, teachers, booksellers, and others interested in books for children. Invitations to speak at local or regional meetings increased, and while I never recovered from the nervous fear of appearing before people, I so loved meeting them that I continued from many years to accept such assignments.

In Lancaster I was invited to come to an old-fashioned church dinner at which I was to be one of the speakers and Elsie Singmaster the other. We were to be the guests of a Mrs. Hostetter and to stay overnight. Elsie met me at the station with her brother in the early afternoon and he drove us to Mrs. Hostetter's.

I met Elsie again in York at a regional library meeting with her friend Alice Eaton, then in charge of the Harrisburg Library. While there it was arranged that we should go to Williamsburg over the Easter weekend. We spent three pleasant days together and a story came out of Elsie's suggestion that I look into the life of Christopher Dock, a Pennsylvania schoolmaster of the early eighteenth century who taught his pupils social grace and gentle manners, since many of them had little opportunity to learn these at home. He knelt in prayer after school, naming those who needed special help. When he died it was in a manner typical of his dedication in living. He was found on his knees at prayer.

Once again a search began for more about early Pennsylvania and the "plain people." My first excursion was to City Hall in Philadelphia and to the office of the Register of Wills. Everyone was helpful and, to my surprise and delight, I was able to see the actual paper on which Christopher Dock's will had been written. It was interesting and a splendid guide to the kind of furnishings in a house of that period. He had allotted each article in his household to a specific person, even to his fourposter bed and his "best iron pot."

In the library I found a summary of his life by Martin Brumbaugh, a former mayor of Philadelphia. This gave me an insight into his character and an understanding of his ideas concerning the education of the whole person, which were far in advance of his time. He believed in rewards rather than punishment and encouraged good behavior by offering awards in the shape of *Fractur Schriften*, religious verses or aphorisms done by his own hand, with birds and flowers, angels and hearts as decoration. He set up a list of rules for conduct such as: "If you must comb your hair, go off into a corner to do it," or "Eat your food at home, not on the way to school," or the one from Socrates, "It is better to do one thing well, than many things badly." I learned that Christopher Dock had lived in the vicinity of Skippack, where his log schoolhouse had been.

As often happens when reading a great deal about a subject and going here and there to see for oneself, I got confused about detail. Being the person I am, I don't always check and double-check. However, this failing of mine leads to new acquaintances, and to the discovery of small details that would otherwise be missed.

For example, I somehow got the mistaken idea that Schwenksville was the site of Christopher Dock's school. I suppose I was taken by the sound of the name Schwenksville.

My husband drove me there and we went first to the library. It was closed that day. I inquired at the nearby store where I might find someone who was familiar with the Christopher Dock legend and was directed to a woman who lived on Main Street and was interested in local history.

The lady was gracious, but, no, she didn't really know anything about Christopher Dock except his name and that he had been a schoolmaster in the 1700s. Perhaps if we went to see the Reverend Schmidt, he could help us. She directed us around the corner and up the hill to a house at the end of the street.

When we arrived at the house his wife greeted us and said, yes, her husband was an amateur historian and knew a great deal about Pennsylvania history, but he was not at home. He was in the apple orchard, just there—gesturing to a still farther rise in the land. We thanked her and set off for the orchard. It was a lovely day in early fall when the Pennsylvania countryside is at its best. We found the reverend trimming his trees amid the fragrance of fallen apples. He too was most welcoming and informative.

"But," he said, "Mr. Dambly, who runs the newspaper in Skippack, knows much more than I about the schoolmaster. His office is right on the main street in Skippack. You can't miss it."

So we went to Skippack, a few miles away, to see Mr. Dambly. We introduced ourselves and I told him my reason for being there.

Mr. Dambly was well versed in local history and told us what he knew about the famous old schoolmaster, where he had lived, the method of his teaching, and his influence on the community. He directed us to Creamery, a village about two miles from Skippack where the school had been and where Christopher Dock was buried. The log schoolhouse had been burned down years before, but a modern school stood almost in the same spot and nearby was the Mennonite meeting. We left Mr. Dambly with many thanks for his help and drove to Creamery, where we walked about the school and visited the monument over the schoolmaster's grave and the meeting house. The following Sunday we drove out from Jenkintown again to attend the morning service in the meeting house.

Later in the fall we attended a church supper in Telford, where I made a sketch of the house and barn where the schoolmaster had lived at one time and where to this day stands an oak with a plaque dedicated to him and his teaching.

So, the story of Christopher Dock slowly evolved. I spent hours in the library refreshing my memory of Pennsylvania history and talked with people who might remember their childhood in that part of Montgomery County, one of whom we met when visiting Richard Ellis and his wife. Richard, a book designer of extraordinary skill, was at that time designing a book on Fractur Schriften, for Henry Borneman, a Philadelphia lawyer. These are the decorated mottoes peculiar to the German culture of the area where Christopher Dock had lived and which he gave as rewards to his pupils.

Mr. Borneman was much interested in the book I was doing and told me of games they had played when he went to school and which would have been played even in Dock's time, with pupils facing outward and with boys on one side and girls on the other, to lessen the disturbances that can arise among children. He made rough sketches to show how the benches were made and later, when his book was published, inscribed and gave me a copy, with permission to use the decorations. Many of them I did adapt as chapter headings.

Because Christopher Dock taught three days a week in the school near Skippack and three days in the Germantown school, riding horseback each way, I thought it necessary to find out how long it would take him to make the journey. Even though the fact might have nothing to do with the story, I had to know. So Dai took me one morning to find out. We followed a milk wagon, horse-drawn and going at a walking pace, and discovered that it went at about four miles an hour.

During this period I was asked to speak at Girard College, and while there I met Dr. Ralph Johnson, psychologist to the orphan boys for whom the school was established. He too was interested in the book I was doing and by then was beginning to illustrate. He told me he thought the school furniture belonging to Christopher Dock was in the Merion meeting near Haverford, Pennsylvania, the oldest Quaker meeting in the state. Then he went on to tell about his own ancestors, who had come to America with the Swedish settlers before William Penn and had lived in caves along the Delaware where Second Street now is. This, of course, led to a visit to Merion Meeting and, later, to two other books.

The morning Dai drove me to Merion Meeting, thinking, of course, that we would have to hunt up someone to let us in, we arrived at the same time as Mr. Bunting, the clerk of the meeting, who had come to see about repairs. He took time to show us around the old building and up to a small attic where there was some school furniture. It was not Christopher Dock's but belonged to the early Friends' school. However, it could be used in my drawings anyway, because it was of the same period.

I loved the touch of the smooth, hand-worn benches, the pegs in the overhead beams where the women hung their bonnets, and the air of solemn peace that pervaded the old meeting house.

When summer came and Nina was counselor at Camp Indian Run, Dai and I drove up one day to bring Nina and Jane Carlin home for their day off, as we did every week. I prepared supper for the boys before leaving and we took ours along, since we had to be at the camp just about suppertime. These jaunts took us over a familiar and pleasant road and were restful and enjoyable.

We arrived at Valley Forge in late afternoon and decided to sit in the grove there to eat our supper. Across the road stood a little schoolhouse that looked interesting. I had to investigate it before leaving.

We found a sign that said LETITIA PENN SCHOOL. It was the

right period! I wanted to see the inside. By holding my hands close to my face to shut out the sunlight, I could make out the interior. It was just right. It was exactly the sort of schoolroom Mr. Borneman had described, with benches and sloping desks along the outside walls and the schoolmaster's high desk at the front. I could hardly believe it. We found a park guard who opened the door and let us go inside, where I made rough sketches to aid my memory.

After that the story went swimmingly. The title didn't come easily, but we finally decided on *Skippack School*.

When it was finished and had been through the editorial process, which meant some changes and reorganization, and galley proofs to be read, there were all the illustrations to be done. This time they were to be done in Wolfe pencil and watercolor.

A day was chosen for me to go to New York to help Peggy "paste up the dummy." That means to cut up the long sheets of galley proof and paste them into a dummy cut to the book size. The type face and general format had already been decided. Now we must discuss where the drawings should go and how much color I could have. Because of the cost of reproduction of color it had to be limited and the pages on which the color would fall depended on how the large sheets were folded and cut as they went into the book. We had several choices, but once decided upon the plan could not be changed.

Usually, I made sketches of the characters so they would have reality in my mind. But often they were elusive and several attempts were made before the characters emerged as I saw them. Story and pictures were to be finished by April if the book was to be published in the fall. I worked steadily and met the deadline.

When the book was published I sent a copy to Hendrik Van Loon, who thanked me with a telegram:

> You have not only brought great joy to the little boy in Hendrik Willem, but you have once more filled the world with so much charm and gaiety that all of us are deeply in your debt. Best wishes and for the sake of the children I hope that your book will find its way to several million homes for God knows we need such a cheerful antidote to make us forget the inexcusable mess we have made of a world that could be such a lovely world indeed.
>
> Hendrik Willem Van Loon

Although a number of other books intervened after *Skippack School,* one more about the Pennsylvania Dutch country had to be done. It was about Yonie and the burning of the old barn, which had stayed in my thought ever since that day when Edith Gaskill and I had gone out Route 23 to Morgantown.

When the story insisted on being written, Nina's first son was about six months old and already curious about the world around him. His father, Alfred, being of Pennsylvania Dutch extraction, called him "Wunnernass," and as all normal children are "wonder-noses," I decided to call Yonie one too. I had already done the research necessary for *Henner's Lydia* and *Skippack School* and needed only to recall it. So, there were now three books for children about the people of Pennsylvania.

I enjoyed every bit of *Yonie Wondernose* and after the book was published in 1944 it was chosen as an Honor Book in the New York *Herald Tribune*'s Spring Book Festival. It was at the presentation in New York, which I attended with Peggy, that I met Ruth Gagliardo, the "book lady" from Kansas.

Chapter Twenty-four

In actual publishing sequence my fourth book, and the one that followed *Henner's Lydia*, was *Petite Suzanne*. The idea came to me one Sunday morning in the late summer of 1936 when my brother Arthur and his wife drove Dai and me to Bryn Athyn Cathedral. As we stood watching the pigeons flying in and out of the tower we talked about their recent trip to the Gaspé Peninsula. They had been fascinated by its old-world quaintness, the charm of the French spoken there. They urged me to go and see for myself, thinking that a story with that background would be a suitable one to follow *Henner's Lydia*.

When I suggested the idea to Margaret Lesser she was enthusiastic, particularly because the French Canadians had, like the Pennsylvania Dutch, kept so many of their traditional customs.

It was late August when I started out, with the understanding that I would be gone for two weeks. My parents had offered to drive me and I would have enjoyed that, but I had the feeling that the close association with the native people I was seeking would come to me more fully if I went alone. It proved to be true.

In Montreal the Canadian National Railroad office arranged my ticket and gave me a letter of introduction to the Convent of Lourdes. Then I took the train to Matapedia, where I transferred to the local that runs along the coast of the peninsula and past all the gates leading to the narrow farms that reach out to the sea. On nearly every gate children stood to watch as the train passed, waving to the passengers as we waved back. That picture of the children stayed with me and is the basis for the cover of the book.

It was night when we reached the village of Gaspé and the hotel where I was to stay until a family could be found who would take me in for a week or so.

When I told the woman in charge of the hotel my errand and how much I wanted to stay with a French family, she suggested I wait until Friday, when the visiting nurse, Anita Le Lievre, would come in on her way home for the weekend. She was of French parentage but spoke very good English, having been trained in an English-speaking hospital in Montreal. The village of Gaspé, I found, contrary to my belief, was entirely English, except for the convent to which I had an introduction.

The next morning I was disconcerted to find that the convent was cloistered, and because the monsignor was away no one had authority to allow me to enter. All this was conveyed to me by a lay sister who stood at the low kitchen window. "But," she said, "I will send a little girl out to talk with you."

The little girl was Berthe La Pierre. Berthe told me about her home life and about Christmas, when she and her brother had crossed the cove to cut a tree in the woods and how they had lost Grandpère's good ax. Whenever I asked her a question, she answered, "Oh, *yes!*" with an upward inflection. She was a charming child of fourteen.

The visiting nurse came in on Friday as expected and, after we had been introduced, suggested that we lunch together. She seemed rather formal at first, but was gracious enough to ask me to ride along with her as far as Roche Percé, where she was to stay overnight, then pick up her aunt and take her home. We began to see country things such as outdoor brick ovens, in which bread was baked, and fish flakes, which were long racks near the shore where fish were dried. I exclaimed over everything and loved seeing the clusters of children we occasionally met. Our conversation quickened. Soon Anita said, "Now, you see! We 'ave jus' met, and now, we are old friends." I agreed.

By the time we reached Roche Percé, Anita had invited me to come to her house as a paying guest, saying that her household consisted of Uncle Arthur, Tante Eugenie, her young sister, Suzanne, and her grandfather, who was very old.

Anita left me at a motel to stay over until Sunday night when she would come for me, saying I must see the pierced rock and, if possible, the bird sanctuary.

I felt very much alone in the cabin where I was to sleep, so I went out for a walk in the afternoon along the shore. I could see the Rock and Bonaventure Island, where the birds had their nests. The wind was cold and the sky was darkening. As I passed I saw people getting into a boat and heard them talking about the island. I stopped. One of the women asked if I wouldn't like to go along with them to see the birds. I said, yes, I would like it very much but had no coat and was afraid I would be cold. "Oh, come along, we will lend you a sweater," she assured. I climbed aboard.

We went out to the far side of Bonaventure and saw the thousands of birds—loons, gannets, gulls, terns, cormorants—flying about above the ledges, which were filled with nesting birds all screaming and mewing, feeding and preening. The baby cormorants reached down into the parents' throats to get the food. Never before had I seen at close range so many or such a variety of bird life. It was very exciting.

By the time we returned to Percé a storm was brewing and I was told later that if I hadn't gone to see Bonaventure Island that afternoon I couldn't have gone at all during my stay on the Gaspé. The storm was so fierce that no boats left the mainland for two weeks.

Sunday afternoon Anita came to pick me up. Her aunt was with her and Lucille Langlois, who lived in Chandler beyond Grand Riviere, where Anita lived. Her father was the proprietor of the hotel there.

That night the Le Lievre family made me welcome, but treated me formally, serving me in their little dining room alone, while they ate at a large table in the kitchen. This didn't suit me at all, and I begged to be allowed to share the table where everyone else sat. How else could I get to know them? They made a place for me and I was one of them.

It was impossible for me to understand all the conversation that went on among the members of the family, although I remembered enough of my high school French to understand a word now and then. But Anita translated for me so I was aware of what was going on. It was mostly about the work of the farm and about the fishing. Once, when we were almost ready to go to bed and the bread had been set to rise beside the stove, a great, sudden, fast sputter of words startled me. What could be the occasion? Then Anita brought her wool culottes and folded them on top of the other coverings over the bread. There was already a white coverlet, a blanket, and something else I have forgotten, but Tante Eugenie was afraid the night chill would keep the bread from rising once the wood fire had gone out. It was not, as one might suppose, a great crisis or a family disagreement that had caused what seemed to me an emergency. It was simply this: What else shall we find to keep the bread from being chilled?

Another such sputter of words happened when we all sat in the shed shelling peas and filling jars with them; the jars would then be processed in a steam bath and kept for the winter. When it had subsided I discovered that something was needed to completely fill the last jar, since the peas had all been shelled. Tante Eugenie once more used her ingenuity and filled the jar with a potato. The crisis was over and talk resumed its normal tempo.

Anita took me with her twice when she attended patients. We drove back into the country and I was allowed to go with her as she visited them, and I saw their joy in greeting her. The furnishings of those small farmhouses were pitifully scant, and the floors bare, but the people seemed quite happy. As I knew well, things do not make happiness. It seemed to me that on the Gaspé the people had the most important elements for the good life, even if it was not an easy life.

I visited the school in Grand Riviere, where the nuns taught and where every available niche held a small bouquet of flowers, where the baseboard, the desks, and even the walls were scrubbed satiny white, and where I was made welcome. The lessons were taught and recited in French, again challenging my faulty memory.

It was a delightful experience to share the life of these people for a week, to see and realize how short and how late was their summer, how swift they must be to gather the fruits of the earth lest frost take them first. Here were spring, summer, and fall vegetables, flowers and fruits all ripening at the same time. Hyacinths three feet tall were still blooming in early September, whereas ours bloom in the early spring. Roses spilled over bushes in great handfuls, and peas in pods eight inches long were just ready for the New York markets. It was as if nature, lying stubbornly asleep, sought to make up for tardiness in abundance and size.

Everyone helped to reap and preserve the harvest, even Grandpère, whose old knees were stiff and aching. "*Mes jambes, mes jambes!*" he said.

As Tante Eugenie said, "If we do not prepare for the winter, who shall care for us?"

At the end of the week Anita drove me to Chandler, where

she had calls to make, but stopped to introduce me to the proprietor of the hotel and his wife, Monsieur and Madame Langlois, and their children, one of whom, Lucille, I had met on the way down from Roche Percé. And there is where I found Cippy and Paule, the two tiny girls. The one called Cippy (Ciprienne) was really named Suzanne, but I already had a Suzanne (Anita's little sister) so I borrowed Cippy's name from her older sister.

By now I was really homesick, so I started back. In Quebec I sent a telegram to ask everyone in the family to be there when I arrived home. I was tired of trying to understand a foreign language so I spent only one day in Quebec, dutifully sightseeing. Then home, home where all my loved ones would be to greet me.

I stopped in New York long enough to have breakfast with Peggy, to tell her about my trip, and to receive from her the encouragement to go on.

At home the family was gathered for dinner as I had hoped. Two of the boys had broken arms! This was our first experience with broken bones. Ted had fallen off his bike and Arthur from a ladder as he was helping to arrange the set for a dramatic performance with his students. But the accidents couldn't spoil the joy of being together again.

Once more I began to do research, this time to acquaint myself with the background and history of the French who had settled on the coast of Canada hundreds of years ago.

Added to the knowledge I had gained from my visit to the Gaspé, and what I had read, was the memory of my father's stories about his life as a boy working in a store in the north woods of Michigan. There had been many French Canadians among the woodsmen. Ol'Batees was one who spoke in French patois. Papa, using his gift for mimicry, imitated him to perfection. Sometimes when he had had enough of something, perhaps too many repetitions of a record, he would say, "I got my sat'sfy dot t'ing."

Through the long winter I wrestled with the text and pictures for *Petite Suzanne*. It was ready for printing by April. The black and white drawings I did on glass as before, but the color I did with a new kind of paint. Supposedly, the new fluorescent paint would eliminate some of the work of an engraver. I managed to use it for the color of that one book, but could not continue with it because of its sickening smell. That was the end of that experiment.

Chapter Twenty-five

In November of 1936, when I had begun work on *Petite Suzanne*, my parents celebrated their fiftieth wedding anniversary. There was a great gathering of friends and family from far and near, and Adelle, my niece, wore Mama's plum-colored silk wedding dress. *Henner's Lydia* had been published, Mama and Papa were very pleased with it, and Papa now realized that I was quite stable with a safe career that didn't interfere with my care of the family and home.

Soon after that Papa died. Gone from our view was his good humor, his zest for living, his genial and comforting presence. For Mama it was half her life gone. She braved it out as best she could and lived to a great age.

As a memorial to him, and as comfort to myself, I began to write down stories he used to tell about his childhood in Lapeer and things I remembered about my own. The smell of apples and spice in Grandmother's kitchen, the tall jelly cupboard, the wooden sink and the pump, the rain barrel where we children tried to turn horse hairs into snakes. I thought of Grandpa's blacksmith shop and the acrid smell of horses' hoofs being burned when the white-hot shoe was fitted, the sound of the hammer on the anvil, the squeeze of the bellows, and dear Grandpa in his leather apron.

Papa had often spoken of Ash Tomlinson, his close friend, and the pranks they had played. Once they had taken a stray calf up into the belfry of the school and tied its tail to the bell rope, causing consternation in the town as the bell rang continually at every jerk of the calf's tail. It was a cruel thing to do, but very funny to the boys, whose sense of humor was like most boys',

149

often cruel until they learned by their own experience how cruelty hurts.

I took the idea to Peggy and she agreed, I had a story. With the other stories of Papa's it became a book, and because as a boy my father had yearned for a pair of copper-toed boots, that is what I called it.

I wanted to hear Ash's side of the story and see if he remembered anything that Papa hadn't told. I wanted to use his name too, because real names are more convincing than made-up ones, so I begged off for a few days and went to Cleveland to see him. He couldn't remember a single adventure that I hadn't heard, but he thoroughly enjoyed the ones I told him and corroborated them and was delighted to have his name used. He had been occupied with business as the owner of a fleet of boats plying the Great Lakes.

From Cleveland I went on to Lapeer to see again the town where I had been born and to visit those of my family still remaining. The strong sense of family bred in us had kept warm the relationship between my cousins and me and I was welcomed as I had expected, driven from one house to another and feted at a hastily planned reunion.

I particularly wanted to see Grandma's house. It was little changed, though the porch was gone. It did not occur to me to make sketches or photographs. Somehow I knew that a memory picture would carry more conviction. It would hold some intangible quality that might embellish or delete but would be the more true for all that.

The whole town seemed shrunken in size; the buildings on Nipsing Street looked as if some giant weight had been dropped on them. Surely that small, brick two-story building opposite Uncle Denny's jewelry store couldn't be where Papa's studio had been! But yes, there at the second-floor level was the studio window, and the store beneath had been turned into a drugstore. (Papa didn't call it a studio, he called it "the gallery.")

Michigan, even in my childhood, was a pioneer state. There were still stump fences confining the fields—tremendous ten-foot-high stumps standing on edge with roots interlaced. What trees must have sprung from such roots! The virgin forest still partly remained and Chippewa Indians lived at the edge of town. They made baskets of reeds to sell from door to door.

As I remembered, farmers came into town on Saturdays to

trade, driving in buggies, with room at the back for their crocks of honey or butter, cheese, or homemade sausage. Or they drove huge drays loaded with wheat to take to Turnbull's mill for grinding into flour, or beans for the elevator. Why it was called an elevator I never knew. There, in a big room, women sat sorting dried beans, the very kind my mother baked every Saturday all day long in a slow oven, rich with molasses, brown sugar, and salt pork.

In winter the drays were put on runners, the buggies were changed for sleighs, and bells jingled on the snowy roads. We children "hitched on bobs" with our sleds, a deliciously scary way to ride gloriously until warned by the driver, "Git off! That's enough." Bobs were great, low, heavy-board vehicles for carrying farm produce or equipment.

Oh, this book would be fun. I could hardly wait to begin. I stayed with my cousins only one night, then left on my long journey home. No plane flights then.

When I had made sketches of some of the characters for the book, I showed them to Peggy. It always clarified them for me and for her and set them in my mind as people in their own right. I told her the gist of the story and set to work.

As it went on I found it one of the easiest books to write because the material was so familiar. It was a family book out of my own experience and memory, as the Ted and Nina books were. Yet, the theme was set back far enough in time to give it a kind of perspective that can be seen only on short acquaintance or by getting far enough away to eliminate cluttering detail. I enjoyed every minute of it and the story was accepted.

Then came the long, grueling task of making the drawings, reversing them, and doing the separations.

It was suggested that toward the end of the drawing I should go to New York and stay at a hotel where I could work intensively on the plates in order to finish them in time for fall publication. I stayed in a hotel overlooking Central Park. I was practically immured and very lonely and worked long hours each day. I was advised by the printer to use a very hard pencil so that my work would print more clearly. As often happens, I thought they knew more than I did, so I followed their advice, to my regret. Because of the way I work, a softer pencil would have been better. When the book was published I was literally ill at the sight of it. A good part of my careful work had simply dropped out.

I went back home tired out completely and determined never again to make separations. And as my books were now selling well, I didn't have to.

After the book was published in October 1938 I sent a copy to Ash Tomlinson and received an enthusiastic thank you and an invitation to take a trip up the Great Lakes on one of his ore boats. It was an eight-day trip from Buffalo to Duluth, where the freighter was loaded with ore. In nautical terms, we went up light and came back heavy. Going through the locks at Sault St. Marie, it was interesting to hear through the early mist the ghostly call, "Sh-i-p- A-h-o-y!" and the answer from our captain, "Syl-v-a-n-ia! Hea-vy from Duluth!"

As I write I can still hear the quiet lapping of the water and dimly see the master of the locks and feel the chill of early morning.

The cruise was restful and luxurious, and a delightful end to the *Copper-toed Boots* experience. My father would have been pleased with the reception the book had in Lapeer. The newspaper gave it almost a page, with photographs of Papa and Ash Tomlinson. There are still discussions about it among the older people because I changed the time the elephant escaped and some other minor details.

Illustration from *Ted and Nina Have a Happy Rainy Day*, published 1936.

Key drawing in reverse from *Henner's Lydia*, published 1936.

Color sketch of the same picture.

Illustration from *Skippack School*,
published 1939.

Illustration from *Thee, Hannah!*,
published 1940.

Illustration from *Elin's Amerika*, published 1941.

Illustration from *Turkey for Christmas*, published 1944.

Illustration from *Bright April*,
published 1946.

Illustration from
The Door in the Wall
published 1949.

Illustration from *Book of Nursery and Mother Goose Rhymes*, published 1954.

It came to pass that God said unto Abraham, "Take now thy son, thine only son Isaac, whom thou lovest, and get thee into the land of Moriah; and offer him there for a burnt offering upon one of the mountains which I will tell thee of."

And Abraham rose up early in the morning and saddled his ass and took two of his young men with him, and Isaac, his son, and clave the wood for the burnt offering, and rose up and went unto the place of which God had told him.

And Abraham said unto his young men, "Abide ye here with the ass, and I and the lad will go yonder and worship and come again to you."

And Abraham took the wood of the burnt offering and laid it upon Isaac, his son; and he took the fire in his hand, and a knife, and they went both of them together.

And Isaac spake unto Abraham, his father, and said, "My father!"

And he said, "Here am I, my son!"

And Isaac said, "Behold the fire and the wood, but where is the lamb for a burnt offering?"

And Abraham said, "My son, God will provide himself a lamb for a burnt offering." So they went both of them together. And they came to the place which God had told him of; and Abraham built an altar there and laid the wood in order and bound Isaac, his son, and laid him on the altar upon the wood. And Abraham stretched forth his hand and took the knife to slay his son.

And the angel of the Lord called unto him out of heaven and said, "Abraham, Abraham!"

Sacrifice of Isaac
GENESIS
35

Chapter head illustration from *The Old Testament*, published 1960. Genesis 35.

Chapter Twenty-six

In 1938, Mama gave us a small lot near Toms River that Papa had owned for many years but had never used for building. A check had come with my royalty statement from Doubleday that was more than I had expected, so we decided to use it to build a vacation cottage. We drove down to Money Island to see what could be done. There we met Kossuth Applegate (Suth), who agreed to help Dai. I planned the cottage and they bought lumber, windows with metal frames, roofing, and bricks for the chimney. Then they set to work.

There was a large room on the ground floor with bunk beds for the two younger boys. It opened into a kitchen, and there was a stairway leading to a balcony bedroom for us and an extra bed for Jack and Arthur. There was no bathroom as yet. We had a sofa bed for Nina when she could come down. The big boys were working and could come only occasionally.

It took most of the summer to finish the cottage and, when the roof was on, Dai and Suth slept in the house. Dai took the small boys with him for several weeks and they had the time of their lives, bathing in the brackish water where the river opened into the bay, eating the kind of meals men get, and having treats of cheap ice cream they liked.

I was doing a third Ted and Nina book that summer, *A Summer Day with Ted and Nina*, so, except for weekends, stayed at home to see how things were going. Once, thinking to be helpful, I gathered empty cement bags and other trash and set fire to it, not realizing how near I was to the house and other flammable material. The fire raced toward the house and the windows waiting to be put in and nearly ruined the whole project. Swift action put out the fire, but not before it had cracked the glass in some of the windows.

The house was suitable for summer only; it stood just two blocks from the river. The street was tree-lined and shady and an eighty-foot spruce grew on our lot, as well as cedars, scrub oak, and slippery elm. It was a delightful retreat for summer.

Nina had graduated from high school in 1936 and was at Beaver College. Jane Carlin too was there and they and their friends spent a great deal of time at our house. We called it Beaver Annex. Jane was almost a second daughter, with us nearly every day, regaling us with hilarious songs and stories. Boys came and went either with our boys or with Nina. She took an interest in some of them as escorts, but the moment they became serious the friendship ended.

In 1939, when Hitler was overrunning Europe, *Skippack School* was published. We were the more distressed when Poland was invaded because of Ed and Hedwig, our dear Polish friends who were a part of our musical world. But what could we do? As Hendrik Van Loon wrote in one of his letters to me, "You and I must just keep on writing our little books." And so we did, trying to push away the horror that would not be pushed away.

More and more requests came for me to speak, at schools, libraries, or women's groups. One of these was from Moorestown, where Hannah Severns was in charge of the library. She had planned a full day for me, first in the junior high school, next at the Friends' school, then lunch with several librarians, some of whom were volunteers. I remember especially Mrs. Richard Wood and Mary Evans. I was amused and pleased when they spoke to each other in the Quaker way of "thee and thou." It reminded me of the Merion Meeting and the story I had hoped to do about a Quaker child. Would such a child resent the Quaker discipline, I asked, or would it be almost born in him?

"Oh," said Mary Evans, "thee ought to meet my Aunt Hannah. When she was a child she kicked her bonnet down the stairs."

With my usual impetuousness I was quick to reply, "I'd love to meet her. May I? Does she live in Moorestown?"

"Yes," said Mary Evans, "she lives here with her niece, Mrs. John Rhoads."

"Do you think I could meet her? . . . Today?"

"Perhaps. I'll inquire. She is ninety-two years old and is very frail. I'll see if she can see you today."

So, after a reception in the library that afternoon, I was taken to Mrs. Rhoads's house to meet Miss Hannah Carter. Mary Evans had brought her some of my books to look at so she would know what they were like, and Mrs. Rhoads had brought from the storeroom some of her aunt's toys—beautifully kept and treasured from her childhood. There was a tiny fourposter bed and twin dolls to fit it. One had belonged to Hannah and one to her sister Sally. Each doll had a tiny straw hat made by one of the sisters and minuscule "worked" slippers in needlepoint. Loving dolls and miniature things as I always had, I was enchanted. But the real enchantment was Aunt Hannah herself, as she so kindly allowed me to call her. She was tiny too, a precious little woman, hair smoothly parted and drawn back, eyes still sparkling with humor, her plain dress needing no adornment but the wholeness of her person. She was feeling quite well that day and told me about all the things Mrs. Rhoads had collected for me to see, and said I might use her name and anything I liked from her life, still making the story fiction. . . . And that was all.

The next time I went to see her, after calling Mrs. Rhoads, she was far away. Very soon after that she died. I felt as if I had lost a long-loved friend. In fact, the whole of Moorestown mourned her. She was much loved.

Before visiting Mrs. Rhoads again, I spent a great deal of time in the Friends' library in Germantown, where Violet Gordon Gray was helpful as always. She directed me to suitable reading concerning the Friends and records of weekly, monthly, and yearly meetings, which were attended by Friends from outlying districts. I read that sometimes, when the house was overflowing with guests, the children had to sleep in the attic, and that once a child had to sleep in the bedding chest! Later, when I visited Mrs. Rhoads, I learned that the child had been Hannah herself.

While I was in the midst of writing the story about Hannah we had a great snowstorm and everyone was housebound. There was no school, no one went to work, and for two days or so we were all together and I was very happy. It was like a picnic. We had so much fun that I wanted to include such an incident in my book.

Knowing the vagaries of Philadelphia weather, which is fickle and likely to change every three days, I had to be sure that there could have been such a storm in the year of Hannah's childhood. I hied myself through the snow from Jenkintown to Germantown to the 'Friends' library and got out the book published by the Corn Exchange Bank about Philadelphia and opened it at random, just to see what I would find. This is the way it went: "The winter of 1856 was a particularly cold and stormy one, the Delaware was frozen from shore to shore and the ice so thick, they built fires on it. . . ."

Just what I wanted! I read on: how pretzel stands were set up, hot soup stands, muffins and fish stands for skaters, but there had been too many fires. One day a sleigh and two horses and several people had fallen through the weakened ice and drowned. Strange as it seems, when I spoke about it to Mrs. Rhoads, she said they had been members of her family.

At one point, when I was writing the story about Hannah, I was tired and had come to a stop because I needed some sort of personal incident, something that would make the family life seem real—a diary or recipe or letter—something.

I decided to go down to the kitchen and make a cake, thus changing my occupation and giving the family a treat. I flipped on the radio as I passed, something I seldom did in the daytime. I heard the voice of Mary Margaret McBride, so sat down a moment to listen and this is what I heard:

> I was in Philadelphia over the weekend, visiting a Quaker family, and came across an amusing recipe for pie crust. Here it is:
>
> PIE CRUST
> Whatever much flour thee has, thee takes a third as much lard—good *leaf* lard, thee knows. Rub it lightly into the flour—so. Then take a small quantity of water—very cold —put it in little by little. Then, thee whacks it out onto the board and rolls it gently. When it is very thin, cover it with dabs of butter and fold over and roll out again. Then, cover it with dots of butter and fold again, so thee can see the dots through the dough. Of course, thee knows that all this time thee's had salt in it!

Here was another of those amazing coincidences that seem to happen with each book. When I need something it seems to come to me.

Because we were so enchanted with the street cries when we

moved to Philadelphia, I thought it would be interesting and typical to use them as chapter headings. Some I remembered, but in an old book I found many more.

The little book called *Thee, Hannah!* went along with less trouble than most. Possibly because I grew to love the characters and their way of life. In a few months it was finished and ready for the pictures, many of which I did throughout the summer in Toms River.

More and more, as time went on and books accumulated, there were necessary trips to New York to confer with Peggy, to speak at authors' luncheons and at library meetings. As always at such gatherings there were people famous in the book world whom I met and some of whom I grew to know well. I didn't allow myself to think how famous were the names on the same program where mine was, lest I be frightened out of my wits. I used to try to allay my fear by saying, "No matter how poorly I speak or how little they like me, they won't kill me or put me in jail. So go on and say what you have to say and sit down."

Dai used to comfort me by saying, "You've got yourself into this—now go on and carry it through."

One of these occasions was a day in Wilmington at the library where Carolyn Field was in charge of work for children. Later I went to Enoch Pratt Library in Baltimore, where Emerson Greenaway was director. I couldn't have known then that, later in Philadelphia, Emerson and Helen, his wife, and Carolyn Field would become our fast friends. More than that, the courtesy and help they have extended to authors and artists is immeasurable.

Wherever I was or whatever I was doing, ideas raced through my head for a book—something I wished to draw or tell about. Why this compulsion to write or draw, I don't know. Perhaps it is to share something or to help remembrance of an interesting or pleasant experience, but it seems as if the book chooses me rather than my choosing it. Who knows why one has this compulsion.

Probably I see things in pictures first, but words too fascinate me, their use and origin, and the way a word passes from one language to another with very little change.

Chapter Twenty-seven

In the late thirties, while I was constantly at work on my books and illustrating others, our family life was going through many changes. Arthur was living downtown in Philadelphia and Jack was in New York, where he had worked for a time at Doubleday and was trying his hand at being an actor, not too successfully, I may add. He had various small parts as a walk-on, one, he recalls, in an opera in which Ezio Pinza was the lead. It happened that, as Pinza made his entrance on the stage, Jack stood exactly in his path. Pinza, striding forth, already singing, simply took Jack by the scruff of the neck, lifted him off his feet, and set him aside.

Arthur came home frequently and Jack occasionally. They brought their friends as always. Sometimes the friend happened to be a girl currently in favor. Usually these attachments were temporary, not because of anything we said or did, but simply because the boys discovered for themselves that the girls didn't fit into the family, and family feeling among us is and was very strong. I remember one girl Arthur brought home who was interesting and amusing but who would have made him miserable had he married her. We invited her to be with us for Thanksgiving dinner and that finished the matter. Arthur saw for himself that she just didn't fit in.

At one point during this period Arthur was timekeeper in a road-building project sponsored by the WPA. Later he and Jack, who came back to Philadelphia and lived with Arthur, were employed in another WPA project in a dramatic group. The sequence of events in those troubled times is impossible to remember, and perhaps the less we remember the better. It was not all grim by any means. There were the evenings of music, the radio program of the Philadelphia Orchestra each Sunday afternoon, the children coming and going, Maury and Ted still in the little boy stage.

While Arthur was counselor in a summer camp he met a girl whom he later married. They lived in a tiny house on one of the old streets of Philadelphia. One winter both Jack and Arthur were in the Federal Theater and there met Edna Silverman. Jack was seriously interested in her and they were married in 1939. She is now a professor of the classics at Lehigh University but she keeps her erudition carefully hidden. Her kindness and gentleness extend to everyone, and her simply offered help in whatever needs to be done is proverbial.

Soon after this, in the fall of 1940, Arthur and his wife moved to Manoa, a new suburb of Philadelphia. They urged us to move there too, and we did.

Arthur had begun working with plastics and was one of the first to develop its use. He began by making table fountains, napkin rings, trays and other small items. Jack Croasdale joined him in the business and Nina became their secretary.

By now Nina was graduated from Beaver and had joined a dramatic club sponsored by Mrs. Grodinsky, who lived in Jenkintown. There she met a young man who was teaching in the high school while earning his master's degree at the University of Pennsylvania.

One night when he drove her home she brought him to meet the family. He stayed only a few moments, but long enough to make an extremely good impression. When he had gone I said to Nina, "Well, if you can get *that* young man, grab him." Half fun, whole earnest.

"But he takes two of us home," she said ruefully.

"See that he takes you home last," I offered, hardly knowing why I gave that advice, which probably came from age-old woman's wisdom.

In a few weeks she announced that she and Alfred Kuhn were engaged. The more we saw of Alfred, the more we loved him. They were married in 1941 and moved to Green Hills near Reading, where Alfred was to work in a theatrical venture in summer theater.

I had not realized until she had left after her marriage how terribly I would miss Nina. Every time I passed her room the pain of loss was almost unbearable. Still, she was happy.

One summer Jack and Edna stayed in our house in Manoa while we were at the cottage in Toms River. It was before their first child was born, and as the summer progressed Edna said, with her usual twinkle, "You may call me 'Your Immanence.'" Shortly after, our first grandchild was born and named Nina after her Aunt Nina.

The house in Manoa had no proper place for me to work. The only good light from the left was at the end of the long narrow kitchen. So there it was that I set up my drawing table and chair, my typewriter, paints, and pencils, and there began the book *Elin's Amerika*.

It was Dr. Ralph Johnson, whom I had met when I spoke at the library of Girard College, who suggested that I write about the Swedes on the Delaware. They were the first permanent settlers in Pennsylvania and were here before William Penn. They lived in caves and huts along the river (De La Warr), and among them were Dr. Johnson's ancestors, the Jansens.

He told me of the settlement in what is now Wilmington, where a church was built and the pulpit handwrought by the settlers, each giving a day's work now and then, "some boards of walnut" and other materials needed. It was also Dr. Johnson who told me about Governor Printz of that settlement and about the carved cherubs sent to the colony by Queen Christina of Sweden and now over the altar in Old Swedes Church in Philadelphia. I thought how a child might react to the strange environment, remembering that our own children were not anxious to leave their familiar home for another when we moved, and how they had not wanted to leave their friends for fear they would not find others.

In searching for books that contained some remnant of personal experience from long ago, I found letters written from America to England with details of life among the Indians. These gave me authority to use a few Indian words and the names for the Indians in the story.

At the historical society I found a long, narrow copybook containing the records of many transactions in the new settlement and accounts of various happenings. It seemed to bring the people of the seventeenth century alive. One account was of a "long, lean-bodied white cow" that had gone astray and was found by the clerk, Luke, who "kept her through the winter." Then she was slaughtered and a certain portion was sent to the governor (William Penn), another portion to the clerk of the meeting, and the rest given to Luke "for the wintering of her." It was just the sort of detailed realism I would like to use in the book, but I couldn't use it in the book about the

Swedish colony because I knew from other sources that every animal in the colony was known, and among them there were only three cows. There *couldn't* have been a *stray* cow.

Still, the incident helped to create an atmosphere of that early time and evoked an image of the kind of loneliness the settlers must have suffered and the concern for food and clothing that must have confronted any new colony. I felt the longing for the ship to come in, which has its analogy in the longing we all experience when something or someone is long overdue. I spent days at the Swedish Museum in South Philadelphia, where there was a *stuga*, a log cabin built by the settlers just as they had built them in Sweden.

Early land grants helped me to reconstruct the period, and a great sweep of jack-in-the-pulpit, growing in a bit of uncleared woodland near us, seemed to say, "We were here when they were here." I brought a handful of them into the house and painted them, knowing that within a few months a contractor's shovel might scoop them up and they would vanish. I had preserved them rather than destroyed them. . . . Then the story began to move.

There was a visit to a log house built by the Swedes in Clifton Heights and to another in Morton, its brick chimney in the loft looking, I'm sure, just as it had two hundred years before. It is a known fact that the Swedes built their log houses so well-fitted that they didn't require caulking and they have stood up under weathering remarkably well.

Our friends Maud and Ben Krieger told me rhymes learned in Sweden in childhood, the rhyme changing slightly from place to place. Memories of Ben's childhood supplied bits and pieces of the story, so tightly woven into it that I can no longer tell what he told me and what I found in the library. He recalled how his father would say to his brother Axel, "Go find Ben and see what he is doing and tell him to stop."

And in the library I had found authentic material that allowed me to finish the story of Elin with the arrival of the longed-for ship from Sweden with its supply of food and clothing, the new colonists, and Brother Axel, and Britta, who was to be Bror's bride, and Gudrun, Elin's new friend.

Elin's Amerika was published in 1941, and at the Feast of Saint Lucia, the Swedish "Little Christmas," I was invited to a reception at the Swedish Museum, which had supplied so much material for the book.

Chapter Twenty-eight

All through these years our main source of recreation lay in our music. The quartets continued to meet at alternating houses, always with the original members when possible, but acquiring new members as one or another dropped out temporarily. Sometimes a guest performer was brought; sometimes a substitute cellist was found. Cellists were rare and seemed to have the most professional engagements. Sometimes we went to the Ryglewicz's in Northeast Philadelphia, where we met their Polish friends. Wherever we met, there was always the renewed anticipation of the music to come after the fiddles had tuned up.

When we met at Ed and Hedwig's we were served Polish food: *galumpke*, *pirogi*, *barszcz*, and *kutia*. We talked over coffee when the music stopped and Ed told us about coming to America from Lovicz, Poland, when he was about ten and how he was teased about his round collar and silk tie, his gentle manners, and his way of speaking English. Right then the idea of doing a Polish book was born. Later, when I really began the book, *Up the Hill*, Ed recalled more of his background, about Christmas customs and the joy of Easter, when people greeted each other saying, "Christ is risen!" and the answer, "He is risen indeed!" He reminded me, however, that most of the traditional customs were practiced by the country people.

He was kind enough to spend the better part of two days telling me these things, and about the language, its origins, and the rules of pronunciation.

Another day he took me up into Pennsylvania to a friend's machine shop, just to get an idea of the variety of things I could use in the story. It was there I learned something I had always wondered about. How are things done the *first* time, before they can be made by machine? For example, the owner of the shop showed me exquisitely fine drilling tools he had made by hand. They were as fine as needles and were used as models for those turned out by machine.

I kept in touch with Ed and Hedwig rather closely at this time. Besides learning the precise rules for pronouncing Polish words and names, I learned a Polish Christmas carol that Ed translated for me and made a copy of the music, which appears on the jacket of *Up the Hill*. He also helped arrange the glossary at the front of the book.

Edward is gone now, but Hedwig and her family are still our close friends. We speak of those evenings together and what fun we had, and in the light of today's unrest we are happy to remember that our children grew fond of each other and their parents and that they too remember with affection those who provided the music to which they fell asleep.

During the early winter of 1941 I had been to the University of Michigan to speak and had stayed with old friends from Lapeer. On their living-room wall I had seen etchings signed with a name that I thought to be Polish. Strangely enough, when Dai took me to Pottsville, where Edward said I would find Polish miners, and I went to the library to ask the help of Miss Patterson, the librarian, whom I had met in York, she took us directly to the home of the artist who had made that etching! His name is Nicholas Bervinchak. Three days a week he worked in the mine and the rest of the week he painted or did etchings, which have an international reputation. Miss Patterson had recognized his artistic ability when he came as a subscriber to the library and had encouraged him to work at it. He found scraps of metal in the mine to make etching plates and tools and had developed his talent with Miss Patterson's help in directing him to reading matter. With his permission I used his experience in the book I was doing.

Those days were full to overflowing with exciting research, with music, not only the quartets but our own singing, violin and piano music.

Sometimes I see myself standing beside the dining table, eager to begin or continue a drawing or a page of manuscript and thinking to myself, If only I didn't have to iron Nina's dress or mend Maury's trousers or sew on that button I could—then sternly reminding myself of a happy day in my childhood, I would think, Perhaps *this* will be one of those days my children will remember. I'd better make it a *good* one!

December 7, 1941, came, when everyone hung over the radio,

listening with unbelieving ears to the reports of the attack on Pearl Harbor.

Ted had been graduated from high school and was classified 1A by the draft board. In no time at all he was called up. I shall never forget the day he left for camp. We drove him to the station, where he begged us to leave him and not go to the train.

It was one of the hardest things I've ever had to do and I'm sure it was as hard for Dai as for me. We drove around aimlessly for a while, then went to my mother's for comfort.

Gradually the pain of loss subsided to a bearable level and we began to look forward to Ted's first letter saying where he had been sent and how he had fared. I worked at my drawing and writing, which helped. Then we began getting letters that were cheerful and funny. Ted made friends easily and soon became adjusted to army life.

Maury was going to school in Oakmont, about a mile from where we lived. We were under wartime restrictions, and as daylight saving was continued throughout the winter it was still dark when he had to leave for school.

One morning, as I stood watching him disappear into the woods on the short cut, I saw coming toward me out of the still gray sky a flock of wild geese. As I watched, one goose detached himself from the end of the flying arrow, flew to the head of the formation, turned the whole flock at a right angle to the way they had been flying, and took off in the other direction. What inborn knowledge had they of the way to go? I stood in the dawning light marveling at the incident. In spite of war and human griefs, the geese still flew their uncharted way, the pussy willow soon would burst its bonds of winter, and spring would come in its time.

Maury, in his boyhood, showed the gift he has for using his mind and his hands. He loved making things, putting together various kits of airplanes and boats, and once a tiny castle with dormer windows and intricate detail. He was meticulous about everything he did at home or in school. It was a joy to have him with us, our last child to be at home.

Sometime during this period we had guests, Henry Beston and his wife, Elizabeth Coatsworth, who were passing through on their way to find a school for their girls. I had illustrated several of her books, most recently *Alice All by Herself*. I showed them where I was working at the end of the kitchen and Elizabeth said she would always think of me sitting there at my work.

As the war progressed we went to Toms River only for weekends. Dai was doing war work for the Signal Corps and was on the middle shift, so he didn't get home until midnight. He rode in a car pool, as most people did, to save fuel, so we were able to use our quota to go to the shore. I prepared everything we needed for the few days allowed us, so we could drive down in the night to make the most of the time.

While I was still at work on the pictures for *Yonie Wondernose*, Earl Schenk Miers, editor of Westminster Press, called me to ask if I would do a book for them. I felt I had an obligation to give any book I did to Doubleday but I had one put away that I had written simply as a memory of an early Christmas in Philadelphia. I had offered it to Peggy but she felt it was not really a children's book and that she would rather have one that was not seasonal, so had refused it. Would he like to see it? Yes, he would, Mr. Miers said. He accepted it.

I had written it in moments of loneliness and nostalgia, remembering how Papa had gathered us together to explain the financial strain he had been under moving from Michigan to Philadelphia, buying new furniture, then having Nina in the hospital with special nurses, where she was still very ill. He asked us to choose between having a few small gifts and having turkey for Christmas. We all chose the traditional turkey for Christmas and that is what I called the story. It was published in the fall of 1944 as a small Christmas token.

My author's copies came when my cousin Kate was visiting us unexpectedly. I had kept secret from my brothers the fact that I had written the book, and hadn't told them about Kate's visit. So I planned a dinner party and invited all four brothers and their wives. Kate and I set the table, and at each place stood a copy of *Turkey for Christmas*. Westminster Press had bound two copies in leather for Dai and me, with our names in gold on the cover.

It was fun to see the look of surprise when the family greeted Kate and again when they were ushered into the dining room and saw the books.

After dinner I proposed that we read the book aloud. It was very short. I asked Dai to begin. He read for about two pages, then, in a quavery tearful voice, said, "I can't read any more," and passed it on to Arthur, my oldest brother. He too read only a few pages, when he had to stop, wipe his eyes, and wordlessly pass it on. And so it went, all around the table. Who ended it, I have forgotten. Not I.

The emotion evoked by recounting that old Christmas had affected me as well, even though it ended happily.

Once more, as I write this, we are having a gathering of the clan tonight. It is a double birthday party for Jack and Knut Krieger. Mimi, Knut's wife, is bringing the whole dinner, down to the last detail. All our children will be here.

As always, when Jack and Knut are together, there will be reminiscences and laughter.

Yonie Wondernose was "in the works" and it too was published in 1944 by Doubleday. Meantime, we had moved to Germantown.

We had lived for three years in Manoa, but it had never seemed the right place for us. Except for Arthur and his wife, and our young friends next door, there were few with whom we felt congenial. The whole development was treeless and bare and at that stage we felt out of our element, so we bought a sturdy stone house on Carpenter Lane in Germantown. It was near the station and was spacious and homelike, with room for overnight guests, a large yard, and good neighbors. The only drawback was the need for cleaning not only floors and woodwork but the walls, which were covered with heavy painted cloth. It was nearly impossible to find help because most women were engaged in war work of one kind or another.

After a year or so of special training, first at Abilene, Texas, then El Paso, Ted came home on furlough. We all went out to Nina's one day, Ted in one of his funniest moods. Nina was awaiting her second child, so Ted asked her when she was going to put that watermelon in the icebox. Then he went on to describe with his inimitable gift for mimicry and gesture the rigors of camp life, especially the twenty-five-mile hike with a pack on his back. He was hilariously funny.

From El Paso, Texas, he was sent to Topeka, Kansas. His manual dexterity had been discovered, so he was assigned to Winter General Hospital, where he made prosthetic devices for the wounded.

While in Topeka the boys were entertained by the citizens, among whom were the Garvins, whose charming red-haired daughter came home from Boulder College at vacationtime and was introduced to Ted. Acquaintance grew into friendship, which led to promises to marry when the war had ended and Betty had been graduated. Ted had spent some of his days off with the Garvins and apparently convinced them that he was worthy to be their son-in-law.

Chapter Twenty-nine

While Nina was still in school, about 1940, my helper in the house was a nice woman whose several children went to the same school as our children. The oldest, a boy, was very dark like his Negro father, but the little ones, though rather dark-skinned, had blond hair and blue eyes. I wondered about this and thought how difficult it might be for them and for their mother. One day it happened as we talked that an opening in the conservation allowed me to speak about the difference in the children and ask if it had caused any trouble.

"Yes," Medora answered, "sometimes it's hard." Always there had been the sadness of belonging to neither one race nor the other. It was near graduation time for the son who was in Nina's class and no one seemed to want to walk with him in the procession. But Nina took care of that. She walked with him.

This sad situation took hold of me. I wanted to write about a Negro child in a white community—a child whose parents were good hard-working people, whose home was pleasant and clean, and whose children were all brought up as Medora's were.

When I first spoke to Peggy about it she looked grave and shook her head.

"Oh, honey, we couldn't do a book like that. Not now. It's too controversial. Just go on with the other book you had in mind. No, it isn't the right time. Maybe later."

So I put it away in my mind. But I still thought about it, and the recurring theme kept popping up. When I delivered the drawings for *Elin's Amerika*, Peggy asked me if I had thought any more about the little Negro child. When I said, "Yes," she said "Well, keep it in mind. Someday we'll do it. Meantime, I think your idea for the Polish book is good, so concentrate on that."

The next fall, when I delivered the last of *Up the Hill,* and Peggy was pleased with it, she said, "Now, believe it or not, I very much *want* you to do the book about the Negro child. I've had several letters asking for just such material. So go to it and good luck." We had our usual lunch celebration and I went home ready to get to work.

Through Arthur's wife I met a woman social worker who was Negro. I invited her to lunch and talked with her about my project, asking where I might go to find pertinent material. She suggested a certain doctor's wife who she thought would be helpful. I had already decided to use the spirituals that I loved as chapter headings, relating the chapter to the spiritual and using as a character in my story an elderly person who would remember slavery. The doctor's wife was against my using the spirituals and against putting in any character who remembered slavery.

"You are twenty-five years too late for that kind of story," she said. "We want to forget all that and begin anew. I think you ought to write about *us.* I mean about those of us who have been educated and have risen above the old idea of spirituals and the memory of slavery." As she talked I could sympathize with her point of view and appreciate the fact that she was better educated than I. She was a concert pianist and had a Ph.D. in music.

But my story was gone, gone completely. I knew then that I must learn a great deal more before doing any book about a Negro child. Again I put the story aside. I decided I would just wait and see what happened. Something would turn up. And it did.

One day I went to buy shoes, and while I waited for the salesman I heard a young woman talking on the phone. I rose to speak to her as she was leaving and explained to her my idea about the book. She was a pleasant, light-skinned Negro who greeted me with a smile when I asked if I could come and talk to her, telling her how long I had been trying to do the book I had in mind. We made an appointment for a few days later when I visited her in her office. She was a public stenographer. Her name was Martha Brown, now Fultz.

As we talked she said she didn't feel qualified to answer my questions, but could direct me to those who could. In passing she asked if I knew Nellie Bright, which I didn't. She named several teachers and school principals whom I visited in turn over a period of two or three weeks. One was Arthur Fauset, then principal of

Singley School. When I told him of wanting to use the spirituals as chapter headings, connecting them in some way with the content of the story, he said, "Don't use the spirituals. The children know nothing about them. They are a symbol of a time we would like to forget."

This didn't seem sensible to me, but I took it into consideration, thinking I would hear what others had to say. Mr. Fauset ended by asking, "Do you know Nellie Bright?" But when I said, "No," he didn't continue with any information about her.

I was so concerned about the spirituals, thinking how I had sung them for years and how much I wanted to use them, that I didn't inquire about Nellie Bright. Through the songs I understood to some extent the sorrow of bondage, the grief of separated families, the hope of a people who were deeply religious. I had read of how the spirituals were sung on the plantations to send messages and signals—"There's a meeting tonight in the big woods," or "Dinah's baby is a boy." They had great meaning for me.

When I asked Mary Chase, the principal of the George Washington School, why no one wanted me to use the spirituals in my book, she said, "Don't you see? It types us. It's as if we had only a sense of rhythm to offer. We have many gifts to contribute." Then at last I understood why I must not use the spirituals. She too said, "Do you know Nellie Bright?" It is strange, but even then I didn't ask further about Nellie Bright.

But the next day, after returning at noon from my search for material, the telephone rang and when I answered it my friend Lora Scott, who was also a school principal, said, "I hear you are working on a book about a Negro child. I want you to meet my friend Nellie Bright, the principal of Joseph E. Hill School in Germantown. I've made a tentative date with her for Friday at one-thirty. Can you go with me? I will introduce you to her, then leave, and you can talk together."

"Of course I can go! Of course." Now at last I would meet the mysterious Nellie Bright. Lora and I went together on Friday, Lora introduced us, then left as she had said.

"Now," said Nellie, as we sat down, "what do you want to know?"

"Just talk," I said. "Begin anywhere in your childhood."

She began, "I was born in the West Indies. My father was an Episcopal bishop. Life was pleasant and uncomplicated, but when we came to the United States, things were different. If we wanted to go on a vacation, we had to write weeks ahead to some friend so we could have a place to stay, because we were not welcome in most hotels. Or we had to go abroad. One time, when we had ridden all night on the train to New York, where we were to take a ship for Europe, we stopped at a Childs' restaurant near the dock to have breakfast. We sat for one hour waiting to be served. Then my father, knowing that we children were very hungry, went to the manager and asked him to serve us. He said, 'You know, we can't serve you here.'

"So, after having been taught all our lives to eat food at home, not on the street, we had to go to a fruit stand and eat our breakfast on the street after all."

By this time I was very much affected by Nellie's recital, but when she told me of her experience in school I was dissolved in tears. The teacher had asked each child what he or she wanted to do when they were grown up. Nellie's reply to the question was that she would like to teach languages in a girls' college. The teacher shook her head and said, "Don't you know you can't do that?"

Seeing Nellie's blank look, the teacher explained about her not being white. Nellie broke into sobs, ran from the school, and burst into the house, where her mother met her. Seeing Nellie's distress, she said, "Oh—it's come."

We wept together. This was new to my experience and heartbreaking.

Another important woman who helped me a great deal was Jessica Cole. She was active in Scouting and had a troup of girls of differing backgrounds whom she kept interested with all kinds of activities. She was imaginative and taught the girls how to make toys out of the simplest things, such as chests of drawers from match boxes with buttons for drawer pulls, flower pots and tea cups out of acorns and thimbles. This appealed to me because I have always loved miniature things. I had liked Jessica from the first when "Griz" had introduced me to her. "Griz" was Gertrude Gold, director of Scouting in Philadelphia and at Camp Indian Run near Downingtown, where Nina spent the summers, first as a camper, then as a counselor.

Mary, Jessica's daughter, was the model for April. I chose her name because I liked it, it was uncommon, and was the name of the niece of a well-known librarian friend, Alice Brooks Mooney. It also expressed the nature of the child who came from my imagination, bright and sunny and stormy by turns.

As I thought about what April's father might do for a living, I remembered the pleasant Negro postman who passed each morning on his rounds, so, thinking how we all have respect for the postman and a kind of affection for one who may bring good news, I made him a postman. It wasn't until much later that I discovered Jessica's husband was a postman! Another one of those strange coincidences.

While I was doing the book my son Arthur assured me that I must be prepared for criticism, and to be called a Communist, or some other unpleasant name, but encouraged me all the same. I cared not a whit. I knew this was something I must do.

There was some discussion about the ending of the book, when April gets into bed with the little white child to comfort her in a storm. Peggy thought I ought to change it, or at least to talk it over with several people whose opinion would count.

I felt the necessity of the power of touch, to show that black skin is as soft and clean as white, to dispel fear of the unknown, to show that to *know* is to understand.

I went to a Baptist minister, whom I knew to be a southerner, to ask his opinion. He said, "Stick to your guns!" So I did. And Peggy came to see I was right.

Much later, after the book was published, I was asked by my friend Charlemae Rollins to speak at Maryland State College, where she was teaching a summer course in library science. The response to my talk from Negro teachers and students was most gratifying.

The drawings for *Bright April* I did from memory, from my walking up and down the streets of Germantown, from the sketches I had made at the Rittenhouse School, and from what I knew of old houses in that neighborhood. April herself is a combination of Mrs. Cole's children and those I had seen in school, and Mrs. Cole would be the first to acknowledge that I didn't get a very good portrait of her. I'm sure she doesn't mind.

From the time I first thought of doing the book until it was published, nearly six years had passed.

Chapter Thirty

While we lived on Carpenter Lane, in Germantown, many changes took place in our lives. Maury had entered the University of Pennsylvania intending to major in chemistry but changed to journalism because it seemed to be nearer to what he wanted. There was the constant fear that he would be drafted for the Army and of our being left to ourselves in that big house with no help. We decided it might be wise to sell the house and move to the cottage near Toms River until something more suitable in size could be found in Philadelphia. But the house at Money Island was not made for year-round use, so Dai got Suth Applegate, our carpenter friend, to do the remodeling and we put our house up for sale, thinking naïvely that the cottage would be well finished before anyone bought the Germantown house. Of course, that is not the way it worked out. A family bought the house hoping to have almost immediate occupancy, and we, happy to have sold so readily, let them have it and moved while the rebuilding was still going on.

Needless to say, there was more furniture than we had room for in the cottage even when it was finished, so we gave things to the children and stored the rest in a garage until the rooms were finished and cleared. The living room was piled high with sheet rock, the bathroom filled with kitchen things. At any moment a saw might come through the floor, a painter look in the window, or a carpenter hammering studding into place. There was not a quiet corner in the house.

Some days only Suth showed up for work. The others had gone fishing. But Suth, the faithful, stayed on and worked, with Dai helping. I couldn't do any writing or drawing, so because butter was scarce during the war years, I decided to make butter, keep the men well fed, and hope they would stay on the job. I had never made butter, but I had seen Aunt Ella make it and the remembrance had been kept alive by the repetition of the butter story concerning Mrs. Desireau. I knew I must be careful about it. I remembered how Aunt Ella's tireless hands lifted the churn handle up and down, up and down, until the sound of the slap-slap changed to a different tone when the butter came. I watched as she gathered the yellow lumps of butter from the whey into a wooden bowl, and with a wooden paddle worked the water out of it, put in salt, and worked it again. Then she formed it into neat one-pound pats, pressed a design into the top, ready to trade at Uncle Steve's store. I thought I too could make butter.

I went up to Mr. Faby's store and bought heavy cream, got out my electric mixer, and set to work. As the cream gradually changed character, which took some fifteen minutes, as I remember, my mind began to wander into the world of imagination, as always when I am doing homely tasks. Suddenly I felt as if someone had plucked at my sleeve and said, "When are you going to do that story about me?"

It seemed that the voice was that of a boy—a Scottish boy, who had been wrecked on Barnegat Shoals. What was his name? I took the butter out of the whey as I wondered at this sudden visitation. It seemed too that he was a Quaker lad and an orphan, coming to New Jersey in the early 1700s. Why not call him Jared Craig, after Dai's grandfather? The story went so swiftly that I had to think to catch up with it. For years I had dreamed of such a tale, sparked by the rumors of buried treasure and Captain Kidd. It was believed that our part of the community was named Money Island because of that treasure. For years it had remained only a picture, unmoving, a boy and a pirate in lantern light stooping over a chest of treasure to be buried. Now it had come alive.

I began the story as it had come to my mind and could hardly wait for the library to open so I could look for authentic material from the period in which the boy had set himself.

Fortunately Mrs. LeCato, the librarian, directed me to a diary and letters written by a New Jersey Quaker in the middle seventeen hundreds telling of the Indians then living in that part of the country. In his diary he had put down words in the Indian language and in the opposite column "the English of it." So I felt safe in using such words as were fitting in my story.

There had been a great storm some fifty years before that time which had changed the course of the Toms River so that ships could no longer go between Money Island and the mainland but must follow the deep current on the other side of the island. All of this I found in old records, other diaries, letters, and maps left by the Irish Quakers who had settled the land.

Naturally the house that became the setting for the book was on the spot where our cottage stood. I think few people realize the amount of thought and work that go into the writing of children's books. In my experience a story is a composite of reality, imagination, and supposition.

While I used the location of our cottage for the house where Jenny and Abner lived, I must build it in my mind according to the way a house would have been two hundred years before. I had to denude the landscape of stores and new houses, telegraph poles and macadam roads, of cars and trains and buses. Because I wanted an old oak tree where Jared could hide the map, I had to imagine that one stood on the top of the hill where Jared could look out to sea. That part of Money Island was covered with scrub oak, so I thought there could well have been an enormous old oak where I wanted it to be.

After the book was published a neighbor who had lived on Money Island all her life read it and asked me, "Who told you about that famous old oak tree?"

"Why, nobody. I just imagined it," I said, wondering.

"Don't you know that there was an old oak of enormous girth which stood just there where you have said it was? It fell only a few years ago!" I was astonished. Once more I had imagined something that was true.

Another incident concerning this book was a scornful attack from a critic because I had allowed Jared to understand the Indian language enough to communicate with the Indians. He could not have been well acquainted with children and their ability to search out ways of understanding each other.

The story of Jared went along fairly smoothly once the research was done. Then came the pictures. But before I had finished the drawings a new idea took hold of me so strongly that I felt I must heed it. So began another book.

Chapter Thirty-one

In April of 1946 Ted wrote us that he was to be discharged from the Army. Dai and I went to Denver to meet him and bring him home. We took my mother with us and thoroughly enjoyed the wonders of the country. Every part of the land seemed more beloved than before, especially because the war was over at last. The vast prairies reminded us of western Canada and we marveled at the deep canyons, the wide rivers, and deep forests and, as always, the mountains were breath-taking.

We stayed at the Brown Palace Hotel in Denver, expecting to meet Ted the next day at the airport. He had gone to Fort Leavenworth to be discharged.

The next day Ted's plane was delayed for two hours, so to pass the time we went to the museum. When we returned to the car an hour or so later we found our large suitcase gone, with my new dress and new suit, new nylons, so carefully saved, and presents we had bought to take home. Fortunately Mama's suitcase was untouched. We had probably frightened off the thieves. Dismayed as we were, and seeing Mama weeping, I said, "Now, we can let this ruin our beautiful trip or we can pretend that it never happened. We can manage with what we have. Let's forget it." And we did. I had a spare white frill for my silk dress in a box in the trunk of the car. We had underwear and night things in a smaller suitcase, so we managed very well, and I can honestly say that decision was carried out—I never gave it another thought.

We met Ted at the airport and spent a few days in Boulder Canyon en route to the college to meet Betty. She was a lovely auburn-haired girl with a delightful sense of humor who was majoring in dietetics. We drove up Mount Flagstaff, where we saw mountain bluebirds, then started back toward home, scarcely believing we had Ted with us safe and sound.

We stopped in Topeka to meet Betty's father and mother and spent the night there. We found them congenial and welcoming and I shall never forget the strawberry pie!

Shortly after he came home Ted entered the Philadelphia College of Art on the GI bill, majoring in industrial design.

In 1947 he went back to Topeka, where he and Betty were married July 9. Arthur went with him to represent the family.

The year of 1947 brought many pleasant happenings and a sad one. Arthur's wife, Muriel, left him after ten years of marriage. There was the publication of *Bright April*, I was working on the book I now called *Jared's Island*, we still had the musical evenings, and the young people still came to spend weekends with us.

Among the guests who had come to our house in Germantown were Vincent and Dorothea Persichetti, both pianists, Vincent a well-known composer of contemporary music whom we had met at the Art Alliance.

I had heard of them and Vincent's sister Nina (pronounced Neena, the Italian way) through a friend I often met on my early morning walks in Money Island. My friends' parents had a cottage next door to Nina's. One night when Vincent and Dorothea were guests of honor and performers at the Art Alliance in Philadelphia, Dorothea asked about the family and I told her of Arthur's lonely state and said I wished I could find for him a girl who would like nothing better than to stay at home and rear a family.

"The nicest girl I know," she said, "is Nina, Vincent's sister. She is lovely."

I had heard nothing but praise about Nina and hoped that someday our paths would cross. They did.

One morning when I stopped for a moment on the hill to speak to my friend Anna, she said, suddenly, "Nina's here! Come, let's go and meet her." She took me by the hand and led me through the tangle of cedar brush to the Persichetti cottage. She knocked, and just as we entered the house Nina came in from the other door in a bathing dress. What a girl!

After a short visit I went on my way back home to get lunch. Arthur was there for the weekend and receptive to my description of Nina. He had met her father once, but Nina had been away on vacation.

"What's she like?" he questioned.

"Like a round ripe peach," I said, remembering her coloring, her perfect figure, and smiling friendliness. "If you don't go down and take her sailing, you're crazy. She likes sailing. She told me so." He went. (I didn't know then that Persichetti means "little peach"!)

In a very short time back he came with Nina for lunch. They went sailing, and that was *it*. From then on they were constantly together and in 1948 they were married at the cottage in Money Island. All the signals for happiness that I had seen in Nina have proven themselves true.

Over the Labor Day weekend of 1947 we gathered the whole family together at Toms River. Families have a way of scattering for one reason or another. We thought it a good idea to have everybody at once while it was still possible. We could take care of most of the children and grandchildren and some stayed at a motel close-by. We arranged that each meal should be prepared and cleared away by each couple in turn. It turned out to be a joyous way for the de Angelis new and old to become better acquainted.

Ted's Betty was a happy addition to our family. Her rich auburn hair and piquant face were charming and her wit matched Ted's. Even now, when we are together, there is constant laughter and warm affection.

Marianne, who was then engaged to Maury, fitted perfectly into the family. She was quiet but merry, reserved but friendly, and she was lovely.

Betty had her degree in dietetics and is qualified to be a dietitian in a hospital. Marianne already had a degree in nursing and sociology and is now librarian at Kimberton School. Betty does volunteer work in our local hospital.

Chapter Thirty-two

Early in the summer of 1947 I had met Ruth Gagliardo again at a Lippincott luncheon at the Art Alliance. When I invited her for the weekend to Toms River she accepted, even when I told her of our remodeling and that there were no doors on the bedrooms and that the work was still in progress. We talked, Dai, Ruth, and I, until two in the morning, drinking innumerable cups of tea to keep us going while we explored our common interests.

Ruth was very much interested in my new idea for a book that had plagued me all the while I was finishing the drawings for *Jared's Island*. She agreed that a book about a crippled child would be helpful to many children who must learn to live with some disability.

It all began while we had been rebuilding our cottage and our old friends the Harmon Robinsons had begun to build next door. Harm played viola in the quartet in which Dai played violin. He was not only a fine musician and teacher, but a gifted cabinetmaker, reproducing antique furniture. Actually, when we knew him, he was past the age to do large pieces, so he made miniatures, such as knife boxes for cigarettes, jewel boxes, mirrors, and small tables.

Harm had been so ill when he was ten that he had been in bed for three years, and when he was able to get up, was frozen in a sitting position, so that in order to walk he had to support himself with his hands on his knees or use crutches. But he was such good company, so well read, so good a musician, that he was always the center of attention. He ignored his disability as far as possible, but gave in to it when it seemed necessary. I think he was always in some pain and he often slept on a small divan, with his feet on one armrest and his head on the other. We admired and loved him.

I wanted to use his experience and character in a book that I would set in the medieval period in England. I had always wished to do such a story and I felt that anything a child could do in that time he could do now. It might encourage some boy or girl who must learn to live with a handicap to know that success in life depends only on what we *do* with what we have.

While I was still illustrating *Jared's Island* I spent my spare time reading about England and studying a book on English castles to learn what the outer and inner baillies were and why the keep was so called. I studied pictures of winding stairs and crenelated walls in that old book of my father's, and almost decided to set the story in the time of Edward III. Still, I had to consider how much history I had to deal with and what period of costume I would best like to draw. My mind wandered over a period of two hundred years, considering just where I would set the story.

When I delivered the last of the pictures for *Jared* I told Peggy about my idea. She was enthusiastic.

"Oh," she said excitedly, "you must go to England! You ought to go right away. We'll go to the travel agent and get transportation for you." She began to shift papers and reached for the telephone.

"*England!*" I gasped. How I had longed to go to England! But it hadn't occurred to me that such a thing was now possible. For years I had had periods of dreaming that I was aboard ship and about to sail for England, but always awoke just as we were about to leave the dock. Was my dream about to come true?

By now I realized that Peggy had just arranged for me to meet Winifred Nerney, Doubleday's London representative, for lunch. Blanche Van Buren, Peggy's assistant, was there too and a gay time we had. Peggy knew that once I had met Winifred I would be sold on the unexpected journey, and I was. She was the sort of charmer who fits into any situation, who made one feel at once that she was your friend. It wasn't that I didn't want to go to England. It was just too good to be true. Besides, how would Dai take it?

When I reached home that afternoon and told Dai we were going to England, he was stunned. He didn't *want* to go to England. He didn't want to go anywhere. What was the matter with Toms River, where we were comfortable, where the swimming was good, and where the children came down for weekends?

I finally convinced him that it was necessary for me to get authentic, firsthand material for the book I planned to do, that plans were already underway, and we must get passports and shots because we were to set sail in less than a month. He was caught up in the excitement of preparation and soon was as eager to board ship as I was.

I have in my journal, "On April 21, 1948, we rose early in order to finish packing, have our breakfast, and be ready to leave for New York with Ted and Betty. Tonight, we go aboard ship for England . . ."

We'd had dinner at Peggy's, then drove to Pier 90, where the *Queen Mary* was berthed. To our surprise, quite a gathering was there to see us off: Mama, my brother Arthur and his wife, Alma, their daughter and her husband, Adelle and Jack. It was a real send-off. We found flowers in our cabin and all the comforts of the great liner.

About four in the morning I awoke, and as I watched out the porthole the engines started and the pier stanchions passed. We were underway. I got up and watched while we backed and turned and Dai joined me to see Old Liberty guarding the harbor. The morning was beautiful, though cold. We saw the pilot dropped, and in no time at all we were out of sight of land.

We rested in deck chairs, we made new acquaintances, we watched the greedy gulls as they fought for scraps thrown from the galley, we looked for whales, and saw dolphins, we ate the delicious meals and enjoyed the excellent service.

Spring was in full bloom when we landed in Southampton. Primroses lined the banks of the railroad, and soon thatched houses appeared. *Real* thatched houses such as one sees in storybooks. The whole English countryside was blooming with color so bright and clear it was as if each bloom had been dipped in sunshine.

There was so much to see that the journey to London seemed short, the Houses of Parliament came into view, and there stood Big Ben. I wept for sheer joy. Dai said, "It can't be true!" But it was.

Winifred was awaiting us at Waterloo Station and conducted us to our hotel, which stood opposite Kensington Park on Kensington Road. Winifred had filled our room with flowers to welcome us. The room was old-fashioned and comfortable, and the adjoining bathroom enormous, with *heated* towel racks.

Days of sightseeing followed, sometimes with Winifred, sometimes on our own when she was too busy.

Contrary to our first plan to go immediately to Ludlow, where I had intended to begin my story of the crippled boy, whom I called Robin after his prototype, Harmon Robinson, we stayed in

London those first two weeks, going by bus to various places of interest.

One day we went to Windsor Castle. It was a special day because it was there that I finally decided the period in which to set my story.

The diary tells about being shown the Curfew Tower, where the mechanism of the clock is. The chimes play only every three hours, but it happened that we were just in time to see the ancient iron arm turn slowly and the great cylinder that played the hymn move. It was deafening in that small place, but thrilling. I looked down at the patched floor where we all stood, feeling a little anxious lest it should break through with ten or twelve of us standing on it. When I asked the verger if he thought it safe, he said, smiling, "I think you need not worry. The floor is fourteen inches thick and has been here for four hundred years."

He then took us through the Royal Apartments, where we saw the originals of the paintings I had loved for so long in reproduction—Holbeins, Van Dycks, Bruegels—then on through a wide corridor leading to the George Chapel, where I knew the ceremony of the bestowal of knighthood in the Order of the Garter takes place. I remembered too that the order was established by King Edward III, and when I saw on the wall of the corridor a great two-handed sword (a claymore), I thought, Yes, I will choose the time of Edward III.

As we stood in the choir of the chapel, with the banners of the knights above us, and listened to some of its history, the verger was saying, "This is the tomb of Edward III. During the time of George III the tomb was opened to make sure it was truly his. They knew it was because some of his clothing still remained and his red hair. Hair, you know, is the most lasting relic." Now I was sure of the period. The verger went on, musingly, "I think there is a lock of that hair somewhere in England, but I don't know where it is." I remember at that point looking down into a money box standing at the end of a pew and thinking, *How I wish I could see that lock of hair*. It would bring the whole period alive. How I wish I could see it!

I'm quite sure that not another person in that group of ten or twelve cared at all where that lock of hair was.

We went back to London and continued our jaunts about the city and by bus to places of interest, one of them an afternoon to Canterbury.

When we reached the cathedral there were crowds of women still entering and a man standing at the door denied us entrance, saying that it was a convocation of county women at a special gathering and that there was no room for us. Just then a young man came along, saw our disappointment, and said, "Come with me. This is a public building and no one can keep you out." He took us around the corner of the building and into the choir, where we had the best view of everything. We sat within a few feet of the passing procession of choir boys, whose sweet, piping voices and perfect diction rose with our hearts to the carved groining of that magnificent cathedral. The dean in his gorgeous robes, the candle and cross bearers, all passed almost near enough to touch. It was a glorious experience.

Another day we went with Winifred to Sheerness, where my Grandfather Lofft had been born. This was not a particularly successful day. People were rude and uncooperative, so we didn't see much of the town or find the baptismal record in the church. Winifred was disgusted and apologized for her countrymen. Years later a woman from Sheerness heard of our visit through some means, or saw my book *Copper-toed Boots*, and wrote me a letter saying how sorry she was that we had not found her. She was of the same ancestry as my family of Loffts.

At the end of that week we went to Oxford as scheduled. Winifred had asked her friend Joan Marsden to arrange accommodations for us at the hotel. She was at the station to meet us when we arrived and took us to sign in at the Randolph, then to her house for dinner. There were other guests as well, a Mr. Jolly, a Fellow at Oxford University, and house guests, Miss Carol Herschel and her sister Mrs. Shorlands, with her two small daughters.

My first thought was to tell about our visit to Windsor Castle, the Curfew Tower, and the paintings in the Royal Apartments, and especially about the George Chapel and how I had decided to set my story in the time of Edward III, then about the lock of hair and how I wished I could see it. Miss Herschel said, very quietly,

"You may see it. I have it." I was so astonished that I must have sat with my mouth open as she left to go upstairs. In a few moments she was back in the room with a jewel in her hand about two inches in diameter. It was of green enamel with a crystal in the center, covering an opal around which was curled *the lock of red hair!* It was unbelievable.

"My ancestor, John Frederick William Herschel, was the organist in the George Chapel when the tomb of Edward III was opened," Miss Herschel said. "This token was given him by the king, George III, and it is so inscribed on the back." She went on to tell us of Herschel's work in astronomy, his home where her aunt still lived, and where the giant telescope still lies in the garden and relics of his many interests fill the house. What an evening! Of all the people of England and all the people in America *I* was the one who wanted to see that lock of hair. And I saw it. How explain it? Guardian angels, that's what.

We went from Oxford to Ludlow, the place I had chosen for the castle where Robin went with Jon-Go-in-the-Wynd in *The Door in the Wall*. I used some of the castle still standing and the church tower in the end paper for the book, filling in missing parts as I knew they might have looked. Having seen the castle and the way the river wound below it I could visualize Robin's escape from it.

During our stay abroad we spent a week in Switzerland and a week in Paris, and very exciting weeks they were.

Chapter Thirty-three

Very soon after settling in at the cottage I began the story of Robin, not, as I had first meant to in the castle town I called Lindsey, but in London. I renamed the town because I was afraid I might make some historical mistake; and because of our stay those first few weeks in London, our visit to Bartholomew Hospital, to Windsor Castle, because of my reading and research at the British Museum and the Bodlean Library in Oxford, the story took a different turn in my mind. The tale began itself in London.

At the point in the story where Brother Luke takes Robin from St. Bartholomew's on his way to Lindsey, I had written, "There were few people on the road because it was not market day." And there I stopped. For two days I couldn't write a word. It seemed as if the whole fabric of my story had fallen apart. Then I thought to myself, Why not say, "There were many people on the road because it *was* market day?" And on went the story! I had simply forbidden a way for the picture that was really in my mind to appear—the teeming men, women, and children streaming to town.

I still had no suitable title for the book, though I thought about it constantly. When a book takes hold one eats it, sleeps it, and lives with it, relating everything to the subject. I seemed to be living in the Middle Ages.

One evening, as I stood in the kitchen washing up the supper things, my husband, who was in the other room, said something to me, ending with what sounded like "the door in the wall." I turned and said, in answer, "*That* is exactly the title for my new book!"

"What is?" he questioned.

"What you just said, 'the door in the wall.'"

"But I didn't say that, I said . . ." And what he said is lost to me, I was so excited at finding my title. It must have come from somewhere in my subconscious, because, as I searched my mind, I remembered that Arthur, calling on the phone about some minor crisis (long before this), had said to me, "Remember, Mother, how you always told us, 'When you come to a stone wall, if you look far enough, you will find a door in it.'" So the title stayed. The book is called *The Door in the Wall*.

By the time I had finished the text and had begun the illustrations it was nearly spring. The jacket and one or two other pictures were to be finished by April so the salesmen could show the reproductions.

By September the report from the salesmen on prepublication sales was excellent, and it was hoped that the book would do well. Dai and I anxiously awaited a review in the New York papers for Book Week. Usually my books had been reviewed in those issues. But when the papers arrived there was not a word about *The Door in the Wall*.

"Are you terribly disappointed about the lack of reviews?" Dai asked ruefully.

"No," I answered, a little sadly, "I have decided I am a success anyway. I have you and all the children, who have turned out well, and have chosen good partners. I have succeeded whether the book 'goes' or not. So there!" We laughed.

In the first week of December that year I went into the hospital for minor surgery. On the way I picked up *The Atlantic Monthly* and when I leafed through it I found the usual column of reviews of children's books for Christmas. There was an excellent review of *The Door in the Wall*. There was also an article on relics by an antiquarian, especially about hair and its being the most lasting relic *and* about a *lock of hair* from the head of the exhumed body of Edward IV! Edward IV? Could there be two locks of hair? I was puzzled. I knew I had heard the verger say "Edward III." My ear had been attuned to that. What was the truth? I didn't remember reading the inscription on that jewel, however. Could I have been wrong? Oh well, it didn't matter. I had chosen the period, the book was done. But had the antiquarian been mistaken? Perhaps.

Some years later, when Dai and I again visited England, we were invited with our friend Joan to visit Miss Herschel, who now lived with her sister. The talk again came around to the lock of hair, and I asked to see the jewel once more. Seeing our intense interest, the ladies brought out not only the jewel with the lock of hair but

Marguerite de Angeli, at the time she won the
Newbery Medal for *The Door in the Wall*.

many other treasures handed down from Sir John Herschel. Carol,
who had first shown it to us, laughingly told us how she had pretended
to be very casual about it, following the American notion that the
English are stolid and unemotional. She said she had been so excited
she could hardly breathe.

Then I examined the back of the jewel and read the inscription.
The lock of hair had been that of Edward IV! But it had served
its purpose as far as I was concerned. They took us for tea to
the ancestral home, where their aunt, Lady Herschel, still lived.
We were shown the giant telescope in the garden, and various other

smaller ones, besides other tokens of Sir John's many interests. He had done beautiful watercolors of African flowers, carefully preserved in yellowing paper. I still have the lilies of the valley Lady Herschel gave me, pressed in my notebook.

In February of 1950 an arrangement had been made between my publisher, Doubleday, and Marshall Field in Chicago, for me to attend a Book Fair to talk, to meet people, and to autograph my books. Peggy Lesser was there as were other representatives of Doubleday.

On our way to Chicago we stopped to see Alf and Nina and the children, near Cincinnati. We arrived at the house about noon, just as David, the eldest, who was six, came in from his morning school. Jeffrey and Henry were still playing oustide. As we entered the house Nina sorted the mail she had picked up from the box on the way. Surprisingly, there was a letter for me. Who could know we had arrived? The letter was from Seattle. *Seattle?* I hastily broke the seal and took out the letter. Everyone watched to see and hear. David too.

The letter began, "Dear Mrs. de Angeli, I am happy to tell you that you are the winner"—my hands shook, I went on—"of the Newbery Award for *The Door in the Wall!*" I couldn't go on. I looked up to see tears in Nina's eyes and tears coursing down Dai's cheeks—not to mention mine. We all had a good cry, dismaying David, who couldn't imagine why we were all crying. We all began to laugh and I went on, ". . . for the most distinguished book for children in 1949. This is to be kept secret until officially announced after presentation in Mr. Melcher's office on March 7. The public presentation will be in Cleveland on June 18, at the Newbery Dinner." The letter was signed, "Ruth Hewitt, Vice Chairman of the Children's Library Association." A secret? And I had been reading aloud with David taking it all in.

"David," I whispered, "can you keep a secret?" He nodded. "Not even your teacher must know. Can you keep it?" He nodded again, and of course never told a soul. Just then the phone rang. It was Peggy. How could she possibly know we had arrived, and that we had received Ruth Hewitt's letter?

She cautioned me not to tell and to be on my guard in Chicago, where someone might question me concerning the medal. Someone did. I innocently said, "Oh, is it time for that now?" and not another word was said about it.

This honor was so far beyond my wildest dreams that I could hardly keep my feet on the ground. I was afraid I would betray my excitement, but I kept the secret and so did Dai.

March rolled around and time to go to New York for the awarding of the medal. We were allowed two guests, so I invited my brother Arthur and his wife, who drove us over in their car. At seven in the morning of the great day our phone rang. It was Arthur (our son) calling to say, "You're another grandmother. We have a little girl and we're calling her Kate."

What a joyous way to begin that happy day! Arthur had for so long wished for a child. Now he had one.

That afternoon, with Peggy, my brother and sister-in-law, and Dai present, Mr. Frederic Melcher presented me with the coveted medal. Then Mr. Melcher took us all to dinner. It had never entered my head that it could happen to me.

Chapter Thirty-four

The booksellers and the librarians on the West Coast got together with Doubleday to send me, with Dai driving, to California, Oregon, and Washington. I was to speak first at a conference of teachers of English in Berkeley, then go down the coast to Los Angeles, San Diego, and various other places to speak at dinners and luncheons, and to a P.T.A. convention program on children's books. Then back to San Francisco, Portland, and Seattle. It was a very full schedule. Leo Politi was with me on several programs. He was the recipient that year of the Caldecott Award for his delightful picture book *The Song of the Swallows*. He is a dear boy. I say "boy" because he is so much younger than I and because he is one of those men who, like Ted, look ever young, because, I think, in spite of sophistication, they retain a certain purity of mind. We had lots of fun together, Leo, Dai, and I. He took us to his home, where we met his wife and children, and to the famous Olivera Street in Los Angeles.

To say that the trip was exciting is an understatement. To say it was also tiring and nervously exhausting is saying no more than the truth. There was the element of time to consider as well. We had to get home and have a rest from traveling before going back to Cleveland to receive the Newbery Medal publicly at the A.L.A. convention in June. Again there would be the strain of excitement, meeting people, being the guest of honor, and giving an acceptance speech still to be prepared.

The National Congress of Parents and Teachers met in San Diego in May, and on the twenty-fourth Dai and I were guests at the meeting, arranged by Ruth Gagliardo of Kansas, the national book chairman. The subject was children's books and gathered on the platform were many authors and artists, I among them. The main speaker was Doris Gates, author of *River Ranch*, and I was to follow her. Ruth Gagliardo introduced me, and was so flattering in her introduction that I couldn't speak for minutes afterward, but stood there like a great oaf, with tears running down my cheeks and my throat aching from the effort to control myself. Finally, in a choked voice, I said, "Well, I guess I'd better tell a funny story." I can't remember what story I told, but think it may have been the one about Yonie and his mother sitting on the river bank fishing.

Yonie said, "Say, Mom, does somesing bite you?"

"No," she said sadly, "nossing bites me."

"Nossing bites me too, let's go home."

Dai's comment was, "Very good theater. You had everybody crying."

The journey up the coast from San Francisco was indescribably beautiful. Each day held a new wonder—the majestic spruces, the redwoods, some thousands of years old, towering into the sky. We were dismayed at meeting trucks carrying the remains of such magnificence, logs so enormous that only one could be carried at a time. How could anyone allow such destruction of a natural resource?

As we were about to enter the library in Portland, a sudden, unexpected sight of Mount St. Helens almost took our breath away. It seemed to hang in the sky, having no connection with the earth.

The most lasting memory is, of course, the dear people we met: Leo Politi, Gladys English, Margaret Girdner, Arthur and Edie Wagstaff, Rosemary Livesay, Gloria Chandler, and many others with whom we would have liked to keep in touch.

We went north to see the Grand Coulee Dam, then down through Spokane, through the Rockies to Yellowstone National Park and beyond to the Grand Tetons, where we saw herds of elk feeding. All along our route the one bird we saw everywhere was the mourning dove. Larks abounded where there were open fields, and once we saw a flock of mountain bluebirds.

One day, as we had been going along a deep canyon for miles and miles, we began to see signs advertising an inn where fresh trout was to be had. We looked forward eagerly to a satisfying lunch. Just as we were about to enter the inn, we looked up to the far side of the canyon and far, far above saw a deer at a salt lick. The trout was as delicious as advertised, and the whole experience at the inn refreshing and delightful.

In due time we reached home, after twelve thousand miles of travel, Dai driving all the way, seeing wonders all across this marvelous country, enriched immeasurably by what we had seen and the people we had met.

There was little time between arriving home and preparing for Cleveland. I had to have new clothes, not only for the Newbery Dinner, but for luncheons and breakfasts as well. I had a black lace, long-sleeved dress made for the dinner, with a wide pink satin ribbon across the breast and under the lace, as was then the style. It was very elegant and the most expensive dress I have ever owned. I had made a gray voile trimmed with lace for lesser occasions, and other dresses that seemed necessary.

There was still the acceptance speech to write and to learn, which gave me flutterings of the midriff when I thought about speaking. I said severely to myself, "If others can do it, you can."

Nina was invited by Doubleday to attend the conference at their expense, and a suite was provided for us at the hotel so that we could receive visitors. Peggy came often and advised me about my talk.

"Don't read it," she said, "just say it in your own way."

Would I remember it? Would I be too frightened to say anything?

Ruth Gagliardo was there at the conference, and many others I had met at regional and state library gatherings; May Hill Arbuthnot, May Massee of Viking Press, Helen and George Papashvily, Alice Dalgliesh, Gloria Chandler, Margaret MacElderry of Harcourt Brace, Frederic Melcher and his wife—oh, many more.

The week was a whirlwind of activity, excitement, and thrills. The climax, of course, was the Newbery Dinner and the presentation of the Newbery and Caldecott Medals. Because it was the fiftieth anniversary of the founding of the children's division of the American Library Association, there was a special celebration. The attendance was unusually large and the atmosphere gay.

As we sat at the table with Ruth Hewitt and other members of the Award Committee and officers of the Children's Library Association, Leo and I found it hard to swallow our food.

"Let's eat the meat, Leo," I whispered, "it will give us strength." So we tried. But the prospect of facing those thousand librarians with our acceptance speeches was too much. We sent our plates away almost untouched. However, when the dessert was brought in by the procession of waiters, with the flaming baked Alaska held high and the lights dimmed, we were able to fortify ourselves with that!

Then followed the introductions and the awards and it was my turn to speak. I remember very little of it except that I know I repeated myself several times and that I sat down with a great feeling of relief. Leo did his part well and we were both happy afterward.

In spite of all misgivings and mistakes, I was surrounded by love and affection, the most essential needs of my life. That week stands out as one of the great highlights of a long life.

Chapter Thirty-five

Because I had been awarded what is considered to be the ultimate prize in writing for children, it was difficult to go on and do another book. Some time elapsed before I began a story for younger children. Time enough so that I could put the honor of receiving the Newbery Medal in its proper place. Then the curiously fascinating theme of a child's relationship to the outside world interested me and I began the story of *Just Like David*. It was sparked by the view, which was a little world in itself, a whole farmstead held in the crotch of a tall maple tree on the front lawn of Alf and Nina's place above a road along the Ohio River. The farm is in Kentucky, on the other side of the river, and looking at it through the tree always set my imagination going. How would it appear to a child, whose knowledge of perspective was even less than mine? Wouldn't he wonder who lived in that tiny house? I wanted to call the story *One House and the World*, but Peggy thought it too long. So we called it by its present name, as being representative of most children's longing to be like an older brother or sister.

In the fall of 1950, when I was working on *Just Like David*, Dai and I bought a very old, little red brick house on Panama Street, one of the kind called Father, Son, and Holy Ghost, because it had only three rooms, one on each floor, in addition to the basement. Panama Street is a small street between Spruce and Pine in Philadelphia, only half a block and around the corner from where Hannah Carter lived as a child and who lives again in *Thee, Hannah!*

While this book was in progress Peggy began to talk of another she and I had discussed for at least ten years, but hadn't done because of the high cost of producing it.

"But costs are not going down," she said. "They continue to rise. Let's do it now."

"It" was a collection of nursery and Mother Goose rhymes, many of which I knew from childhood and had repeated to my own children and grandchildren.

We began, Dai and I, by reading through a number of accredited collections, comparing them with our own remembered versions to see which seemed the best, marking the ones to use. Then Peggy came down to Philadelphia, bringing several other collections and her favorite choices. We talked over plans for design of the book, how much color I could have, and how long it would take to do the drawings.

"Take your time," Peggy said. "There's no hurry. You will enjoy it more if you don't have a deadline and it will be better. Do the drawings any way you like. Use any period that suits you. If it takes five years—it takes five years. We'll publish it when it is ready." What an assignment! No deadline! I set to work, and for three and a half years had the time of my life, drawing whatever took my fancy. Certain rhymes took me back to my childhood and my mother's comforting arms. Some recalled the early years of our own children. One,

Marguerite de Angeli in 1952.

which I read in the *Oxford Book of Nursery Rhymes*, was considered to be one of the oldest on record and was the first one Nina had learned. She had her own version of it in her lisping voice: "One Mithty, moithty morning—when a-cyowcy wath the waether . . ." which endeared it to us forever. Another came suddenly to my inner ear in the voice of my grandfather: "Theophilus Thistle, the Successful Thistle Sifter . . ." How odd! For a moment it seemed as if Grandpa Lofft was at my elbow.

What delightful days I spent recalling my thoughts and the pictures they evoked as one by one I read or remembered each rhyme. Many of the drawings were done during summers at the Toms River cottage, where I worked in the apartment we had built over the garage. One summer my mother was with us. She was very old then, lonely without Papa and forlorn. We tried to make her feel at home and wanted, but her mind was already set on another land and on those who had gone before. She had been many years without Papa and never ceased missing him. It happened that she appeared in one of my drawings as a bewildered woman tossed up in a basket. I was not really aware that I was drawing her likeness, but she recognized it herself.

"Did you mean that drawing for *me?*" she questioned.

For another illustration for "Boys and Girls Come Out to Play," I went out into the small street just a few steps away from our little Panama Street house to study the roof lines of the old brick houses, then went back to my drawing board and made a sketch from memory, never thinking anyone would recognize the place. But after the book was published, several people made such comments as: "Oh yes, there's the house Al Bendiner lives in," or "Oh, Iseminger Street!" It surprised me.

Many of the rhymes suggested an English background, for which I called upon my memory with help from various sources to get the proper detail. Had I known what I learned several years later, the background for one of the rhymes would have been Danish rather than English. The rhyme is the one described earlier, "One Misty Moisty Morning." In an issue of the *National Geographic* there was an article about the discovery of bodies buried in peat about A.D. 700 in Jutland. A photograph showed the head of a man, perfectly preserved, though darkened by the peat, "clothed all in leather with a strap beneath his chin," just as described in the nursery rhyme! Probably a ritual rhyme says the *Oxford Book of Nursery Rhymes*.

I saw the Muffin Girl, lilting along a London Street as if she had been there before my eyes, and the children in "Banbury Cross" practically drew themselves.

While I was doing the pictures of the "Old Woman Who Lived in a Shoe" and "Mary Had a Little Lamb" I thought of all my grandchildren, and while their parents wouldn't have recognized them, perhaps, to me each child represents a certain one. Kate, being the right age and of great appeal, dances through the whole book, partly because I saw more of her at that time than I did the other younger ones.

Little by little through the three and a half years the drawings accumulated and were finally complete. The book was published in 1954.

During the time when I was illustrating the nursery rhymes there were several additions to the family: Michael, Maury and Marianne's oldest son, was born in August of 1951, and Ted and Betty's Sarah, their first child, in December of that same year. Maury and Marianne's second son, Peter, was born in 1953. Just before the publication of my book a son was born to Ted and Betty and named Dailey after his grandfather. Each new child added to the richness of our lives and the joy of being grandparents. They all grew and learned with such incredible swiftness, and were so responsive to our affection, that it was like having our own dear children again, only without the full responsibility.

In August of 1951 the boys consulted us about buying an automatic metal-working business set up in an old barn near Skippack, Pennsylvania. Neither Jack nor Ted was satisfied with what he was doing; Maury wanted to get into something more rewarding to him than news reporting, and Arthur, whose idea it was, felt it to be a good opportunity for them all. With our help they bought the business and, keeping the same foreman, Elmer Boohar, they set to work, learning by doing how to program the machines to make all kinds of spare parts. Ted and Maury, especially, had a natural bent for mechanics; Jack was well equipped to take care of office work and correspondence and Arthur, besides contributing financially, had his own free-lance business and did some of the selling for the new shop. Then Maury heard of an opening with the Knoll Furniture Company. He applied for the job and was accepted.

Chapter Thirty-six

When I had delivered the last of the drawings to Peggy for the nursery rhyme book she suggested that Dai and I take that long-delayed vacation to Scotland and to Skye. I had wanted to go ever since hearing Elizabeth Vining talk about Skye and Flora MacDonald. So it was settled, and in two weeks we sailed for Plymouth.

Our regular physician had retired, so we had gone for our health certificates and shots to a neighborhood doctor. He didn't tell us, but told a friend after we had left, that Dai was so ill he should never have set foot on that ship. I realized that he seemed tired and at times was confused, but I had no inkling that it was due to a failing heart. I too was tired from the long siege of drawing and painting, and we both found the boat trip restful.

When we arrived at Plymouth the Devon countryside was at its springtime best, and swift acquaintance with a lady in our railway compartment contradicted the legend of English reticence. She invited us to visit her for a few days, which we would have enjoyed, but as time went on we were shy of calling to ask if it might be convenient, and to our regret we never saw her again.

Our first stop was in Salisbury, where we stayed with Carl and Stella Persichetti, Nina's brother and his wife, who made us most welcome and guided us about the cathedral. My notebook says, "The cathedral gave us the same otherworldly feeling we'd had in Canterbury. But no other cathedral we have seen is set as Salisbury is set—free all round, so that its majesty can be viewed from all sides." It was especially beautiful from the water meadow as we walked by the stream where wax-like flowers elbowed up from the water plants below. We walked to Harnhem to see the ancient mill there and saw the view of the cathedral painted by Constable. Lovely.

Carl and Stella took us to Stonehenge, where I had wanted to go all my life. What manner of engineering lifted those stones? What do they mean? I have now been told how it is believed it was done, but to me it remains a complete mystery.

Winifred met us at the train as she had done years before, and guided us to the hotel near Piccadilly. Wonderful Winifred. She was at home in any society and completely herself always. She is gone, but her kindness to us, her thoughtfulness and generosity, will never be forgotten. We didn't see Winifred as often as we would have liked.

From the hotel on Half-Moon Street we wandered into unfamiliar corners of London, yet they were familiar through books: Curzon, Clarges, and Bolton streets, and Berkeley Square. We stopped in a small eating place where we had the most delicious stewed oysters I have ever eaten. We searched for bookstores, hoping to find two Polish books for Edward Ryglewicz to add to his collection, but no one even knew the titles. They were old and rare books in any case.

A great deal of our time was spent in art galleries, as before. Dai was able to sit down while I still wanted to look. We saw the new portrait of Queen Elizabeth by Augustus John. It was beautifully done.

Joan Marsden invited us for three days to Oxford, giving us the luxury of tea in bed, a lovely evening of music with her friends, and a jaunt in her car to Burford and Rolling Stones.

June 2, 1954, we left for Scotland, stopping over in York and Durham to see the cathedrals. We spent the night in York, giving us time to explore the Shambles, the old walls, and the splendors of the cathedral, especially the rich color of the great window, to hear its history and imagine the stream of time and the ghostly hordes who had passed through its doors.

How new everything in our America seems as compared to the antiquity of England. The awesome height of Durham, with its Saxon pillars, its archaic records and artifacts. I remember seeing among the treasures we were shown a strip of hand-woven material that may date from Roman times. Such homely things carry one back to the time when they were made and in use, to the woman sitting at her loom or the artist at his bench.

We went on to Edinburgh, where we stayed for ten days.

On June 4 it was my brother Arthur's birthday, and because he had told us to be sure to see the Firth of Fourth Bridge, we went on that day. As he had said, one couldn't visualize its height and length unless one had seen it, either by standing close to it or taking the ferry across the river. It was a thrilling sight, but *cold!* The wind coming off the North Sea is piercing and shudderingly cold.

My diary says, "The mists came doon and it was cauld." And so it was, the whole time we spent in Scotland and in Skye, but as in England, flowers garlanded the fence corners and doorways, covered the fields, and even grew out from the rocks and boulders. At one place where we stopped for tea while on a bus trip a great stone in front of the tea shop held a whole nosegay of miniature flowers in yellow, pink, blue, and violet in a depression no larger than my palm. It was exquisite. We sat on a bench nearby to enjoy it while waiting for the bus and made friends with an Irish wolfhound who came up to greet us.

Before we left home the receptionist at Doubleday had recommended that we go to Oban on the west coast of Scotland before leaving for Skye. When we took the train we didn't realize that we had made no provision for lunch or that it would take us several hours to get there. But two young women in our compartment who were going to Oban on "holiday" were kind enough to share their lunch with us, so we didn't starve.

We were housed in a pleasant seaside hotel in Oban. One day, as we walked along by the shore, watching men unloading fish, I saw two little boys about four years old tussling with each other, laughing and punching each other as boys do to show their affection, not as girls do, walking with arms entwined. I was reminded of our own boys and stopped to watch, as I always watch children. Then I discovered that they were identical twins.

"Oh," I said suddenly to Dai, "I have an idea!"

"What is it?" he asked.

"I can't tell you. It is too vague and might get away." He laughed, knowing me.

That afternoon Dai went to get his hair cut and I went along.

It happened that the barber was a woman, so I sat with them and we talked as she worked. Then I told her about the two little boys I'd seen on the dock that morning.

"Oh, they're my sister's children," she said. "They often tease people by making believe one is the other. They are full of tricks and sometimes fool even their mother."

Ah, I thought, now I *do* have an idea. But I kept it to myself. From then on I kept thinking about those boys—only they grew in my mind to fourteen instead of four. They became mixed up with the Scandinavian place names we kept hearing, Skeabost House, Dunvegan, and interwoven with the tales we heard about the feuds among the clans, the MacDonalds and the McCleods, the barbaric treachery and bloodshed.

On one of our bus trips we had seen an enormous flat rock edging into the loch, where, our driver told us, the funeral processions of the kings of Scotland embarked in boats for the Isle of Iona, where the kings are buried. We went there one afternoon.

As I recall the scene, clear in my head to this day, I see the clumps of yellow iris in fence corners as we passed. I see the great rock and the shadows of trees on the water of the loch, and I see the procession of the king's men carrying his body for burial. How I wanted to have that procession in my book! But it just didn't fit.

After leaving Scotland we went again to Oxford to visit Joan Marsden, and while there I bought books at Blackwell's to help fill in the background of the book I was going to do. I bought *Scottish Border History* and one on Scotland from earliest times. The only way I could make sense of it was to scan it quickly so that the meaning of the words would emerge partially, as one peers through a veil at an image. Two other books I bought after returning to Philadelphia were also in what seemed a Scotch version of Chaucerian English, *Wallace* and *The Bruce*. They were no less difficult, but they gave me a feeling for antiquity, the violence, treachery, and intrigue of those tenth-century times. Intrigue is not my strong point—I am a fairly straightforward person—so I found that the history of Northumberland helped me to build the plot I needed. The names over a period of years were so similar that I had difficulty in remembering who was whom. There were Edwin, Edwy, Edmond, Ethwynd, and more. I took six or seven clothespins and printed names on them, drawing a crown for the king. Probably none of those names are in the book, but I had to have a clear picture of the time in my mind. I read and read and read for nearly a year before attempting to begin writing. Finally I decided it was time. I sat down at the typewriter and tried to think of how to start. I sat for quite a while, then started to go downstairs, thinking I wasn't ready yet. But my inner voice said, Get back there and begin. This happened three times. Then, I thought, Well, I'll put down the first thing that comes to mind. I did and off went the story.

I wanted to call it *The Jewel of Lorne* (the county of Lorne being the area where we had stayed near Oban). But, I thought, perhaps there *is* a jewel of Lorne.

I wrote to the Duke of Argyle and asked. I had a reply from his wife that yes, there was, and it was housed near the ruined castle we had seen beyond Oban. That settled the title. I used a brooch that is in the Metropolitan Museum in New York, found in my costume book as a part of the plot. When the book was well along I settled on the title, *Black Fox of Lorne*.

It wasn't until the book was published that I realized I had really used as models the twin fair-haired boys who had moved into the house next door to us at the Toms River cottage and who were Latvian! I scarcely knew them, but saw them passing as they went down to the river to swim.

Chapter Thirty-seven

Soon after returning to Philadelphia, and while I was doing research on the *Black Fox of Lorne*, we went out to visit Alf and Nina in Cincinnati. Dai drove, as always, and when we stopped overnight on the way he noticed that his left leg was quite swollen. In fact he said it was so heavy he could hardly lift it. It was alarming, but we had not the slightest inkling of how serious a matter it was. Dai was seventy-four at this point and found the driving more tiring than ever before. He was exhausted by the time we reached the Kuhns' and the swelling was no better.

Nina, feeling sure the swelling indicated heart trouble, called the university to ask the name of a specialist. The doctor's diagnosis was heart occlusion and he prescribed complete rest, telling Dai to sit with his feet up as often as possible and to see his own doctor immediately upon returning home. Dai took it with his usual attitude of acceptance, and because I was ignorant of any kind of heart condition, I too accepted the situation without too much anxiety. Since then I have wondered how we managed to drive home without a disaster.

At home again I tried my best to get Dai to the doctor, but with no success. The swelling had gone down and Dai felt there was no cause to worry.

I talked to Arthur and between us we arranged for him to have his own physician call Dai and insist on his coming for an examination. He called and ordered Dai into the hospital as soon as there was a vacancy. He told Dai not to do *anything*, to keep very quiet. I was frightened.

I had ever so many appointments to autograph the *Book of Nursery and Mother Goose Rhymes*, and Dai had always driven me to such affairs and was a source of encouragement as well as a great help in the sheer nuisance of getting around. I had been so well looked after that I scarcely remembered how to buy a ticket at the railroad station.

One such morning, when I was expected in Allentown to autograph books at the Leh Company store, I had to start out early, leaving Dai in bed with no one to look after him. The doctor had warned me that he was in very serious condition. My spirits were at their lowest ebb.

When I had found a seat in the train I realized that I must not appear in Allentown with such distress evident in my looks and bearing. I closed my eyes and tried to realize the presence always of God, and, as I believe, his care for us. I faced the fact that my dear husband might die, that I might have to face the remainder of my life alone. The desolation that flooded my being was complete. Then I said to myself, "Many women lose their husbands, and when they do they must take up life as it is—not as they wish it were." Suddenly the most extraordinary thing happened. I felt as if a thick curtain had been raised from my eyes and from above my forehead. I felt free of all anxiety and a great sense of security surrounded me.

From that day on, until after Dai had gone to the hospital and was home again, I never worried. I simply knew that he would recover. And he did, completely.

Marguerite and her husband, Dai, sharing their love of music.

Maury and Marianne took me to stay with them and Marianne drove me to the various schools and stores where I was expected to be, besides taking me often to see Dai. He was in no pain or discomfort and seemed better than he had been for months.

But that ended his driving, not only for his own sake, but for the safety of others. It was not easy, after forty years of having a car, to be dependent on public transportation or upon relatives and friends.

When I delivered the last of the work for *Black Fox of Lorne*, with the usual trepidation for fear it was not good enough, Peggy laughed at me and called in the office staff to see the drawings. Then at lunch she asked what I would like to do next.

"I would like to make selections from the Old Testament and illustrate them," I said. "Perhaps you won't think it a good idea."

"I think it is a wonderful idea!" she said enthusiastically.

"It seems to me," I went on, "that very few people know much about the Old Testament, and I would like children to understand that its history and prophecy are our heritage. It would give them a sense of the continuity of family, of Abraham and Isaac and Rebecca, Jacob and Joseph. They would learn about the prophets and the promises. It seems to me it is a necessary part of education to know the Bible, if only because of the constant references to it one finds in reading."

"I agree," Peggy said. "Now, let's plan your trip to the Middle East, because of course you must go."

My eyes must have shown my astonishment. *Middle East?* I had never thought of such a thing.

"But Dai isn't able to take such a trip," I protested. "And I couldn't go alone, partly because of the language barrier, but well, I just couldn't."

"What about Nina?" Peggy asked. "Couldn't she go with you? I'm quite sure we could help you with expense. I don't know exactly what can be done, but we'll find out. Meantime, you see what can be done about Dai and whether Nina will be able to go." I was soon caught up in Peggy's enthusiasm.

"Now," she continued, getting up energetically, "we must go see Bill Cade, who has arranged trips for various Doubleday people, and find out what he suggests."

"Right now?" I gasped.

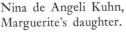
Nina de Angeli Kuhn,
Marguerite's daughter.

Alfred Kuhn, Nina's husband.

"Right now," she said, laughing at my disbelief. "You must go in early fall."

I couldn't believe that so big an undertaking as a journey to the Holy Land could be planned on such short notice, in spite of my native impulsiveness. How would Dai take it, being left for so long?

When I carried the news to him at home he was philosophical about it as usual, though incredulous. Well, there were about three months for him to get used to the idea. Nina must be asked and Alf must give his consent. I would have hesitated more than I did about asking him, except that I knew how efficient he is in whatever he undertakes. He can cook if it is necessary, and the boys—David, Jeffrey, and Henry—were all in school then and pretty self-reliant. They were twelve, ten, and six or seven.

Alfred taught at Cincinnati University only a few hours a week, preparing his work at home in the study, so there was no lack of supervision for the boys. However, knowing how devoted he and Nina were, I did hesitate to ask him.

We had already planned our annual visit to Alf and Nina's family. We now went by train, leaving in the early evening and arriving in Cincinnati about seven in the morning. Nina met us, and after our greeting, I said, "How would you like to go with me to the Middle East in September?"

Nina's eyes widened. *"Middle East?"* she said. "What for? Are you joking? Isn't there a war going on there? When and for how long?"

"About ten weeks," I said, and went on to tell her about the itinerary and that Doubleday was prepared to assume half the cost.

"Of course I want to go. But how will Alf feel about it?"

When we arrived at the house and the bear hugs were exchanged, I put it to him immediately.

"Can Nina go with me to the Middle East? We would be gone about ten weeks."

Alf's comical look of disbelief was very funny. His jaw slackened and his eyes popped. Then he said, "What can I say? I couldn't deprive her of a chance like that. I have to let her go, certainly. But oh, *ten weeks!*"

"Can you manage? Nina says she can get a woman she knows to come in and keep the house clean and cook things ahead for you. Besides, you're a good cook yourself."

"I guess we'll manage," he sighed. "When do you have to leave?"

"The twenty-second of September on the American Export Line—the *Excambion*. It will be a wonderful trip."

Once the plans for the trip had been made I began selecting parts from the Old Testament to illustrate, rereading and choosing what should go into the book.

Peggy sent her assistant, Ann Durell, to help me in the selection. She had majored in Bible at Mount Holyoke and was more familiar with some of the books of the Old Testament than I.

It is interesting to note that, after I had made my selection of material from the Old Testament and Ann Durell came down to assist me, I would say, "Begin at verse so and so in such and such a chapter, and go down to verse—then turn to the middle of chapter— and begin again at 'and' in the twenty-second verse . . ."

Ann would say, "That is exactly the place I have marked!" It happened again and again.

But there were books of the Bible with which I was not so familiar: Amos, whose poetic prose I had sung in anthem and solo, but had not studied or read; Ezra and Nehemiah, which I scarcely knew at all.

Besides the stories in Genesis, which I loved, I tried to keep those parts that showed the continuity of the whole, so I sought out places that carried on the thought, adding no words of my own. I tried to avoid the repetition and deleted such phrases as seemed unnecessary and unsuitable for a child's reading without changing the sense of the original.

When, with Ann's help, the text was complete, it was given to Dr. Samuel Terrien, Auburn Professor of Old Testament, Union Theological Seminary, for approval. He arranged it according to chronological order, but did not change any of the selections.

By the time the text was finished and off to be set in type, it was late spring of 1956. I was very tired and bothered by a bronchial infection. Our Dr. Hershey had given up private practice because of his health and I was at a loss to know what doctor to choose.

Just at this time the Kabuki Dancers were in Philadelphia. Elizabeth Vining gave a luncheon for the wife of the director and invited me. Next to me at the table was Dr. Emma Bevan, to whom I took a great liking. After the luncheon Elizabeth invited Dai and me for Sunday night supper at her house and when we arrived we discovered that Dr. Bevan was there too.

When I asked her if she would take me as her patient she agreed, and Elizabeth and her sister laughed. This had been the idea all along. They knew I needed a physician and hoped I would choose Dr. Bevan, who had been theirs for so long.

It wasn't long before Dai too acknowledged her superiority in her profession. She has been our friend and medical adviser, surgeon and life preserver, ever since.

Through Emerson Greenaway, our director of libraries in Philadelphia, and his wife, Helen, Dai and I had leased a flat for the summer in New London, New Hampshire.

It was in the center of town, where stores and the post office were nearby, as we could no longer drive, and was not too far from where the Greenaways and our friends the MacKaughans lived. Nina and Arthur and Kate drove us up and stayed with us for a few days.

That summer in New Hampshire was one of the most pleasant I remember, mostly because of our happy association with the friends we already knew and our acquaintances with Eunice Blake, her mother, and her sister. Eunice I had known years before when she was with Macmillan and I was illustrating books for their Junior Classics. At that time she had been assistant to Louise Seaman.

There were happy days when we visited at the Blakes' with Helen Greenaway, or days at the MacKaughans' house in the woods on Lake Sunapee. Sometimes Helen or Betty took us on jaunts through the countryside. It was cool and delightful and altogether beautiful.

Mornings, in the flat above the barn, I worked on designs for the pages of the projected book, trying out various ideas, hanging them on the wall to consider which was best. Always I came back to my first one, which was to have the folio number and a few words indicating the subject matter in the text on the page, at lower left, and printed in sepia. Also in sepia was an illuminated initial as a chapter heading.

I spent several days drawing in pencil the head of Abraham as he had always appeared to me and as it is shown in the first pages of the book.

Rest, and the treatment prescribed by Dr. Bevan, soon cleared up the bronchitis that had plagued me for weeks, and the necessary shots for going to the Middle East were given me by the local doctor. My brother Arthur and his wife, Alma, came up to see us for a few days and we explored the country farther afield.

At the end of August, Ted and Betty, with Sarah, came to take

Ted de Angeli, Marguerite's son.   Betty de Angeli, Ted's wife.

us back to Philadelphia. Not the least of our enjoyment of the summer was the company of our young ones to and from New London.

Nina arrived in Philadelphia several days before our departure to see all the family. There were gatherings here and there to bid us "Godspeed," then Betty and Ted drove us to New York, where we were given a farewell party by Doubleday. A good number of friends attended, most of whom Nina was meeting for the first time. She is remembered by some because at one point she said, as she stood talking, "I've got my standin'-up girdle on and my sittin'-down shoes."

It was all a part of the excitement of our journey, which we felt might be canceled at any moment because of the Suez crisis. Yet, we continued to be hopeful and, because there was nothing we could do about it, somewhat fatalistic.

One day, before I had left Philadelphia, I had called on Julia Williamson, a retired librarian who was housebound because of arthritis. Mary Cole was there, the daughter of Jessica Cole, who had allowed me to use her name in *Bright April*. As I talked of our projected journey, she asked what line we were taking and then exclaimed, "Friday?" I nodded. "So am I! I'm going to Ceylon for the government on the same ship."

Just after we sailed, my last book, *Black Fox of Lorne*, was published, but I didn't see it until we came home. It was a runner-up for the Newbery Medal.

Chapter Thirty-eight

We sailed the day after the Doubleday party and found the whole family assembled at the dock to see us off. It was hard to leave them, especially Dai, but the boys had promised to look after him.

As the ship began to move away from the pier Nina and I decided that a retreat would hide our feelings best, so we moved toward the stern of the ship to be out of sight of those we had left. Soon we were engaged in conversation with others and able to look ahead to the trip.

The whole voyage was refreshing and pleasant: the weather good, the service, all that could be wished. It was a happy coincidence for us to have Mary Cole as a traveling companion and tablemate. The feeling of complete relaxation that takes possession of one aboard ship is almost magic in its effect. One seems enclosed in a capsule of fairy-wrought air, cut off from telephone, from the trivial matters of everyday life, from anxiety and from responsibility. There is nothing one can do about any one of them.

Nina and I, knowing the rather strenuous days ahead of us, walked around the deck three times each morning, much to the amusement of the other passengers, who teased us about our regime. But it paid off. We withstood the rigors of going down five hundred feet into the tombs of the kings in Egypt all the better for having kept our leg muscles in condition.

As we passed through the straits of Gibraltar, Nina and I leaned over the ship rail and peered at the lights offshore.

"Nina," I said, incredulously, "that is Africa. Can you believe it?"

A wave of homesickness came over me. Where was Dai? What was I doing thousands of miles away from home? Soon the excitement of what was to come, the thought that we were entering the Mediterranean, canceled out the momentary uneasiness. I remember how satisfying it was to have Nina with me and that tomorrow we would be in Barcelona to discharge cargo and to take a two-day excursion, first to the ancient monastery of Montserrat, then a day's exploring of the city. When Nina and I were on our own, we drove to see the Gaudi cathedral, fashioned after the pinnacles of Montserrat and still being constructed.

Our next stop was Marseilles, where we took a bus and rode through the countryside to Avignon, stopping near the bridge to sing the old song "Sur le pont d'Avignon."

Then on to Arles, where we had lunch in a coffee shop where Van Gogh used to eat. We walked where he had walked and saw the scenes he had painted.

We visited the coliseum, a counterpart of the one in Rome, then were led to the Palace of the Popes, also a relic of the Roman occupation of southern France in the first century. In the great hall our guide explained a remarkable architectural feature, so well planned that when the procession of choir boys sang on entering the echo of the first few bars made harmony with those that followed.

Our next stop was Genoa, where we were at liberty, as our schedule was marked. Instead of going with the group from the ship, Nina, Mary Cole, and I went shopping. We poked around in little leather shops, buying gloves for gifts and for ourselves. Then back to the ship.

We met our first rough sea going down the coast of Italy. There seemed to be no storm, but all night long things slid back and forth in our cabin, drawers opened mysteriously, and we rolled in our bunks. By morning ropes were stretched in strategic places to keep passengers from falling, and at the table the hinged edges had been turned up to prevent the food from sliding off. Luckily we were not seasick.

Off the coast of Turkey, at Latakia, we stopped offshore to discharge freight and a few of us went ashore for an hour. Along the ancient streets were open shops with bags and baskets filled with seeds and spices familiar to us from childhood Sunday school lessons, anise and cummin, mustard and caraway. When I lifted my camera to photograph the scene, the guide grasped my hand.

"Put that away! Quick!" he half whispered. "They don't want the old ways pictured. They want the new ones shown, the corrugated tin roofs and such things." But who would want that? There was plenty of that ugliness at home.

Afterward I was careful never to take a picture without first asking our guide, except through a car window where it wouldn't be seen. One I took that way, of a tiny mosque in a village, is among the best I have. It is perfect, pictorially. The pictures I took were a great help in my work later. The all-pervading light, which, in the East seems almost shadowless, is one of the wonders of Eastern countries. I had not expected such beauty.

After Latakia, in Syria, we stopped at Beirut to discharge cargo. A guide with a car was at the dock to meet us, calling us by name. He was a pleasant young man, a Christian Arab who spoke excellent English. He took us first around the city, showing us the university, the shopping center, and the pigeon rocks on the Mediterranean, then out to the highway leading to Damascus. The day was perfect, cloudless except for a tiny white one above the Lebanon Mountains. It followed us all day, its only function to emphasize the intense blue of the sky.

The Bekaa Valley, on our right, as we followed, then passed a camel caravan, was rich and fertile, covered with grape vines that lay along the ground to feed upon the springs below. Bekaa means "valley of weeping," and refers either to the springs below the surface of the earth or perhaps to the weeping captives who had traversed the land.

Baalbek, with its imposing ruins of temples variously dedicated to the worship of Baal, to Jupiter, to Bacchus, and to Venus, depending on the time of occupation, was filled with interest and beauty. The immense size of the ruins, the elaborate carvings, done after the building had been erected, were cause for wonder. Nina and I stood beside a piece of the cornice, fallen from the hundred-foot column, and could scarcely believe that the tremendous fragment had fitted into the small space, which showed, empty, where the column soared into the sky.

The deep hole in one ruined altar, which the guide said was dedicated to the god Baal, led into sluices beneath the stone floor that had carried away the entrails from sacrificial animals. It reminded us of the story of Elijah, the prophet, who defied the god Baal and called down fire from heaven and his own God to lick up the water in the trench around the altar. *Here* was the very place! I had never thought to see it.

The successive possessors of the place of worship had each built their own version of temple and altar, and each in turn had been destroyed by earthquake, fire, or battle.

We were tired from the excitement of travel and sightseeing, but were rested and refreshed by the excellent lunch served us in the hotel. There was fresh water fish and the best, most satisfying and delectable bread we had ever eaten. We couldn't stop reaching for it. It was paper-thin Lebanese bread baked on top of stone ovens.

We visited a shop where antiquities were sold and were shown the contents of a Roman lady's jewel box, recently found when digging for a sewer. The box, of course, had dissolved into the earth from which it had come, but the rich gold ornaments remained: bracelets, necklaces, and rings, one of which I bought. It was set with an intaglio of a lady's figure, to be used as a seal. When I wear it I think of the Roman lady who wore it two thousand years ago.

After lunch we drove on to Damascus. As we entered the most ancient city in the world we rode alongside the Abana River, well known from the biblical story of Naaman, who was cleansed of leprosy by washing in its waters. The river ran right in front of the hotel where we were to stay and could be seen from our window.

That evening we were taken by the guide through the ancient, narrow streets, houses, and shops, shuttered and mysterious in the moonlight. A small door led us into a tiny hallway, pitch dark and a little frightening, and through another door to a room where a man sat at a loom that almost filled the small space. One glaring light showed his dark but smiling face and the exquisite brocaded fabric on which he was working. Except for scattered bits of cloth, there was nothing else in the room. We stayed only a few moments to watch the shuttle moving in and out, over and under, magically weaving the complicated pattern as it had been done for centuries. Then we were ushered again into the tiny hall and through another door that opened into a lovely garden filled with moonlight, with the fragrance of jasmine and the sound of water rising and falling in a fountain. Much later, when I was making the illustrations for the book, this garden scene came fresh and clear to my mind.

Surrounding a courtyard were stagelike platforms, which, we were told, had been the male and female quarters of a harem. Now they were given over to the demonstration of various enterprises such as brasswork, embroidery, or the making of inlaid tables, trays, and chairs.

Our feeling of strangeness had vanished. These were friendly people like ourselves, differing only in the way they spoke, the way they earned their living, and the way their skin was darkened by the sun. Their needs were the same, their smiles evoked the same response as smiles do everywhere.

We returned to the hotel, wondering why nations find it so hard to get along peacefully together. Perhaps we were naïve, but we felt that it takes very little effort for people to understand each other.

The next day we visited the "street called Straight" of biblical fame. It was lined with bazaars filled with enticing things to buy. We recognized some of our shipmates buying inlaid tables, camel saddles, and oriental rugs. We bought small tokens such as coins, sheep bells, and a length of silk. Unknown to me, Nina bought a glass vase, which I received months later for Christmas. According to the experts at the Corning Glass Works it is of the period of A.D. 700. Later, in the Philadelphia Art Museum, when I asked a representative from the Cairo Museum about the authenticity of the age of such objects, he said, "Do you enjoy them?"

"Of course," I answered.

Then he replied, "Well, isn't that enough?" So I enjoy them in the belief that they are as old as they are said to be.

A chapel has been made of the house of Ananias and Sapphira, where Paul was hidden. It brought alive to me the reality of Paul's illumination on the way to Damascus, his conversion from the harrier of Christians to their champion, and I caught myself singing the recitative of "The Lord Is Mindful of His Own," which I sang often at church services. The mosques and churches, Saladin's tomb, all were fascinating to see.

Chapter Thirty-nine

Our next stop was Alexandria. Because of the Suez Canal crisis, which was still very much alive and in the news, we were a little doubtful of our welcome in Egypt. However, our fears proved groundless and our welcome cordial. We were greeted by our assigned Sudanese guide and taken on the prearranged tour of the city and the coastal road, to the palace and gardens of King Farouk, the date palms laden with fruit, the vegetable gardens and flowers flourishing. The guide told us of at least one reason for the immense size of the dishonored king—for breakfast he demanded the condensed broth of at least thirteen chickens!

The three-hour stay in Alexandria came to an end, and we were on our way by train to Cairo. The journey took only a few hours. Through the train window I caught a picture of a village mosque that should take a prize. It is clear and sharp and beautiful, and was of use later in illustrating the Old Testament.

In Cairo, as in Damascus, the hotel was called Semiramis, as in the *Arabian Nights*. There was a balcony from which to view the Nile and the embankment where women gathered to gossip, holding the token veil across their faces.

In our view was the bridge leading to an island, banyan trees, and Farouk's yacht, tied up and used as a restaurant. We sat for breakfast in the cool of autumn mornings, took pictures, and at night sat under the stars before going to bed. Never in my wildest dreams (of which I'd had quite a few) had I thought to be eating breakfast beside the Nile.

The next day a guide came to take us to the pyramids. Much to our surprise they were not far away and soon loomed up over the horizon. Camels awaited us, and the sneering beasts kneeled for us to climb aboard. Nina and I stood the rocking motion of the camels remarkably well. It recalled my first ride on a camel when I was four at the World's Fair in Chicago.

Dinner at the Semiramis was served on the roof, where the stars shown down soft and bright. Fresh dates followed dinner, delicious and sweet and twice as large as those we have at home.

The citadel mosque, with its pillars and high pulpit and oriental rug, was impressive, but what I remember most is the triangular, lovely face of an Arab woman, her smiling dark eyes and waving hair, her dimpled cheeks, her thin veil not covering her face as was usual but held beneath her pointed chin. She was with her husband and child, sightseeing as we were. She smiled at us as we all stood admiring the magnificent view from the citadel wall, from which we could see Cairo and the distant pyramids.

We took the train that night for Luxor, en route to Thebes and the Valley of the Kings, four hundred miles up the Nile. The beds were comfortable and we slept well, arriving at Luxor in the morning. In the excitement of arrival I had left my watch hanging on the hook provided for it and realized it only after the train had gone.

A guide drove us to the Winter Palace Hotel, enormous and almost empty, not only because it was off season but because of the Suez crisis. There were only ten guests, including ourselves.

Breakfast was served to us by a little round man in a turban and a long galibeah, with a cummerbund at the waist. He was gentle and kind and named, of all things, Ali Baba. His English was perfect and his manner most respectful. He urged Nina to eat well. "Madame," he said, "eat your bread, you will need it." And we did need it. Our two days of sightseeing were strenuous, viewing the Temple of Karnak, the obelisks, the Avenue of Sphinxes, and climbing to the top of the pylon familiar to me from early childhood in looking at that old book of Papa's.

Ali Baba had not exaggerated the drain on our energies. Now we realized how wise we had been with our shipboard morning walks. After lunch we were only too glad to rest on the linen-sheeted beds with their net canopies.

We visited the Temples of Luxor, with their magnificent pillars, some, we were told, large enough at the top to hold fifty men. All were inscribed with hieroglyphic cartouches extolling the virtues of the kings, which the guide interpreted for us. Once more I harked back to my father's book and its accompanying steel engravings of the Temples of Luxor and the wonders of Egypt.

The next morning we arose at 6:30 to be ready for our journey across the Nile to Thebes and the Valley of the Kings so that we could return before the heat of the day. We crossed the Nile in the native felucca and were met upon landing by a horde of children begging for pennies. They were having some sort of celebration in the village that seemed to be a welcome to us.

We passed the Colossus of Memnon, ancient reminder of man's feeling of superiority over women. There sat the great statue of a pharaoh with his knee-high queen beside him. There was still evidence of the receding spring flooding of the Nile in little bays and pools. Exotic birds flew about in the small trees growing in the narrow band of green bordering the river that is the life of Egypt.

The descent into the tombs was an experience I shall never forget. Down, down the stone steps cut into the wall for five hundred feet to view the wonders of the ancient world. Walls and ceiling were covered with paintings of kings and queens, hunting scenes, with water birds, lotus flowers, and papyrus filling in the background. Sometimes a figure was drawn from the base of one wall, up across the ceiling, and down to the base on the other side. All figures were drawn in the stiff, formal manner characteristic of Egyptian art.

Nina and I had the guide take our pictures in the palace of Hatshepsut, the queen who called herself a king, because no queen was allowed to reign in Egypt. But like the tale of the donkey in Lincoln's story, calling herself a king didn't make her a king.

Coming up those five hundred feet from the tombs was even more difficult than going down. I paused several times on the way up. Then the guide took my arm to help me and said, "Cour-ahge, madame, Cour-ahge!" I finally made it.

It was time to leave the tombs of the beautiful Nefertiti, the fabulous Tutankhamen, Set, and Rameses, and again board the felucca for Luxor across the Nile before the great midday heat. We were more than ready for our afternoon rest. At the station, as we left for Cairo, the station attendant handed me back my watch.

Back in Cairo we visited the American Embassy library, where, to my surprise, we found my Ted and Nina books on the shelves.

Our guide took us to the Coptic Church and to an ancient synagogue in old Cairo where we saw original hand-lettered parts of the book of Isaiah and held in our hands the book of Esther, twelve hundred years old.

Chapter Forty

From Cairo we were scheduled to go to Jerusalem by plane, and due to certain regulations in that time of tension we had to enter on the Jordan side. The two-hour flight was made in a rather small plane, but we had a perfect view of the country, most of it barren and dry. We were met by a taxi and driven to the American Colony Hotel, recommended by our friend Besse Howard. We had reservations and an introduction to Mrs. Bertha Vester, owner and director, a woman of great charm and ability and beautiful at eighty-six. She was pro-Arab, but that is understandable. She had lived among the Arabs since babyhood and had done a tremendous amount of work in establishing hospitals and clinics. We had tea in her apartment and were shown watercolors of the flowers of the Holy Land, which were later published in a book.

Here, in Jerusalem, we spent the better part of a week. Our room was pleasant and comfortable, the ceiling rising to a dome about twenty feet high.

David, the guide assigned to us, kept us in a state of merriment, not only at his jokes, but by his amusing way of expressing himself. When we asked if such and such a place was truly what it was purported to be, he asked, "What is your religion?" We answered that we were more or less neutral, so he said, "Well, it is supposed to be. Nobody really knows. Most of the holy places were chosen arbitrarily in the fourth century by Queen Helena, mother of Constantine. Nobody really knows."

Nina and I sometimes felt in our bones that *here* was the place where some event had happened. Other times we felt very strongly that it was *not* the place. For example, the Church of the Holy Sepulcher is built on the site of the supposed tomb of Jesus. Yet, it didn't seem to us as real as the garden tomb near the Hill of Calvary. There we entered the low door cut into the side of the mound and sat facing the two empty tombs hollowed out of the native rock. I definitely felt a presence and we both felt it to be the real place where Christ was buried. And so it was as we walked the Via Dolorosa and the paving stones of the crypt beneath the convent kept by French nuns, which had been the courtyard of Pontius Pilate's palace. We even saw the scratched stone where the soldiers played their games of chance the night of the betrayal and trial of Christ. It all came alive. Each place had its own association in connection with our early teachings.

We removed our shoes before entering the mosque enclosing the Dome of the Rock, sacred to all religions, where Abraham took Isaac for sacrifice and where, instead, he found the ram caught in the bushes.

After hearing all my life about the Valley of Kidron, the Pool of Siloam, where at the troubling of the waters people were healed, the temple where the money changers were cast out, the Via Dolorosa through which the cross was carried, I could hardly believe I was seeing the actual places.

While we were being driven to Jericho we stopped where a deep ravine divided the mountain. Just opposite where we stood a stream of water burst from the earth to flow down and replenish the brook far below. There Elijah had been fed by the ravens at brook Cherith.

Another day we went to the Garden of Gethsemane, where the ancient olive trees in tortured shapes of silvery gray have kept watch for two thousand years. The garden is tenderly cared for by the monks, who grow flowers in profusion. Then we followed the supposed route of the disciples and Jesus with his captors, ending at the palace of the High Priest Caiaphus, where Peter denied being one of the apostles. We saw the threshing floor and the underground caves where the disciples spent the night.

The afternoon that we visited Bethlehem we went to the church built over the birthplace of Jesus, entering by a narrow, low door. The manger is so covered with decorations and hanging lamps that it was disappointing. We would have liked to see the crude manger that served as the cradle of Christianity as we pictured it and as it must have been. As I remember there was a small chapel adjoining, where, just at the time we were there, it was the hour of vespers. The service was conducted by the monks. We stayed through the service, then from the cavelike chapel were led through passages to the cell where St. Jerome wrote the translation of the Bible called the Vulgate.

Our last day in Jordan Jerusalem we spent walking about the city by ourselves, staying a long time in the museum, where we saw artifacts thousands of years old and a cave unearthed and set up as it must have been before biblical times. I remember particularly a skull with two rows of beads imbedded in the forehead.

It was difficult to realize as we walked through the streets, recalling the Bible stories, that the street level is about forty feet higher than it was in the time of the Caesars. The Pool of Siloam was far below the street level, as was the courtyard of Pilate's palace beneath the convent.

It was time to leave Jordan and go into the Israeli part of Jerusalem. For some reason I cannot explain I was nervous about entering Israel. We had been warned before leaving home that we might be unwelcome in some places. Too, there was the tension caused by the Suez crisis. As we had been treated exceedingly well everywhere we had been, I suppose I thought that we must meet unfriendliness *some*where, and as Israel was the last of the Middle Eastern countries for us to visit, I was sure it would be there. Nothing could have been further from the truth, but it took a day and meeting Isaac to find that out.

As we neared the Mandelbaum Gate on that Friday morning, the Muslim Sabbath, I began to suffer from nausea and extreme discomfort. The Mandelbaum Gate, which I had pictured as large and imposing, was nonexistent. There were simply two small buildings where we had to identify ourselves by showing our passports. Then we were taken from one building on the Jordan side to the one on the Israeli side. A small boy accompanied us, carrying our suitcases. We were asked about the length of our stay and told to wait a little while until our guide came. Finally a car arrived for us, driven by a woman who said she was in charge of public relations and was substituting for the guide we were supposed to have because he had been taken suddenly ill. She was very kind, took us to her office and gave us tea, and asked us to wait again till Isaac could get there. It seemed as if the whole episode bore an air of mystery, which didn't help my discomfort. It wasn't until nearly a week later that we discovered our intended guide had been called into the army and that a battle was imminent. However, as soon as Isaac appeared to take over the driving for us, I settled down and felt that all was well. He told us that we must allow several people to ride with us because of the emergency. We accepted of course. A Mr. and Mrs. Friedman and a Mrs. Singer rode with us, but didn't stay in the same hotel.

As we passed through the towns and villages of Israel we often picked up soldiers and took them to some other place on our way. There was no "by your leave." It was simply announced by Isaac, "They *must* be picked up." We passed large camions of army matériel. I always sat in front with Isaac, the Friedmans in the back, and Nina and Mrs. Singer in the middle seat, where the soldiers also sat when picked up. The mystery increased, but Isaac, although he listened to the radio intently, never translated the news, and by his casual manner and agreeable conversation kept us calm.

We rode all afternoon through the Judean Hills listening to Isaac as he pointed out places with familiar names: just beyond that rise had been the palace of Ahab; there, over that field, was the village of Endor, where the witch had lived in the time of Saul; these were the plains of Yezdrael, of Esdraelon; there, a few miles beyond, the village of Bashan. By evening we arrived at Tel Aviv and the Hotel Ramat Aviv, where we found good accommodations and a good dinner awaiting us.

The next day there seemed to be no tickets available for a concert and we were too tired to do much walking, so we went to the museum. It just happened that the rooms were filled with an exhibit of children's drawings illustrating the Old Testament. All captions were in Hebrew, but we tried to decide what each drawing was meant to depict. All were exceptionally good for sixth and seventh graders, and one we felt was surely meant to represent the Creation. Just as we were discussing it a man came up to us and, with gestures, asked if he could be of help. He had few words of English, but spoke Hebrew, as all citizens of Israel are expected to do. We told him we thought the picture was a very good representation of the *Crea*tion—the *Begin*ning—emphasizing the words as we are all inclined to do, hoping it will make the word more easily understood. Light dawned on his face. He nodded vigorously. "Yes!" he agreed. "*Yes*, Cr-r-r-e-ation!" Once more we had penetrated the barrier of language and felt the thrill of communication.

We went back to our hotel ready for our accustomed siesta.

The next two days were spent traveling north toward Nazareth. There have been recent discoveries of caves that are thought to be similar to the one that served Mary and Joseph, Jesus and his brothers, as a home. A little farther up the rise a church covers the supposed carpenter shop where Jesus learned the trade with Joseph. The caves are cool, and in the one we entered through a narrow passage there was a great air vent at least twenty or thirty feet high and six feet across. There was a tiny shelf jutting out from the wall to hold the oil lamps then in use. Here in these airy caves one feels the presence of former inhabitants and can visualize the Holy Family in its proper setting. It was a moving experience.

We passed through Cana of Galilee and on to Tiberius on the Sea of Galilee. From there we could see Capernaum and the Mount of Beatitudes, where Christ preached the Sermon on the Mount. Nearby is the site of the miracle of the loaves and fishes.

We were taken to a little restaurant on the edge of the lake in Tiberius, where we ate fish freshly caught. It was very good, even though I found it a little disconcerting to see the fish's eye staring up at me. But I put the head aside and made believe it wasn't there. Mrs. Friedman said, emphatically, "You are a good sport! I know you are not used to having fish served that way." Nina and I had agreed that when we stopped for food we would have whatever the Friedmans and Mrs. Singer chose to have. They were all Orthodox and didn't eat butter with meat, so sometimes we had a meat meal, sometimes a dairy meal, and sometimes a fish meal. We liked them all.

We drove on to the River Jordan, wondering at the new green growing in Israel in contrast to the desertlike hills of the Arab countries. The Israeli have cleared off large areas of land and replanted them. The top rock, fallen from the hills, is gathered at the edges of the fields, leaving good land for cultivation. It is forbidden to keep black goats, because they forage so eagerly that they destroy the roots of the grass.

As we crossed the plain, Mount Tabor, hallowed by all Christians, rose majestically against the sky. The day was over, so we didn't stop there but went on to Haifa and the Hotel Zion. On our arrival we learned that Mrs. Huyum had called to say she would expect us at her house for dinner the next evening. Mrs. Huyum is the sister of our friend Mrs. Bettauer of Toms River. While in America she had visited her sister there, we had become acquainted, and Dai had driven her to New York to register as an alien. At that time she said we must come to see her if ever we came to Israel. Little did I think I would ever take advantage of her invitation.

We continued our expedition the next day, seeing the new industry in Haifa, its improved housing and highway, then up the height of Mount Carmel, from which we could overlook the bay and see, beyond, the hills of Syria. Far up the mountain we came upon the gold-domed chapel of Bahai, with its lovely gardens, where we rested. Then down the mountain and along the shores of the Mediterranean to Acre, where Crusader walls and citadels still stand, and on to Upper Galilee. When we paused to see the remains of a Roman palace, with its statues of heroic size, I walked along the shore hunting for shells to take home to Johnny, my nephew. But I found none, to my surprise.

We wound our way inland to Meron, where a famous rabbi lives. It is now a study center for boys and for scholars, where the Torah, the Talmud, and the Cabala are taught. Old men sat in deep study and never lifted their eyes as we passed. It seemed rude to me until Isaac explained that one must never look upon a woman when studying the holy books.

From Meron we went to Safad, a village occupied by Jews from time immemorial. It lies at the top of a steep hill, so we had to leave the car and walk up to a garden and a café where we had lunch, where Isaac teased the seventeen-year-old girl who served us, where we sat in the sun under olive trees as ancient, as twisted, and as gray-green as those in the Garden of Gethsemane. It was a delightful pause in the pure air, and the food was good.

Back in Haifa we had just time to take a taxi to Mrs. Huyum's home part way up Mount Carmel. Mrs. Huyum met us at the door with her new daughter-in-law and apologized for the absence of her son, who was in the army, and for her husband, who had gone to Galilee to pick up cots for the hospital in Tel Aviv. As we ate dinner he stopped in to greet us but didn't stay. There was little mention of the need for the stretchers, but by now we were pretty well aware of the gravity of the situation. Excitement, or rather apprehension, began to build up in us, although the conversation at dinner was kept at a cheerful level and no sign of anxiety appeared. We marveled at the courage and self-control of these women, especially the bride of two weeks, who in the face of all-out war were so calm, so cheerful.

After leaving our friends' apartment we found it impossible to get a taxi. It was dark and the road was very steep. Mrs. Huyum accompanied us as far as the main street, where, as we stopped long enough to rest, we saw soldiers standing guard at store entrances. Lights were dim and a general air of tension added to our excitement. Nina excused herself to go and try to find a newspaper. As we were getting ready for bed I said, "Well, we might be bombed tonight. Perhaps this is the time to take those pills Dr. Bevan gave me for a time when we might find ourselves in a tense situation." Nina agreed, but I didn't know until much later that she had gone down to see what information she could gather. She learned about the battle in the Negev, but kept it to herself.

Before we had started to undress we were called by our travel agent in Tel Aviv. He said he was afraid our Sabena plane would not get in for our one o'clock flight to Athens the day after tomorrow. We had better plan on a later one and talk to him when we arrived in Tel Aviv the next day. We took our medicine and went to sleep. Isaac arrived on time in the morning, bringing our traveling companions. After a dairy meal in a small village about one o'clock Isaac said, "Now, we'd better get to Tel Aviv and talk to your agent." And so we did.

He pointed out various places of interest, but went speedily on to Tel Aviv, stopping at the office of the agent before going to the hotel. He advised us to pack and be ready for an earlier flight than we had planned.

We were due to fly to Athens the next day, where we had reservations. "The flights are irregular, due to the emergency," the agent said. We were still not frightened, only excited. We packed our things, talking breathlessly, sorting out the summer things from clothing we would need in the cold November of European countries. We packed carefully. Just as we had all in order and suitcases closed, the telephone rang.

"This is your agent in Tel Aviv," came the message. "I think you had better call your American Embassy and see if they will fly you out tonight. The flight I had scheduled for you has been canceled and I am not sure there will be another. The number is—" and I wrote down what he said.

A voice answered immediately when I called the embassy. "Yes," a man's voice said, "we can fly you out tonight. You may have one suitcase each. You must be at the airport at six-thirty this

224

evening. Please eat something before leaving the hotel and bring some food with you."

Now we were really excited. We were to be refugees! We repacked, leaving all unnecessary things behind. What would happen to them? We worked feverishly until nearly 5:30, leaving all summer things and weighty presents such as camel-skin bags and most of the things Nina had bought.

It was early for dinner, but we asked to be served whatever was ready and for extra food to take with us. We ate by the light of small oil lamps such as had been used in biblical times, and a bag of sandwiches was given us to take along. Our bill had just been attended to when Isaac arrived to take us to the airport. He promised to send us the things we had abandoned as soon as the situation quieted down.

It was dusk as we left for the airport and dark when we had driven the fifteen miles with our lights dimmed and covered with blue paper. No lights shone on the road, but still we felt only excitement, no fear. This has always mystified me, because from childhood I have always been timid about the unknown.

We were among the very first to arrive at the airport. There was a round pillar where we chose to sit. We were on time and hoped that the American plane would leave soon. It didn't.

More and more people came as time went on, many with children. As dark came only one dim light from a lantern was allowed. It stood on the floor at the entrance to the restrooms. By then all the seats were taken.

As the night went on the building became jammed with people. They were sitting on suitcases, on the floor; children were sleeping on coats, on laps, anywhere. None of them cried or made any disturbances. They seemed to know that this was an occasion for their best behavior. Children are wonderful.

The coffee shop ran out of food. We had eaten our sandwiches dry, because we had no Israeli money to buy coffee. About midnight one of the men introduced himself to us. He said he was from Montana and had been in northern Israel teaching the farmers to raise pigs. He said he would get us some coffee. He collected enough from the crowd to buy it at seventy cents a cup! From where we sat for coffee we could see the planes being loaded by flashlight. Our new acquaintances on the round seat promised to keep our places. I was one of the oldest in the crowd, so more in need of a seat than most. Nina, I suspected, retained hers because everyone liked her and because she was my companion.

It seemed incredible that we sat there from six-thirty in the evening until four the next morning. But we did, and because of the new experience and the interesting people the time passed reasonably well until the plane was ready to fly out. When we saw the mountain of luggage to be cared for, and counted the number of passengers, we could understand. Besides, there were people coming in all through the night. While we were waiting for our passports to be processed we stood in the outer room of the building. I complimented a young couple on the behavior of their two small children through the endless night. Then, introducing myself as Mrs. de Angeli from Philadelphia, I introduced Nina as Mrs. Alfred Kuhn of Cincinnati. The young man's eyes popped.

"You're not Al Kuhn's wife, are you?"

"Yes," said Nina. "Why?"

"Well," said he, "I'm the last one to read proof on your husband's book! I'm an economist, stationed here for two years. To think that we'd meet in Tel Aviv at four o'clock in the morning!"

By this time our passports had all come through and we were shepherded out onto the field and into the great maw of the transport plane. We were seated not far from the opening because we were almost the very last to go aboard. The plane was tremendous, with two floors, and not pressurized. The mountain of luggage took up nearly half the space on the lower level. Several splendid young army men took care of our comfort, even to warming a bottle for one of the babies.

The noise of the plane was deafening; it was impossible to talk, so Nina and I simply endured it. Sometimes I looked behind my seat and below where the window was to see what I could, and at last dawn came, and with it a view of the islands of the Aegean Sea in the rosy light.

Four hours after leaving Tel Aviv we arrived at the airport near Athens. There we disembarked and were taken to a seaside summer hotel, opened to receive us, where we were given breakfast as guests of the United States. How proud and happy we were to be Americans.

While we had breakfast an American Embassy official welcomed us to Greece, then offered money to anyone in need, saying it could be repaid later.

Chapter Forty-one

While we waited for our driver to take us to Athens and the Hotel Grand Bretagne, where our reservations were for that day, I began to fall asleep wherever I was. It didn't matter whether someone was talking, or what was going on around me, I was completely helpless and committed to sleep. It seemed that Nina and I were the only ones of that two hundred or so who had a definite plan and place to go. Some, especially those with young children, looked anxious. They had no idea where their paths would lead them, or whether they would ever again see their homes in Tel Aviv or recover their household goods.

About 10:30 our driver from Athens arrived and we were mercifully taken to the hotel. The concierge handed Nina two letters from Alf. There were none for me. I hadn't heard from Dai in two weeks. I was afraid he was ill and that the boys were keeping it from me. Later I found out that the post office had given him the wrong information as to the length of time a letter would take to reach me.

"Now," said Nina, when we had been to our room, as if she had been the mother and I the daughter, "don't lie down, Mother, until you've undressed. We're going to bed." That woke me for a moment. "Going to bed at eleven in the morning!" Bed was always my last resort.

"Going to *bed*. We've been up all night, remember? And we've been through an experience that would exhaust anybody." She was pulling down covers and undressing at the same time. How glad I was to be told what to do! I undressed, fell gratefully into bed, and went to sleep.

When we awoke eight hours later, it was dinnertime. I, the poor sleeper, had slept eight hours in broad daylight! Incredible.

We dressed and went down to dinner, expecting to stay up for the evening to see a bit of Athens. Did we? No, we went straight back to our room and sleep again, not to wake until morning. By then we were refreshed and ready for the planned schedule, which included, naturally, the Acropolis and the Parthenon, which we had glimpsed from our balcony. We marveled at the hold it had upon us. The guide had a pleasant, triangular, tanned face and long-toothed smile and a way of twisting his fingers as he spoke in broken English that kept us amused and interested. He described the symbolism of the eggs in the baskets on the heads of the maidens supporting the roof of a temple, and the meaning of the vine decoration around the door, the egg and dart motif around the cornice of the ruined temple to the God of Fertility. "Athes to athes," he lisped, rubbing fingers and thumbs together, "And dutht to dutht." It was very funny. Nina and I kept it as a joke between us. It still evokes a chuckle when we say it, but we didn't insult the poor man by letting him see our amusement.

One ancient landmark I loved is the church at Daphne, where we saw the magnificent mosaics and where we sat in the lovely garden on a round bench encircling a tree. The view through the gateway was enchanting and that is what I remember best.

After a day of shopping and looking about the city on our own, we were scheduled to go to Sunion and the ruins of the Temple of Poseidon, high above the ocean.

At Sunion we ate fresh fish for our lunch, just as Besse Howard had said we would. We saw the temple against the westering sun and the blue of the sea peopled with ghosts of the past. But my picture of it shows only Nina with her kerchief fluttering in the wind.

The next day, on the road to Corinth, we went on through olive groves and vineyards where women were heaping grapes into baskets. We continued over the constantly rising ground to the ruins of the city of Corinth. There stood the ruin of a temple, small but perfectly proportioned; nearby, market stalls in outline. Over against a wall, the place where Paul preached to the Corinthians. It seemed to echo his denunciation of sinners and perhaps it was here that he preached his gospel of love as we know it in the Epistle.

It had been a beautiful day, steeped in the past. On our last day at liberty in Athens, Nina and I went to the museum, which proved to be a high point in our stay there. As we entered, an archaic statue of Apollo greeted us with his eternal smile. It had been discovered recently and was thought to be the oldest sculpture yet found. With Apollo, in the entrance to the building, was a statue of a woman, also of an archaic period, and like others of that time it was rather stiff in concept, but charmingly smiling as if good will had carried down through the ages.

The greatest impression and perhaps the one best remembered is the heroic statue of Poseidon. Its perfection stays with me, and with it I recall the "little jockey," both fairly recent finds. The whole experience of the museum is one of excitement, of inspiration, and lingering beauty.

Each time we returned to the hotel the concierge handed Nina a letter. "Didn't I give you a letter just a while ago?" he teased. "Yes, you did," replied Nina airily. "This is another one." There were four from Alf one day and none at all for me. Dai had always written me every day when he traveled. What could be wrong?

Our stay in Athens came to an end. We left with regret, although we were both beginning to long for home.

The flight from Athens to Rome was about four hours. Rome proved to be almost as beautiful as Athens. Here too business stopped for the long siesta. Shops pulled down their blinds, pedestrians vanished, and the city went to sleep. So did we.

The Hotel Flora, where we were registered, was within walking distance of the Via Veneto and the smart shops, famous landmarks, and delightful sidewalk restaurants such as Doney's.

Nina begged off from going to the Coliseum and I agreed that we had seen the one in Arles and that one can have enough of sightseeing. Instead we went out the Appian Way to the Catacombs by taxi. It was interesting to find that the guide assigned to us was a young priest from Ireland with the most delightful lilt to his rich brogue.

There were ten or twelve people in the group assembled to go down into the depths of the earth. At first we moved along with them, but there were so many interesting things displayed along the passage that we hung back until we began to feel lost. One was the form of a girl, cast in plaster, who had been caught by the volcanic ash of Vesuvius, which moved us deeply. Then we hurried on to catch up with the others in time to hear our young Irishman saying, as he pointed out one of the rather small embrasures in the wall, "It is here they buried them that died, and they had a little smoothin' iron to level off the plaster."

One memorable day was spent at the Vatican. The vast interior diminished us to the size of children. The fonts, at eye level, were supported by cherubs of heroic proportions, and as we advanced down the nave, the great altar rose, with its twisted columns, to an immense height, and beyond was the choir, as large in itself as a good-sized church.

We were impressed by the chapel of lapis lazuli, but most moving and beautiful of all was the *Pietà*, carved by Michelangelo and signed by him in the night so that no other artist could claim it.

We sat in the Sistine Chapel and marveled at its perfection, the incredible immensity of its conception, and the persistence and physical strength of its creator.

We loved the Borghese Gardens and the museum there, filled with sculpture, the Bernini *David*, the handsome heads of the Caesars, the richness of porphyry, the soft smoothness of alabaster. How the vastness of the Pantheon diminishes one's ego! It is breath-taking.

We left Rome by motor coach and drove through the hill towns to Assisi, where we stopped overnight. Far down in the valley we saw white oxen working in the olive groves. On the hills, castles and towers and churches. As we had neared Assisi we had passed the church of St. Maria de Angeli. How odd to see one's name on a church in Italy.

Assisi is a town straight out of the Middle Ages, not only in the ancient look of the houses, but in the way things are still done; hand embroidery is still pressed with a charcoal iron, which is taken into the street and swung back and forth to get the charcoal burning.

A young priest who guided us through the Church of San Francisco was an American and a homesick one from his tone of conversation. He accompanied us as we stood in awe before the Giotto paintings; he told us about Saint Francis and the dedication of a worldly young man to Christianity and his vow of poverty. The whole experience of Assisi was very moving.

In Florence the one thing Nina wanted to see most was the Baptistry and the Golden Doors by Ghirlandaio. We went there immediately after settling in at the Hotel Luchesi on the Arno. Some special ceremony was going on so we couldn't enter the building, but we could enjoy the Golden Doors as long as we liked. I, of course, wanted to see most the Michelangelo *David*. It is magnificent, but other sculptures of Michelangelo's touched me more; the Prisoner, half released from the stone and the self-portrait. Yet, as I remember the excitement of that afternoon, the *David* is the most clear and impressive.

The weather those few days in Florence was cold and rainy. The picture galleries were unlighted and unheated so that our anticipated joy in seeing the original long-loved paintings was somewhat diminished. However, one could not deny the thrill of just *being* in Florence, walking along the Arno, shopping on the Ponte Vecchio, eating dinner in a vaulted room that, during the fifteenth century, was the basement of the Villa d'Este. Rain or no rain, we walked through the narrow streets, across the Piazza Signorina.

We left for Paris on the Simplon Express and I couldn't help the feeling that there might be government agents or international spies aboard searching for political escapees. I was determined to wake through the night and look out to see the Alps climbing the sky, but I slept.

Morning found us in Gare Lyon answering the call of our new guide and driver, "Mrs. de Angeli?" We were taken to the Hotel Duminy and left for the day to our own devices.

In Paris several of Dai's letters finally caught up with me and I was reassured as to his health. The knowledge that all was well somewhat allayed my homesickness, and in any case we had our itinerary to fulfill as scheduled. Nina too was ready to go home, but eager to see both Paris and London, so we made the best of it.

It was November in Paris, cold and gray, but we had our winter clothing and we took advantage of every opportunity to have coffee.

The longing to go home became more and more insistent. We curbed our impatience and looked forward to the Paris to London flight next morning. It seemed unbelievably short. Winifred Nerney met us and, after settling us in at the Hyde Park Hotel, took us to lunch. Her charm won Nina at once, as it had Dai and me, so long ago. And before leaving us she made sure that we would spend Thanksgiving Day at her home. She realized the special need for consolation we would have for spending that day away from home and family.

The next day we went with Winifred to Didcot by train. There, we were met by Joan Marsden and taken to her newly acquired house in Blewbury. On our way, shortly before we arrived at Didcot, I was looking out over the frosty fields with the borders of naked trees, when suddenly it seemed as if a Shepard drawing from *The*

Wind in the Willows had come alive. Yes, Nina and Winifred agreed, it did look like a Shepard drawing.

After Joan's greeting at our arrival a few moments later, as we turned to go into the village of Blewbury, Joan said, "You know, this is where Kenneth Grahame lived, and where he wrote *The Wind in the Willows*." And there, just as we turned into the street where Joan's house is, was the Grahame house beyond the gate. Was this some form of extrasensory perception? If not, how could one account for it? We were charmed with Joan's house, once an inn, and so arranged that it could fairly easily be turned into three units, one to let, one for guests, and one for Joan's living quarters.

Nina's delight at being in a real country house in a real English village was, in itself, a delight to me. But more, here was Winifred, a most special kind of person, and Joan, her old friend and now, ours, to talk on every subject, to enjoy the still-blooming garden, the house, and the eleventh-century village church. It was a perfect day and one to remember.

The following day, Thanksgiving Day, was our last in England. We spent the morning getting our things in order, and in the afternoon went to Wandsworth Common, to Winifred's. She lived on the top floor of her house and rented the other two floors. Although it meant going down three flights of stairs, she felt no need for a refrigerator, but kept her perishable food in the cool cellar. She served us a royal roast beef dinner, and with her warmth and interesting tales, dispelled our homesickness.

As we rode down to Southampton next morning to board the *Queen Mary*, the fields were white with frost. The compartment was cold and with all our efforts we could not keep warm. But nothing daunted us. We were going home!

Customs seemed endless, but we were aboard at last.

When we learned, or remembered, that we were going home by way of Le Havre it seemed like Marianne's joke about her father's way of going anywhere, as she said, "By way of Eaglesmere," and absolutely senseless from our point of view. But it had to be, that was the schedule. We resigned ourselves, thinking, Oh well, by midnight, according to plan, we should have left the coast of France and be on our way across the Atlantic. But were we? No.

When we awoke in the morning the ship was ominously quiet. We were still in the harbor. The propeller shaft had broken and men had worked all night to repair it. At about nine in the morning we were underway and thanked our stars it had been no later. The steward assured us that we would probably make up the lost time anyway.

We tried to make the most of our return voyage and to enjoy whatever entertainment was offered. I made a feeble attempt to draw, we took long walks and long naps, but our thoughts were turned homeward and to those we had left for so long. We waited impatiently for the end of our journey, which finally came the evening of November 28, 1956.

To our surprise there was quite a delegation to meet us. Two of my brothers and their wives, with my mother and Dai, were there, and of course, Peggy. We all had supper together somewhere near Pier 90, then Nina left for Cincinnati and home to Alfred and the boys. Our ten weeks' journey was over.

Now the work was to begin on illustrating the Old Testament. It was to take more than three years.

Chapter Forty-two

After being away so long from my work there was, as always, a period of frustration and inability to produce anything. This usually lasts about a week, while I try sketch after sketch, or line after line of writing, convinced that I shall never draw or write again. The period finally ends when some small incident or thought triggers an idea too interesting to ignore. It must be put down. Then at last the work goes forward.

Peggy and I had agreed upon the format for the Old Testament book before Nina and I left for the Middle East. According to my usual custom, I made the drawings about one third larger than the reproduction would be, following the same proportion throughout.

There were to be thirty-two pages of color and sepia decorations around the initial letters opening the chapters. Knowing that the color drawings take longer to reproduce than the black and white, as well as longer to do, I began at once to work on the first color page in the book, Adam and Eve in the Garden. How could I picture it? There must be animals and the serpent as well as the figures of Adam and Eve. There must be an apple tree because it is traditional.

So began many trial sketches, several trips to the zoo to see animals at close range: to study how the angle of the shoulder leads into the leg; how the vestigial thumb interrupts the line leading into the paw; how the eyes are set in the head; how, in walking, the legs move. I had to consult my file of animal photographs to help memory when the sketch faltered, and to clarify ideas and composition, keeping in mind the all-pervading light that illumines the countries of the Middle East.

For a month I worked on the watercolor painting of the Garden of Eden, loving each minute of it, eager to begin work each morning.

In the Pennsylvania University Museum I found tiny animals of gold, exquisitely made, and amulets, or talismans, which I used in the chapter decorations. I found a book picturing flowers that grow in the Middle East, a terebinth tree to use in the drawing of Cain and Abel, and a scythe and dagger from the Stone Age.

For Noah's Ark I had to draw upon my imagination, my memory of concepts I had seen, and, as well as I could, follow the specifications set forth in the Bible for the building of the Ark—so many cubits high, so many cubits wide, and so forth. This drawing was in black and white, done with carbon pencil. With many trial sketches, this also took me a month to do, but I loved doing it.

The romantic story of Abraham's wanderings with Lot is the beginning of a family saga I have loved since before Sunday school days when I used to lie on my stomach to look at the Doré Bible. When and how I went from pictures to text I don't remember. Probably my parents led me from one to the other.

I have pictured the part where Abraham and Lot go their separate ways, each with his flocks and herds. I could imagine the anguish of the women leaving friends and sisters to go to an unknown land. I remembered as I drew them the lovely triangular face of the Arab woman I had seen and sketched in a mosque in Cairo where we were both sightseeing.

I thought it hard that Sarah should turn Hagar out into the wilderness with her child, and tried to show in my picture the conflict between the two women, Sarah wrinkled and old, and Hagar the young and beautiful Egyptian.

How the stars must have shown in the desert as Abraham considered their number and wondered at the promise of innumerable descendants. What awe must have struck him when three men appeared out of nowhere and announced the birth of a son to Sarah in her old age. Sarah laughed.

For the next chapter about the son, Isaac, I drew for the heading the ram provided for sacrifice in place of Isaac, and pictured Rebecca with the water jar as I had seen women carry them at the well in Jericho thousands of years later, walking with grace and dignity.

The picture of Laban's hospitality to Abraham's emissary, washing his feet and caring for animals and servants, gave me an opportunity to use the artifacts I had seen in the East and in the museum. I used the water bottle and basin that had been in the room Nina and I had had in Jerusalem, because it was like the ones we had seen in the museum, which might well have been in use in Abraham's time.

Although the deception planned by Rebecca and Jacob to obtain the father's blessing always troubled me, I rationalized it, thinking that perhaps Jacob was the more worthy to receive it than Esau, the elder brother. The dream that appeared to Jacob seemed easy to imagine, and his devotion to Rachel romantic. That he was deceived by being given Leah for a wife instead of Rachel seemed only fair after his own deception. I have pictured the two wives, Rachel and Leah, as they might have sat over the cooking fire, each trying in her own way to entice Jacob with his favorite food, Leah tender-eyed, Rachel beautiful and well-favored.

The story of Jacob and his many wives, the gathering of "all the souls gotten in Haran," is the subject for the two-page color drawing used as a jacket for the book of selections from the Old Testament, and it also appears inside.

In Damascus, Nina and I had seen a tent set up as an exhibit to show how the tribes of Israel lived, as indeed the Bedouins still live, the skin bottle hanging from the tent pole, the jars for meal and oil in the cooking place, the skins and robes in the sleeping place.

The only sons of Rachel, Joseph and Benjamin, hated by their step-brothers except Reuben, Leah's son, carry on the saga. How I loved as a child the story of Joseph's coat of many colors. How I grieved at his being put into a pit, then sold to a caravan going to Egypt. It was because of this story that we went to Egypt, to see the pyramids built by the enslaved Hebrews, the sea of reeds, corrupted by translation into the Red Sea, the tomb of Rameses, and the temples.

I tried to show in my picture of Joseph, as a man of authority, the abjectness of his brothers begging for grain and Joseph's power to give or withhold it, and in another drawing his tenderness toward Benjamin, his young brother.

As I review the pictures of Moses I recall the title and meaning of this book, of the earnest effort to do everything as well as possible and the sometimes disappointing result. Once again, "Butter at the old price"; Moses was quite a challenge. If my interpretation of him differs from others, it must be so.

I thought of him as rather young, perhaps forty, tending his father-in-law's flocks, which might have been the black African goats that we saw often in the Middle East, except in Israel.

David has always been one of my favorite characters. In his youth he was so brave, so appealing, as he soothed the savage humor of King Saul with his harp. And what child is not thrilled at the idea of a giant overcome with a pebble slung from a boy's shoulder? Or at the boy's rise from shepherd to king?

I loved the story of Solomon and his just decision about the child claimed by two women. For a background to this I remembered spiraled columns set in niches high above the altar in St. Peter's in Rome, said to be from the Temple of Solomon. As I sketched the purple robe I remembered reading how royal purple was gotten from sea creatures, trodden out by slaves.

In a tailpiece for the book of Amos, I remembered the felucca in which Nina and I had crossed the Nile at Luxor.

Each drawing was a matter for thought, research, and numberless sketches. I loved the poetic book of Isaiah, but how could one picture it? I followed the description of the seraphim, each with six wings. Over and over I tried to visualize them. Then one morning, while my husband and I were on vacation in New Hampshire, I made a sketch with colored pencils from which I did the watercolor for the book.

Beginning the Psalms, I wanted to draw a branch of a fig tree, but could find nothing among my books to guide me. It seemed out of the question to go to the library that day, but after dinner I went to a neighborhood gathering in a small street called Fawn Street, where our mayor was speaking. From where I stood I could see into the backyard of the house facing Twelfth Street. There, just inside the fence, was a *fig tree!* The next morning I went armed with paper and pencil and asked permission to draw some leaves from the tree. It seemed symbolic to use a fawn as the little animal in the decoration at the head.

When I came to the part of the Old Testament where men were sent to the land of Canaan to see "if it be good land, fat or lean, whether there be wood in it and to bring back fruits" the drawing almost did itself. To think of a cluster of grapes that would be so heavy it would take two men to carry it!

When I came to the story of Esther, I wanted to show her in rich clothing as she was about to enter the presence of the king. I went to a well-known dry goods store in Philadelphia, asked the young man to show me some brocaded material, and told him I wanted it for the story of Esther. He brought out a bolt of handsome red silk, just what I wanted—but it was woven in an ecclesiastical pattern and was the only one he had. As I handled it it fell into such rich folds, with the lamb and cross half in shadow, that I decided I could use it, disguising the pattern.

Arthur's wife, Nina, posed for me while I draped the lovely stuff around her, then painted the figure of Esther. (It was Nina who had posed for me as the figure of Robin's mother in *The Door in the Wall.*)

In the drawing of Esther, I used only flowers that grow in the Middle East, and, around the fountain, pots I had seen in the museum in Jerusalem.

And so with some of the Psalms, the story of Daniel and part of Proverbs, ended my selections from the Old Testament with verses from Isaiah, comforting and hopeful. I used the passion flower in the decoration and a dove with the olive branch as a kind of colophon. The drawings had taken me three and a half years. The book was published in 1960.

Chapter Forty-three

Dai and I were nearing our fiftieth wedding anniversary. It was becoming difficult for Dai to travel by public transportation and neither of us was able to drive, so when Maury suggested that we buy a small house not too far from where he and Marianne and the boys lived and on the same road, we took his advice. It was very pleasant to be near them, to have Marianne take me shopping and to have tea afterward. We intended it to be our permanent residence and to spend at least eight months a year there. It stands on Upper Ridge Road back of a small wooded area near Sumneytown and Green Lane, about halfway between Quakertown and Pottstown in Pennsylvania.

All of our sons and their families live within a six-mile radius. All are helpful in getting us from one place to another, the girls no less than the boys.

Willow trees and evergreens separate us from our neighbors at the back, and at one side it is thickly wooded. Across from us is property belonging to the Boy Scouts, and on our other side the dearest of neighbors, the Bockiuses.

We moved there in October 1959, in time to enjoy the beauty of the fall countryside when the dogwood berries are red-ripe and the smell of autumn fills the air.

For furniture (we decided not to give up our Panama Street house after all) we gathered things we had loaned to various children, distributed among them when we sold the Money Island house. Twin beds from Arthur and Nina and the old bureau that had been my grandmother's, a chair that Ted and Betty had recovered for us, the drop-leaf Michigan table from Jack and Edna, the needlepoint chairs from several of the children. We bought a lovely corner cupboard from the antique store across from Yoder's in Green Lane and a desk from somewhere near New Hope. It began to look like home. What special quality makes a home individual? The girls all declared that if they had walked into the house without knowing who lived there they would have known immediately it was ours!

The language draperies, which I had seen first in Emerson Greenway's office at the Logan Library, were all in place and the other curtains hung. The language drapery is quite a conversation piece. It had been designed originally for a synagogue, and the Hebrew line of text printed in sepia on a neutral ground says, "Oh, Lord, our God, You are One." It is assumed that the other lines of six different languages say somewhat the same. They are Egyptian, Slavic, Scandinavian, archaic Greek, Amharic, and Arabic, each in its own characteristic calligraphy. One can make out "Fadr," in the Scandinavian.

The draperies hang at the two wide windows facing each other, giving us the view of the blue hills and in front the stone walls, the immense black oak, and the woods.

For the first time in years, now that my mother was gone and we had room, it seemed right for us to have the Thanksgiving dinner. We invited all the available family. The girls were to bring vegetables, rolls, casseroles, and pie for dessert, while I provided the turkey. I stuffed it in the old-fashioned way with bread, onion, sage, and butter as my mother used to do, and put it into the oven at midnight, hoping it would be all right. I had never before cooked a turkey so large. It was thirty-five pounds.

At seven on Thanksgiving Day I awoke and remembered the turkey. I flew to the kitchen, afraid that it was ruined. It wasn't. It looked simply perfect. Dinner was set for two o'clock, so I turned off the heat for a few hours, putting it on again at eleven, basting the turkey at intervals and testing it as I'd been taught by thrusting a fork into the wing muscle.

By dinnertime the family began to arrive with their various offerings. A borrowed table had been added to our two drop-leaf ones, silver, some of it also borrowed, had been laid on the white cloths, and dishes assembled, Marianne's blue ones added to my Spode. The turkey was done to a turn and looked beautiful. It was the purest chance, but successful.

There were twenty-one of us at the long table. John, Maury and Marianne's baby lay asleep on the bed. Only one family was

Arthur de Angeli, Marguerite's second son.　　Nina de Angeli, Arthur's wife.

missing, Nina and Alf's. They were at home in Cincinnati with their friends.

At Christmas we followed our custom of gathering for a Christmas Eve party, but not at our house as it used to be. The old fellow with the scythe was beginning to catch up with us, so we went to the young people's for these occasions. Nowadays my contribution to the feast is a large molded fruit gelatine salad.

After the holidays Dai and I began to think about our Golden Wedding, coming up in early April. It seemed right and proper to have it there in the country, where the large living room with dining area adjoining is spacious enough to hold many guests.

We made lists and lists, which lengthened by the day, until we had 125 names. We sent out invitations on which I had sketched two lovebirds and had had printed. With the invitations we sent a map I had drawn showing how to get there. Then we hired a caterer to come from Philadelphia.

I was as sure as sure that someone would be left out and a number were, for which we were sorry. Those of my family who lived in California I knew would not come, although they were invited. We also made arrangements for the following day, April 3, at a restaurant for dinner so that all of our children and those of my brothers' children could be included.

Some of Alf's family came from Lancaster and Newark and the office staff from Doubleday, but my dear Peggy couldn't be there. She was in the hospital recovering from an operation. All of our children and our thirteen grandchildren were there. The big girls and boys looked after the little ones, keeping them out of doors most of the time. There were Nina and Alf's three, David, Jeffrey, and Henry; Jack and Edna's Nina and Tony; Arthur and Nina's Kate, Ted and Betty's Sarah, Dailey, and Tom; and Maury and Marianne's four, Michael, Peter, Daniel, and John.

Alf and Nina arrived the day before with their three boys. Alf and Nina stayed with us and the boys stayed with uncles and aunts. Many of my library friends came, as, of course, did my four brothers and their wives. So did several of our author and artist friends and a sprinkling of those I had known in childhood. One was a friend whom I had known as a girl when we were both

Maury, the youngest de Angeli son, and his wife, Marianne.

Jack de Angeli, Marguerite's eldest son.   Edna de Angeli, Jack's wife.

pupils of Madame Suelke. She was an excellent accompanist as well as a singer and we shared happy memories of gatherings both at her house and ours. She begged as a special favor that I sing one of my old songs and that Dai play the obbligato as we used to do. My voice by then was of uncertain quality and Dai's hands were stiff, but we played and sang together on our fiftieth wedding anniversary. Quite an accomplishment, even if not up to standard. It was a very happy occasion.

That morning, when we awoke, on April 2, 1960, Dai had called over to me, "Well, Mama, we made it!"

Epilogue

Perhaps the most fitting title for this roundup of events since the golden wedding is a quote from the de Angeli *Book of Nursery Rhymes:* "Lawk a mercy on Me, This is none of I," for to this "lady from Philadelphia" honors and awards are not only unexpected but unbelievable. And in the years since 1960 they have accumulated.

Although she neglected to mention it she was made an honorary life member of the Philadelphia Booksellers' Association in 1956, and in 1960 the same group awarded her a scroll to honor her twenty-fifth anniversary as a writer and illustrator of books for children.

In 1958 she was made a member of the Daughters of Pennsylvania and in 1966 Governor Scranton presented her with a special citation for her contributions to the state.

The Lit Brothers' Good Neighbor Community Service Award went to her in 1963 and that same year at a large reception in her honor the Drexel Institute of Technology, Graduate School of Library Science, awarded her a citation for her "distinguished and lasting contribution to the World of Children's Books."

She is an honorary member of Theta Sigma Phi, national journalism fraternity, and the recipient of two scrolls from the Philadelphia Arts Festival. The first scroll was given in 1962 and the second in 1967, when she received the award for literature as "one of Philadelphia's foremost authors in residence."

In 1968 the Regina Medal, presented annually by the Catholic Library Association, went to Mrs. de Angeli, and in the fall of 1969 the mayor of the Borough of Collingswood, New Jersey, proclaimed September 23 as "Marguerite Lofft de Angeli Day" to

Marguerite receiving a special citation from Governor Scranton in 1966.

be celebrated annually with friends of the Collingswood Library "in honoring a former citizen of our community" for her many contributions to the youth of the country through her books and illustrations.

Along with the many honors, books have continued to come. In 1961 she made a special selection for very young listeners of rhymes from the big *Mother Goose* book, *A Pocket Full of Posies*. For the next two years she turned again to her music and collected and illustrated hymns she had loved as a child and had sung during her years of choir work. This was *Marguerite de Angeli's Book of Favorite Hymns*. While this was in progress, she began to work on the retelling of one of Grimms' fairy tales, *The Goose*

246

Girl, a story that she had always wanted to illustrate. It was published in 1964 and that same year she began the illustrations for a story written by her son Arthur, *The Empty Barn.* This was followed in 1969 with a dramatization of *The Door in the Wall* done by Arthur with illustrations by Marguerite.

As always, the pattern of family life continued side by side with books, paintings, and honors. When the circular stairs in the little house of Panama Street became a trial for Dai, following his heart trouble, they sold the house and moved to an apartment with a tree-top view of the Philadelphia Museum of Fine Arts. Summers they took refuge in the little cottage not far from Red Hill where the three older boys had moved their expanding machine shop business to larger quarters. In a few years enlargement was again necessary and they added a series of offices over the shop and increased their working force. They do a great deal of work for the Knoll Company and are thus closely associated with Maury, their youngest brother.

Marguerite de Angeli in 1968.

Maury, after ten years with Knoll, branched out with a business of his own, the making of harpsichords and clavichords. He had built one of each and sold them to friends, and then, encouraged by his parents, he decided to try it full time. The first year he made five harpsichords and five clavichords and sold all but two clavichords. After he had completed six more harpsichords, doing all the work himself, he decided that his business would have to be a sideline, and returned to Knoll.

Because the boys and their families all live within a six-mile radius of Red Hill, the summers and holidays are times for family gatherings made even more exciting with the coming of the first great grandchild, Deborah, daughter of Nina, the first grandchild. The gatherings will continue as always, but in the summer of 1969 the long struggle with his heart ended for Dai, barely eight months before what would have been their sixtieth wedding anniversary.

Margaret Lesser

INDEX

marriage, 159; photo of, 243; and theatrical activities, 117, 118, 158

De Angeli, Kate (granddaughter), 73, 188, 196, 207, 242

De Angeli, Kate Craig (mother-in-law), 47, 49–50, 66, 109–10ff., 115

De Angeli, Marguerite Lofft (*see also* specific relationships, works): and breakdown, 112–13; childhood, family background, 1–45; and church, 15–16, 33, 115–16; and death of sister, 83–84; Golden Wedding, 241–43; meets future husband, engagement, 46–48ff.; and music, 14, 39–42, 46, 51–53, 70–71, 74, 75, 99–100, 162, 163, 203, 243; photos of, 5, 14, 15, 39, 52, 89, 186, 194, 203, 245, 246; pregnancies, births of children, 56, 64–66, 72, 73, 74, 75ff., 86, 98, 104–5; and sales job, 42–43; trips abroad, 179–82, 197–201, 204–33; wedding, early married life, 54–55ff.

De Angeli, Marianne (wife of Maury), 177, 196, 204, 230, 232, 240, 242

De Angeli, Michael, 196, 242

De Angeli, Maurice Bower (son), 109, 111, 112, 117, 119, 138, 158, 164, 196, 204, 239, 246–47; birth, 105; children of, 196, 240, 242; in choir, 116; in college, 172; engaged, 177; and *Henner's Lydia*, 135–36; photo of, 242; sketch of, 127

De Angeli, Muriel (wife of son Arthur), 159, 176

De Angeli, Nina (daughter). See Kuhn, Nina de Angeli

De Angeli, Nina (granddaughter), 160, 242, 247

De Angeli, Nina Persichetti (wife

of Arthur), 176–77, 238, 239, 241, 242

De Angeli, Peter, 196, 242

De Angeli, Ruby Catherine, 77–78, 80–81

De Angeli, Sarah (granddaughter), 196, 208, 242

De Angeli, Sarah Daugherty (Dai's grandmother), 49

De Angeli, Tom, 242

De Angeli, Tony, 242

De Angelis, Jefferson, 49

Desireau, Mrs. (butter-maker), 11–12, 173

Detroit, Mich., 23–24, 82–83

Dinsmore, Miss (art editor), 102

Dock, Christopher, 138–42

Door in the Wall, The (about medieval England), 178–83, 184–88, 238, 246

Doubleday, 107, 153, 165, 187, 189, 191, 209, 242. *See also* Lesser, Margaret (Peggy); specific books

Dove in the Eagle's Nest, 101

Drexel Institute of Technology, 244

Dukhobors, 59

Durell, Ann, 206, 207

Durham, England, 198–99

Eaton, Alice, 138

Edinburgh, Scotland, 199

Edmonton, Alta., 62–63, 72

Edward III, 181, 182–83

Edward IV, 185–86

Edwards, Jonathan, 10

Egypt, 215–17

Elin's Amerika, 160–61, 167

Elliot, Frank, 50

Ellis, Richard, 140

Empty Barn, The, 246

England, 178–83, 185–87, 197–99, 200–1, 231–32

English, Gladys, 190

Evans, Mary, 154, 155

Everett, Walter, 32, 90, 102

Nina and Tony de Angeli,
Edna and John de Angeli's children.

William W. Walls,
Nina de Angeli's husband.

Deborah Walls, Nina and William W. Walls' daughter,
Marguerite de Angeli's great-grandchild.

Kate de Angeli, Nina and
Arthur de Angeli's daughter.

Henry, David and Jeffrey Kuhn,
Nina de Angeli and Alfred Kuhn's sons.

Julie Kuhn,
David Kuhn's wife.